Hospitality Service and Product

HOSPITALITY SERVICE AND PRODUCT

Atul Shrivastava

CENTRUM PRESS
NEW DELHI-110002 (INDIA)

CENTRUM PRESS

H.O.: 4360/4, Ansari Road, Daryaganj,
New Delhi-110002 (India)
Tel: 23278000, 23261597, 23255577, 23286875

B.O.: No. 1015, Ist Main Road, BSK IIIrd Stage,
IIIrd Phase, IIIrd Block, Bengaluru-560085 (INDIA)
Tel: 080-41723429

Email: centrumpress@gmail.com
Visit us at: www.centrumpress.com

Hospitality Service and Product

First Edition, 2013

ISBN 978-93-81293-97-3

PRINTED IN INDIA

Printed at Balaji Offset, Delhi.

Preface

The hospitality industry is composed of a variety of sectors. As stated in earlier sessions there is the food and beverage sector, the accommodation sector, the entertainment sector, etc. At this point it is also important to note that the hospitality industry is divided into two categories. These are the commercial category and the non-commercial category. To put it simply the commercial category includes establishments that operate for profit. The non-commercial category comprises establishments that operate on a not for profit bases. The non-commercial establishments are usually subsidised by governments and in many cases supported by private enterprise. An example of a non-commercial organisation is the Salvation Army. The hospitality component in assisted living is by comparison much larger, and the healthcare component much smaller, than in any other segment of the healthcare industry. This may explain why, in recent years, firms in the hospitality industry, such as Marriott International and the Hyatt Corporation, have been expanding into assisted living.

Hospitality firms are especially well positioned to compete in this field. They are experienced in creating value and ensuring quality service through customer satisfaction. However, anyassisted living facility (ALF), regardless of whether it is affiliated with the hospitality industry, should also focus on creating value and ensuring quality service through customer satisfaction. Some suggestions for accomplishing this follow.

In an attempt to fill units, many ALFs have tried to cut costs and reduce prices. Decreasing prices to increase occupancy, though, can lead to an erosion in quality of service. ALFs should focus instead on providing exceptional quality, ensuring quick recovery from any service failures, and training and empowering employees to respond efficiently and effectively to customers' needs. By using a marketing philosophy as their orientation, ALF operators can earn profits by serving their customers "better than the next guy. This would include: Enhancing revenues with ancillary services. The movement toward aging in place will provide opportunities for ALFs to sell ancillary services. One approach is to offer the services of assisted living but in the seniors' own homes. In 2001, Sunrise Assisted Living began offering "At Home" Assisted Living by Sunrise. This includes an in-home aide to help the senior dress and/or bathe, and technology to provide assistance in taking the right medications at the right time, or to call for help in times of emergency. Besides home health services, ALFs can offer other services in the home, including rehabilitation services and geriatric assessment. By offering such services at seniors' homes, ALFs can maintain operating margins while virtually guaranteeing a source of future residents. For example, when seniors who subscribe to Sunrise's "At Home" Assisted Living become too frail to stay at home (even with assistance), they are likely to move into a Sunrise ALF. Already familiar and comfortable with the service and personnel provided by Sunrise, a senior will find it easier to make the transition to an ALF setting.

Maintaining occupancy by focusing on resident health and wellness. Health and wellness programs are important to ALFs because they help residents to age in place, and thus help the ALF to maintain satisfactory occupancy rates. As one analyst has noted, "Managing acuity means managing costs, and managing costs will help to preserve assisted living's value and capacity to compete with providers of other health sectors." Managing the medical needs of residents through health and wellness programs can help ALFs address financial issues.

This book will prove beneficial to the students, teachers and researchers in the field of this subject.

—Author

1

The Distinguishing Factor of Hospitality

Introduction

County Louth has a tradition of entrepreneurial flair and industrial innovation. Over the course of the *County Development Plan 2003 – 2009*, the county shared in the benefits associated with the Celtic Tiger and has become well positioned as a major manufacturing, commercial and service centre catering for both domestic and international markets. Louth Local Authorities have proactively engaged with the private sector and other agencies to create strong economic partnerships. This has been coupled with the development of a holistic approach to economic development which involves educational institutions, cross border engagement and the establishment of concrete targets for job creation and economic development.

The key economic strengths and drivers in County Louth include, inter alia, its strategic location, high quality infrastructure, people resources, education and skills of its work force and the high quality of life available to its residents.

Louth enjoys a very favourable location along the Dublin-Belfast corridor with close proximity to Dublin and the related advantages of easy access to Dublin Airport, Dublin Port, third and fourth level educational institutions and domestic and international markets. It is also very accessible to Belfast and the highly urbanised north east including proximity to Belfast International and City Airports and the sea ports in Belfast and Larne. The A1/M1 motorway linking Dublin and Belfast runs through the heart of the county providing high quality access to national roads and motorway infrastructure. The improved level of rail infrastructure and services provide an alternative and sustainable transportation option for both goods and passenger traffic. Louth is highly urbanised and has a high density of population compared to other rural counties. This is primarily as a result of having within its boundaries two of the largest provincial towns in the country, namely Dundalk and Drogheda. This generates critical mass and a large and well educated labour force pool, which is an essential resource for economic activity and expansion. The high quality of life enjoyed by the residents of County Louth and which is available to potential investors is regarded as a major economic strength of the county.

County Louth Economic Development Strategy 2009-2015

This report presents an economic development strategy for County Louth for the period between 2009 and 2015, which coincides with the timeframe for the Plan. It focuses on the following:

- Assessment of the economic strengths and weakness of Louth
- Identification and making of recommendations on economic opportunities that can be successfully delivered
- Identification of current and future challenges and threats facing the county
- Making of proposals for a unique County Louth brand and a supporting marketing strategy
- Identification of potential funding sources and mechanisms

Whilst it is accepted that the majority of employment growth will be focused on the two principal urban areas of Dundalk and Drogheda, the Strategy also recognises that there is considerable scope for new economic opportunities in rural County Louth.

Key Development Opportunities for Louth as identified by County Louth Economic Development Strategy

Louth is ideally placed to capitalize on the advantages afforded to the county arising from its approximate location to Dublin along the Dublin Belfast economic corridor.

People Resources

The significant commuter population in County Louth points to an opportunity to leverage the high skilled labour pool to market Louth as a location for future investment.

Economic Sectors

Existing and emerging strengths would suggest that there are potential significant development opportunities for Louth in foreign owned and domestic owned high value industry and internationally traded services, including high end, specialised manufacturing, financial and business services and other commercial activities, including retail.

Louth has particular advantages such as high quality visitor attractions, easy access to Dublin Airport and accommodation which indicate significant opportunities to further develop the county as a high quality destination for overseas and domestic holiday and business visitors. The following recommendations for the promotion of economic development of the county are contained within the Strategy.

1. The county development plan should target an increase in the population of the county and its main towns to approach 150,000 persons in the county and around 190,000 persons in the wider economic area surrounding the county by 2020.
2. The county development plan should facilitate commercial and other development to provide additional employment of between 17,000 and 22,000 jobs in the administrative and economic areas respectively, to support the targeted expansion in population.
3. County Louth should develop a diversified economic base to reduce its vulnerability to any one sector or a limited number of potentially vulnerable sectors.
4. A labour and skills strategy should be implemented which supports the required growth in the work force while addressing the specific skills required to support the sectoral economic strategy.
5. Continued and intensified efforts should be directed as a priority at addressing specific challenges faced by the

county in the areas of unemployment and social exclusion.

6. Deficits in important key infrastructure, such as high quality broadband availability should be addressed in the county to facilitate economic and population growth.
7. Town centre development should continue to focus on ensuring the development of attractive centres for the county's main towns.
8. A marketing and branding strategy should be implemented which capitalises on the strengths of Louth and its constituent main towns as locations for investment and tourism.
9. A coordinated and consistent approach to the implementation and delivery of the development strategy is required, supported by appropriate structures at local authority and agency level.
10. A range of public, private and public private partnerships (PPP) funding options should be explored to support the delivery of infrastructure and other priorities. Economic development strategies have also been prepared for the towns of Dundalk, Drogheda and Ardee. The Plan will support the implementation of these in addition to the economic development strategy for the county.

Policy

To capitalise on the location, natural and people resources of County Louth in the pursuit of the economic development priorities identified in the *County Louth Economic Development Strategy 2009-2015* and *Economic Development of Ardee 2009-2015* and support the implementation of similar strategies for Dundalk and Drogheda.

Employment Opportunities in smaller Towns and Villages

The main centres for employment within county Louth are Dundalk, Drogheda, Ardee and Dunleer and the council supports the role of these towns as the primary locations for employment generating activities within the county. However, the council also acknowledges the need for greater employment opportunities in smaller settlements and in rural areas. The spread of employment opportunities throughout the county is considered necessary in order to revitalise and sustain rural communities where traditional employment sources, such as agriculture, are in decline.

The following settlements are identified as suitable for small scale businesses and enterprise and it is proposed that lands for employment activities will be identified and zoned in the review of the local area plans.

- Clogherhead
- Castlebellingham / Kilsaran
- Greenore
- Louth Village
- Collon

Policy

To protect and enhance the status of Dundalk, Drogheda, Ardee and Dunleer as the principles centres of employment, industrial and commercial activity within the county.

To secure a spread of employment opportunities at key strategic locations throughout the county and facilitate the development of local based micro and start –up enterprises.

To identify and zone additional lands, if required, for employment activities in the review of the local area plans for Clogherhead, Castlebellingham/ Kilsaran, Greenore, Louth Village and Collon.

It should be noted however that the above policies do not preclude the location of industrial and commercial activity elsewhere in the county, where consideration will be given on the merits of each individual proposal.

Development at Motorway Interchanges

The M1 has the potential to act as a major stimulant of economic development and activity by providing high quality road infrastructure and connectivity to air and sea ports and thereby to domestic and international markets. Motorway interchanges are strategic locations much sought after by developers due to the desirability and benefits of having immediate access to the primary road network.

However, uncontrolled and poorly regulated development at interchanges can often be problematical. This can be due to such development being solely dependent on roads transport, the possibility of traffic congestion on national routes, the impact on rural landscapes and environments and the costs involved in the provision of other infrastructure such as piped services, electricity and gas. Such development can also detract investment from existing towns and settlements that are badly in need of renewal and development.

In order to maximise the benefits accruing to the county from the motorway and to regulate development in a sustainable and appropriate manner along its route, the following policies will be applied.

Policy

To promote and facilitate development at urban–related* interchanges in accordance with the zoning provisions of the *Dundalk and Environs Plan* and the *North Drogheda Environs Local Area Plan 2004.*

To resist development at rural-related** motorway interchanges.

Urban –related interchanges are Ballymascanlon, Castleblayney Road, Dundalk South interchange and Drogheda North.

Rural –related interchanges are Carrickcarron junction, Drumleck, Charleville, Mooremount and Woodlands.

Cross Border Economic Co-Operation

The emergence of a lasting peace in Northern Ireland presents significant opportunities for cooperation between local authorities, community groups and the private sector in the promotion and development of the region on a cross border basis for the mutual benefit of both.

To this end, the International Centre for Local and Regional Development (ICLRD) has developed a number of concepts which include the Newry-Dundalk Twin-City Region and a Newry-Dundalk International Services Zone. It is considered that a twin-city region would have the capacity to facilitate an integrated approach to the strategic planning and special needs of the area and to promote a sustainable central corridor strategy on the eastern seaboard. The International Service Zone concept is based on the Derry- Letterkenny modal. Newry-Dundalk is considered a prime location as a centre for internationally traded services due to its location at the centre of the Dublin-Belfast economic corridor.

Consideration will also be given to the carrying out of an economic analysis and development strategy focusing on the M1 corridor extending into Northern Ireland and to the counties of Meath and Fingal.

Policy

EDE 7: To support joint initiatives between local authorities, community groups and private sector for cooperation and promotion of the region on a cross border basis for the mutual benefit of both.

Adoption of a Partnership Approach

A key facet of the economy in County Louth has been the adoption of a partnership approach towards growing the economy. This is manifested in the work of organisations such the County Development Board, Louth County Enterprise Board, DKIT, Fas, the Chambers of Commerce and Louth Leader Partnership, Enterprise Ireland, the IDA, and the Newry-Dundalk Business Linkage Programme. The partnership approach has been most successful in the work undertaken by the Dundalk Economic Development Group. The DEDG was established by the Louth Local Authorities in 2006, as a partnership initiative bringing private and public sector leaders together to promote Dundalk as an ideal place to live, invest or visit. Its work has been recognised at a national level.

Policy

EDE 8: To work in partnership with development agencies within the county to promote economic development, enterprise and employment.

Employment Trends and Opportunities

County Louth has traditionally had a strong employment and industrial base centred primarily on the towns of Dundalk, Drogheda, Ardee and Dunleer. The significant foreign direct investment in new enterprises supported by the Industrial Development Authority (IDA) has taken place in county Louth in more recent years and this has made a very valuable contribution to economic development and employment opportunities. The Dundalk Institute of Technology (DKiT) provides a range of high quality third level diploma and degree courses in the sciences, engineering, building and construction and the number of highly qualified graduates passing through the college each year is a major strength and opportunity for the county. The changing employment profile of Ireland has been manifested locally in a shift towards information, communications and technology (ICT) based industries, specialised engineering and food processing. Today, the county is rapidly becoming one of Ireland's principal industrial centres and has attracted new growth in the engineering and IT sectors, principally to the two major towns.

The quality of infrastructure in terms of road, rail and access to sea and air ports in addition to the high quality of the environment and quality of life, makes the county an attractive location for investment and as a place to live.

Employment Sectors

The breakdown of sectoral employment within the county is set out. Currently the majority of employment in Louth is in commerce (31.1%), education, health and social work (22.3%) and manufacturing (17.9%). A relatively low proportion of the county is involved in farming or agricultural activities, reflecting the highly urbanised nature of the county and the general decline in agricultural employment in recent years.

As might be expected, the economic boom of the past decade has resulted in significant increase in employment opportunities within the county and a corresponding decrease in the unemployment rate from a peak of 22.3% in 1996 to 11.1% in 2006 (*CSO 1996 and 2006*). However the 2006 figure of 11.1% is significantly higher than the national average of 8.5%, which is reflective of the existence of high social exclusion and high unemployment within the RAPID areas of the towns of Dundalk and Drogheda. The deteriorating economic climate that has emerged in late 2008 and is continuing, could have serious implications for employment in county Louth and it is likely that the unemployment rate will increase, if temporarily, until such time as there is a sustained economic upturn.

Policy

To work in partnership with national and local economic development and employment promoting agencies to support employment generating initiatives within the county.

Development Management Standards for Industrial and Commercial Developments

The council will require that industrial and commercial lands be developed to a very high standard in campus style settings combining aesthetics with enterprise and attracting high calibre business occupiers. In spatial terms this will mean the development of a series of innovative landmark buildings set in attractive landscaped grounds. New development proposals should aim to provide design excellence realised within a hierarchal road structure and a hard and soft landscaping framework.

Landscaping and Amenity

Commercial and industrial development should present a pleasant aspect aided by a high quality of landscape design, including tree planting, within both public and private domains. The existing landscape framework and its associated topography should be respected.

Landscaping should be such as to ensure that the buildings will not be dominated by extensive areas of parking, hard standing and roads, thereby detracting from the quality of the environment. A detailed, high quality landscape plan, planting schedule and planting programme will be required with all applications. Planting shall include semi- mature trees in order to reduce the visual impact of structures on surrounding areas.

The provision of a buffer zone of not less than fifteen metres in width will be required where industrial and other land uses adjoin to ensure amenities of adjacent properties are not adversely affected.

There should be no significant amenity loss (by way of noise, smell or other nuisance) to immediate neighbours or the area in general resulting from the nature of the proposed business, the amount of traffic generated or the servicing arrangement.

Surface Water Drainage

Adequate measures should be taken by commercial/industrial users and developers in the treatment and disposal of surface water to prevent pollution, including the adoption of the principles of sustainable urban drainage systems (SUDS) in designing surface water management arrangements.

Sustainable Design

All commercial and Industrial development should adopt a sustainable approach to design and building methods including passive design, use of solar energy, low energy performance buildings and the use of renewable energy supplies, in association with Sustainable Energy Ireland and having regard to the Guidelines for Sustainable Design and Energy Efficiency in Buildings as set out in paragraph 9.7 of the Plan..

Car Parking, Loading and Unloading Provision

All surface car parking areas should preferably be located behind the building line, out of view of the general public. Where this is not practical, parking areas should be suitably screened and landscaped. All car parking areas should be suitably surfaced and illuminated. Individual parking spaces should be permanently marked and shall not be less than 5.0m X 2.5m in dimension and shall have appropriate access and circulation aisles.

Sufficient loading and unloading bays should be provided. These should be of sufficient size to accommodate loading and unloading operations without encroachment onto any public road, footpath or interfere with the safety and free flow of vehicular traffic or pedestrians.

Design

Where two or more commercial or industrial buildings are being developed, a uniform design for boundary treatments, roof profiles and building lines is recommended. The scale and design of proposed development should be in keeping with the surrounding area and adjoining developments.

Site Coverage and Plot Ratios

The maximum site coverage permitted in industrial areas shall be 50% and the maximum plot ratio shall be 2:1.

Open Storage

Any open storage areas shall be located behind the building line and be adequately screened from public view.

Roads and Footpaths

The width of all internal industrial estate roads shall, generally, not be less than 7.3 metres with minimum radii of 10.5 metres at junctions. Visibility splays shall not be less than 70m x 4.5m x 1.05m within speed control zones and 160m x 4.5m x 1.05m elsewhere. Footpaths shall not be less than 1.8 metres in width.

Nuisance

The 'good neighbour' principle should be applied in respect of all industrial and commercial developments where possible conflict could arise with other established uses. In particular, noise emissions, whether from plant, machinery or traffic, shall comply with the provisions of Noise Regulations (S.I. No. 140 of 2006).

Foul Sewerage

All discharges of trade effluents to sewerage networks or receiving waters shall be subject to a Water Pollution Act Discharge Licence. Specified appropriate pre-treatment of trade effluents shall be required prior to discharge to council sewers.

Public Water Supplies

All supplies to industrial developments shall be metered and consumers shall be charged on basis of usage in accordance with guidelines set out in the *Water Services Pricing Policy.*

Fire Prevention

Adequate storage and hydrant capacity should be provided in consultation with the fire department of the council.

Building Regulations

Designers, developers and owners should ensure that all buildings and structures comply with the requirements of the *Building Regulations 1990.*

Signage

Signage shall be kept to a minimum. In order to ensure high

quality signage and to safeguard the amenities of the area, a uniform signage scheme should be devised and submitted as part of the planning application for the development to which it relates. Billboards or free standing signage will not normally be permitted.

Public Artwork

Public art should be provided within an open space or focal point within new development schemes, through the *Percent for Arts Scheme* administered by the Department of the Environment, Heritage and Local Government. The council should be consulted on opportunities for permanent art.

Commerce and Retail

Introduction

The level of commerce and retail activity is reflective of the overall economic well being of the economy. County Louth, by reason of its border location, has suffered as a result of different pricing structures, monetary and taxation regimes, north and south of the border. This is particularly evident in recent months and is being further exacerbated by the current economic downturn. The importance of commerce and retail in County Louth is evident from the proportion of the total labour force, some 31.1%, employed in the sector.

Traditionally, the main destination for shopping has been town and village centres. These also acted as the focus for a variety of other activities including business, social, leisure and residential uses.

Recent trends have seen the decline of small independent grocers and the emergence of larger supermarkets, franchise based local convenience stores, discount food stores and retail warehouses at out-of-town locations. These emerging trends in the retail sector have increasingly influenced shopping patterns and have created a demand for large shopping centres at locations where extensive car parking facilities are available. The council recognises the importance of retaining the primary role of town centres for commercial and retail activity. Therefore, the retail policies outlined in the Plan aim to preserve the viability and vitality of the town and village centres of the county whilst also recognising the need to provide for new retailing formats to meet consumer demands.

Louth Retail Strategy 2009

The *Retail Planning Guidelines for Planning Authorities 2000* were issued under the provisions of *Section 28 of the Planning and Development Act 2000* and were subsequently revised in 2005. The purpose of these guidelines is to:

- Promote a healthy competitive retail environment.
- Promote forms of retail development which are easily assessable by public transport.
- Protect the role of town centres and resist large scale out of centre shopping malls
- Resist large retail centres close to national roads or motorway interchanges
- Assist local authorities in the preparation of retail policies for incorporation into development plans

In order to comply with the guidelines planning authorities are required to prepare retail strategies.

The *Louth Retail Strategy* was prepared and adopted in 2002 and subsequently reviewed in 2009. The 2009 Strategy has informed the retail policies of this development plan. The purpose of the *Louth Retail Strategy 2009* is to:

- Promote a healthy, vibrant and competitive retail environment within County Louth
- Identify the core shopping areas in Dundalk, Drogheda and Ardee
- Formulate policies to protect the vitality and viability of existing town and village centres
- Ensure the provision of appropriately scaled convenience retail outlets in new residential areas
- Establish a county retail hierarchy
- Define criteria for the assessment of future significant retail developments

The Strategy has confirmed that there has been a 127% increase in the retail floor space available within the county since the previous strategy was completed in 2002, with increases of 170% in Drogheda, 108% in Dundalk and 49.2% in Ardee. This represents a very significant increase and is reflective of the progressive development of the county over that period. One of the important functions of the retail strategy was to establish a county retail hierarchy which is set out. The primary positions of Dundalk and Drogheda at level one is recognised whilst the local importance of Ardee places it at level 2. Other important local centres of Blackrock, Dunleer, Collon and Carlingford are included at level 3 and all other villages are at level 4.

In terms of retail warehouses and retail parks the strategy suggests that there is considerable existing floor space and that there is unlikely to be any additional need or demand over the period of the Plan. The also concludes that Ardee should continue to develop its convenience retail offer in tandem with its expanding population and that there is a current need for an additional convenience retail store up to 2500 square metres.

However, it considers that there is no justifiable need for retail park development. Furthermore, the development of Ardee's retail comparison offer should be closely linked to the evolution of the town's untapped tourism potential.

In the other towns and villages, the priority is to cater sufficiently for the basic convenience and lower order comparison requirements of their existing populations, and the aim is to facilitate retail development commensurate with their population sizes, location and traditional built environment.

The retail policies as set out below are inclusive of those recommended in the retail study.

Policy

To promote a healthy competitive retail environment within County Louth and to maintain the vitality and viability of town and village centres and their role as primary retail core areas.

To ensure that applications for retail development comply with the provisions of the *Retail Planning Guidelines 2005* and the *Louth Retail Strategy 2009*.

To support the development of Dundalk and Drogheda as important regional shopping centres and to maintain the role of Ardee as a sub county retail centre and the retail function of all other settlements, commensurate with locally generated needs.

To resist the provision of large scale retail developments outside town centres subject to the application of the sequential test and demonstration that the existing town centre will not be adversely affected.

To promote the provision of local retail centres serving small, localised catchment populations in new residential areas, commensurate with locally generated needs.

To generally discourage permission for change of use from retail or service (including banks and similar institutions with over the counter services) to non- retail or non service uses at ground-floor level.

Town and Village Centres

Rural town and village centres have traditionally been at the heart of the economic commercial, social and cultural heart of rural communities. They were bustling centres of activity which had a complex mix of uses including residential, retail, professional and other services, leisure and cultural activities. The advent of the motor car and changing consumer demands have resulted in a decline of the role of town and village centres as both the residential and commercial functions sought to relocate to more desirable and accessible out of town locations. This has had a negative impact on the fabric and environment of many towns and villages, resulting in a loss of vibrancy and activity particularly outside of business hours.

The council recognises the important role that rural town and villages play in the social and economic life and therefore considers it necessary to devise policies that will protect the vitality and viability of these settlements. The retail policies outlined above which are derived from the *Retail Planning Guidelines 2005* and the *Louth Retail Strategy 2009* seek to preserve the retail function of town and village centres. It is considered that, though important, retail policies alone will not be sufficient to protect the broader range of essential town and village centre uses.

Town and Village Centre Environments

It is important that town and village centres are attractive, safe and easily accessible to all. A number of town and village improvement schemes have been carried out during the period of the last plan, in cooperation with local Tidy Towns Committees. The success of Louth's towns and villages in the Bord Failte sponsored Tidy Towns Competition bears testimony to the improvements made.

Improvements to footpaths, street lighting, street furniture and landscaping make a valuable contribution to the attractiveness of the environments of town and village centres. The council will continue to co-operate with local groups towards further improvement in towns and villages throughout the county.

Policy

To promote the improvement of the environment of town and village centres through good design in all development, landscaping, street furniture and public art works. To improve traffic mobility through traffic management, improvements to pavements, provision of access for mobility impaired and public transport waiting facilities. To co-operate with local Tidy Towns Committees and other community groups in the implementation of environmental improvement schemes.

Architectural Conservation Areas and Protected Structures

Many of the towns and villages within the county have designated architectural conservation areas (ACA) and a number of protected structures. Any proposed developments within an ACA or involving modifications to a protected structure shall comply with the requirements.

Living over the Shop

The council will promote the provision and modernisation of residential accommodation over commercial premises in towns and villages in order to improve the vibrancy of their centres. This will be subject to the provision of good quality accommodation with separate and safe access from the street and the protection of residential amenities from any possible conflict with other uses.

Policy

To promote the provision and modernisation of residential accommodation over commercial premises in towns and villages in order to improve the vibrancy of their centres.

Shopfronts

The towns and villages of County Louth contain numerous examples of traditional shopfront design together with large numbers of more modern design, much of which reflects a certain amount of corporate harmonisation. The council will encourage the preservation of authentic, traditional shopfronts and the provision of good quality contemporary designs.

Design criteria for shopfronts should ensure that:

- Entrances are fully accessible to all people with mobility difficulties.
- Where a shopfront involves two or more units, that it is divided with separate fascias and columns to reflect the separate units.
- The shopfront respects the building's elevation and architectural details. Period shopfronts on protected structures and in ACAs should be retained.
- The design takes into account adjacent shopfronts where they make a positive contribution to the streetscape.

Policy

To encourage the preservation of authentic, tradition shopfronts and good quality contemporary designs.

Security Shutters

Whilst the council recognises the need for the sufficient security for commercial premises the installation of security shutters can detract from the appearance, visual amenity and safety of town and village centres particularly at night and weekends. The council will discourage the mounting or location of rollers on the exterior of shop premises where such shutters would detract from the streetscape and ambience of the town. However innovative solutions involving tradition wrought iron window guards or shutters which provide a high degree of transparency which allows the window display to be visible will be considered.

Policy

To discourage the mounting or location of rollers on the exterior of shop premises where such shutters would detract from the streetscape and ambience of the town or village. To consider innovative solutions including tradition wrought iron window guards or security shutters which provide a high degree of transparency which allows the window display to be visible.

Canopies and Blinds

Blinds were traditionally incorporated into the shop front fascia and designed be retracted into it when not in use. This is still the best way to handle a blind where one is required. Curved and Dutch style canopies are unsympathetic to the traditional streetscape will be discouraged.

Policy

To encourage the incorporation of blinds, where required, into the shopfront fascia so that they are capable of being retracted when not in use. Curved and Dutch canopies will be discouraged.

Signage

The size, shape and position of signs should reflect the scale and facade of the building on which they are located. Hand painted signs or illumination by bracket or wash lighting are preferred to internally illuminated fascia signs. In general signs should not be located above fascia level.

Signage forms an integral part of most shop fronts and commercial areas. However, the proliferation of insensitive displays of advertisements can seriously detract from the visual quality of the area and have implications for public safety. The following guidelines should be applied in the design of town and village centre signage:

- Signage should be kept to a minimum and be of a size, design, scale and degree of illumination which is compatible with the surrounding area.
- Signage above fascia level, free standing signage and billboards will not normally be permitted.
- Only one projecting sign per unit will be permitted at fascia level.
- Signs should not adversely affect the safety or free flow of traffic, including pedestrian traffic.

- The location of free standing advertisements and other objects shall be discouraged in the interest of pedestrian safety. Any such objects shall be subject to licence under Section 254 of the *Planning and Development Act, 2000.*
- In new development a uniform signage scheme should be prepared and submitted with the planning application for the relevant development.

Policy

EDE 24: To discourage a proliferation of signs within town and village centres which would detract from the visual amenities of the streetscape and which would interfere with the free flow and safety of vehicular and pedestrian traffic movements.

Site Coverage

Site coverage shall not exceed 80%.

Height

The height of proposed buildings should respect the height of adjoining structures on either side. Normally buildings in excess of four storeys in height will be discouraged except at key locations or landmark sites where taller buildings might be acceptable. The height of new developments should not detract from views of existing protected structures and landmark buildings.

Overshadowing and Overlooking

Where three or four storey buildings are proposed adjoining lower buildings, the council will require that the developer submit daylight and shadow projection diagrams and demonstrate that the adjoining properties will not be unduly affected by the proposed development.

Windows and balconies of new building should avoid overlooking of adjoining property, particularly residential property.

Tourism

The *Economic Development Strategy for County Louth 2008* identifies the potential of tourism to contribute significantly to the economic development of the county. The attractions of

County Louth as a tourist destination include an unspoilt natural landscape, areas of outstanding natural beauty, clean uncluttered beaches, a pollution free environment, a wealth of historical and architectural heritage and a range of high quality tourist attractions and facilities.

The county is conveniently located to the heavily populated areas of Greater Dublin and the north east of the island, centred on Belfast, which provides a large population mass within a one hour drive of the county. The improved road and rail infrastructure which has been put in place, both north and south of the border in recent years and accessibility to east coast air and passenger ferry ports makes the county very accessible to the international tourism market.

Tourist Attractions

The broad range of tourist facilities and attractions of County Louth include, inter alia, the following:

- Historic towns of Dundalk, Drogheda, Ardee and Carlingford
- Areas of Outstanding Natural Beauty
- 120 kilometres of clean coastline and blue flag beaches
- Marina, sailing and sea adventure centres
- Clean air and water
- A large number of archaeological sites and monument
- Historic Boyne Valley and Battle of the Boyne Site
- A large number of historic houses and landscaped gardens
- Equestrian based activity
- High quality golf courses
- Identified cycling and walking routes
- Cultural based activities
- High quality hotels and other accommodation
- Places of recreation including theatres, cinemas, pubs and restaurants
- All weather racing track and international standard ice rink

Regional Tourism Policy

Failte Ireland East and Midlands Regional Tourism Plan 2008-2010 provides a road map for both national and local agencies, local authorities and other public bodies to contribute to the sustainable development of tourism in the region.

Louth is one of eight counties included in the remit of this plan which aims to deliver increased tourism benefits to the region by providing better hospitality, greater appeal and an improved quality of visitor experience. It notes that visitors are attracted to the region because of the diversity of tourist attractions. Within County Louth the Cooley Peninsula has proved attractive as a natural base for outdoor pursuits, whilst the major heritage and historic sites such as those at Monasterboice, Mellifont and the historic towns of Dundalk, Drogheda, Ardee and Carlingford combine to provide a rich heritage menu.

Tourism Plan 2008-2012

Louth Hospitality, which is a local authority supported partnership with the private tourism sector in the county, recently published the *Tourism Plan 2008-2012*. The mission statement of this action plan is *'to attract tourists to County Louth by providing a quality experience'*. It aims to offer compelling reasons to motivate tourists to visit Louth and to make attractions more accessible and tangible. To facilitate the development of Louth's heritage sites as top class visitor attractions, it is an objective of the action plan to provide the necessary infrastructure, visitor services and promotional material to market the sites.

Policy

To support the implementation of the *Tourism Plan 2008-2012* and the *Failte Ireland East and Midlands Regional Plan 2008 – 2010.*

To promote the sustainable development of Louth as a quality tourist destination themed on heritage, culture and an unspoilt natural environment.

To assist in the development and marketing of County Louth in conjunction with the local authorities north and south of the border.

To support the development of community festivals, cultural activities and other outdoor activities.

Co-Operation with other Bodies

The council is aware that the development of tourism in County Louth would benefit greatly from a co-operative approach with other local authorities and relevant agencies both north and south of the border. Such initiatives could involve the co-funding of tourism infrastructure, product development and marketing. Cooperation on a number of projects has already taken place and it is proposed to pursue and bring to fruitation these initiatives during the course of the Plan.

Cross Border Ecologically Themed Project

During the period of the Plan, the council will explore with the relevant authorities north of the border the development of an integrated themed cross border project based around the common themes of a high quality landscape and natural heritage. This is most strongly manifested in the geological underpinnings which characterize the Cooley Peninsula, Mourne Mountains and Slieve Gullion. This common bond has left a legacy of great beauty and economic potential which can be harnessed to greatest effect by the respective local authorities adopting a collaborative approach to the development of the regions natural wealth.

Much of Cooley, the Mournes and Slieve Gullion comprise of dramatic mountainous areas where the visual impact is increased by proximity to both the open sea and Carlingford Lough. The open moorland of the higher areas has a variety of undisturbed flora and fauna together with large pockets of coniferous forest In human terms, the area is rich in archaeological items and renowned in legend and folklore. These factors together with the isolation and tranquillity combine to give a very broad appeal for visitors and locals alike.

Policy

To pursue the development of an integrated themed cross border tourism project including joint marketing, promotion and where appropriate and viable, infrastructure provision.

Narrow Water Bridge

The provision of a road link through the construction of a bridge between the Cooley Peninsula in County Louth and the southern portion of the Mourne Mountains in County Down at

Narrow Water would make a valuable contribution to the development of tourism in Louth and the Mournes. Initial funding for the project has been provided in the *National Development Plan 2007-2013* and preliminary design work commenced.

Policy

To co-operate with the authorities in Northern Ireland in the provision of a road bridge between Cooley and south County Down.

Oriel 2012

Oriel 2012 aims to promote the Newry and Mourne and the Louth region as a base for pre-games training camps for participants in the 2012 London Olympic Games. Given the region's proximity to London, the cluster will also put in place strategies to attract teams and spectators to the region in their pursuit of leisure and recreational activities. Membership of the Oriel 2012 cluster is open to businesses, sporting organisations, schools and support organisations that are keen to tap into the opportunities that will inevitably arise from the training camps. The council is fully supportive of this initiative.

Policy

To support the Oriel 2012 project and co-operate with relative authorities, business interests and stakeholders north and south to advance its implementation.

Boyne Valley

The historic Boyne Valley, Bru Na Boinne, is a world heritage site. It also contains the site of the historic Battle of the Boyne. The Boyne Valley falls partially within the functional area of Louth County Council, Meath County Council and Drogheda Borough Council. The heritage town of Drogheda which is located on the Boyne Estuary is the gateway to the historic Boyne Valley.

The council recognises the significant contribution and potential of the Boyne Valley for the development of tourism in County Louth and is keen to participate in a joint approach with Meath County Council and Drogheda Borough Council in its protection, development and promotion.

Therefore it is proposed to co-operate with Meath County Council and Drogheda Borough Council in the preparation of a strategy for the protection, development and promotion of this important heritage site.

Policy

To co-operate with Meath County Council and Drogheda Borough Council in the preparation of a strategy for the protection, development and promotion of the Boyne Valley heritage site.

Tourist Accommodation

Growth in the tourism sector will result in a corresponding need for more visitor accommodation and facilities across the county. The council is keen to ensure that there is a range of high quality and affordable accommodation provided in order to meet the needs of visitors and tourists to the county. However, care will be needed to ensure that the unspoilt natural environment and landscapes of the county which have been identified as a major reason why tourists come to County Louth are not compromised by inappropriate tourist accommodation development.

Hotel, Guest House and Bed and Breakfast Accommodation

The number of hotel beds within the county has increased significantly over the period of the last county development plan as a result of the construction of new hotels in Carlingford, Drogheda and two in Dundalk. The council will encourage the provision of additional hotels including leisure and conference facilities, within the county in order to attract more visitors and to boast employment.

Custom built guest houses should be located within existing towns and villages to avail of and support existing services. Bed and breakfast accommodation is normally provided within existing dwellings and can be accommodated in both urban and rural areas. Low cost, high quality guest houses and bed and breakfast accommodation are an important component in the range of accommodation choice required for a vibrant tourism industry.

Policy

To encourage the provision of additional hotel, guest house bed spaces and bed and breakfast accommodation in County

Louth in conjunction with leisure, conferencing and other associated facilities and amenities, subject to the protection of the unspoilt natural environment and landscapes of the county.

Holiday Homes and Self-Catering Accommodation

Holiday homes are defined as '*purpose built self-contained residential units, which provide accommodation on a short term basis for visitors to the area*'. The council will resist the proliferation of holiday home developments in rural areas except where the development would involve the conversion or restoration of existing vernacular buildings and derelict dwellings.

In order to manage the provision of tourist accommodation in a manner that meets the needs of the tourist while at the same time supports the local economy, it is considered important that the provision of holiday homes and self catering accommodation should, by and large, be provided within the network of existing settlements and be of a scale that the settlement can sustain. Therefore the council will resist proposals for the development of holiday homes and self catering accommodation in the countryside, except where existing stone buildings of character are to be converted or where the restoration of vernacular dwellings is proposed.

Policy

To facilitate the limited provision of holiday homes and self-catering accommodation in locations within existing towns and villages, of a scale that the settlement can sustain. To resist proposals for the development of holiday homes and self catering accommodation in the countryside except where existing stone buildings of character are to be converted or where the restoration of vernacular dwellings is proposed. To limit the floor area of all holiday homes and self catering accommodation to a maximum of a 100 square metres.

Caravan Parks

The provision of caravan parks which are popular, particularly in coastal locations, can have a serious detrimental impact on the amenities of the coast unless they are sensitively located and properly managed and maintained. Proposals for new caravan parks will only be favourably considered where they are located within a secluded and a mature landscaped setting and where there is an adequate road network to serve the development.

The focus of the council's policy in relation to caravan parks will be to secure the upgrading of existing parks particularly in relation to wastewater treatment, general facilities and amenities.

Policy

To permit new caravan parks only where they are located within a secluded and a mature landscaped setting and where there is an adequate road network to serve the development. To encourage the upgrading of existing caravan parks in approved locations.

Budget Hostels

Hostel accommodation, catering primarily for those travelling on a limited budget, occupies an important niche within the tourist accommodation market. Whilst the individual spend on accommodation is by definition, low, there can be considerable ancillary spending by such tourists on local services.

Policy

To facilitate the provision of budget hostels within existing urban centres or close to public transport facilities.

Tourism Related Signage

The provision of directional and promotional signage is important in facilitating tourists and enhancing their overall experience and enjoyment of their visit. The provision of finger posts and other directional signs is a function of the local authority and is provided under the roads capital budget. Significant improvements in this area have taken place in recent years and the council will continue to improve road signage where required and subject to the availability of adequate funding. In addition to the road signs provided by the council, Section 254 of the *Planning and Development Act, 2000,* makes provision, under license from the planning authority, for additional road signage to facilitate existing significant activities including tourist related attractions and amenities.

The council will favourably consider the granting of licenses for Failte Ireland approved finger post signage where appropriate.

However, it should be recognised that excessive numbers of signs is counter productive as it leads to clutter and confusion which detracts from the appearance of buildings and rural landscapes and may conflict with essential local authority directional and safety signage. Such a proliferation of signage will be resisted by the council.

Tourism related promotional and advertisement signs are also important for the industry. Such signs should be suitably designed and appropriately located on the building or within the curtilage as appropriate so that they do not detract form the visual amenities of the area.

Policy

To continue to improve local authority directional road signage to facilitate visitors to the county.

To facilitate the licensing of Failte Ireland approved tourism related signage subject to a demonstrate need and the avoidance of clutter and confusion with existing road signage.

To ensure that tourism related promotional and advertisement signs are suitably designed and appropriately located so that they do not detract from the visual amenities of the area.

2

The Important of Distribution Channels

The Regional Economic Strategy *('East of England 2010 – Prosperity and Opportunity for All')* (RES) was published by the East of England Development Agency (EEDA) in June 2001. It sets out how sustainable economic growth can be achieved throughout the East of England. Government guidance states that RSS should assist the implementation of Regional Economic Strategy (RES) and that the RES must sit within the spatial planning framework provided by RSS. In effect the two regional strategies must be complementary.

EEDA is currently reviewing the RES, with a consultation draft published in Autumn 2004. The synergy between the two documents is based on work undertaken to align the draft regional spatial strategy with the regional economic strategy 2001: "prosperity and opportunity for all". This work developed to give a spatial distribution of job growth required to achieve the regional economic strategy and other spatial policy objectives, such as directing growth to deprived areas in order to facilitate regeneration. As a result of this work, RSS14 proposes total job growth across the region, for the period 2001 to 2021, of 421,500. The RES shares this proposition.

EERA and EEDA have jointly researched the land use implications of the RES. This concluded that some growth could be achieved in the Region through gains in productivity and policies such as promoting skills development and innovation, overcoming key transport bottlenecks and facilitating higher participation rates within the Region's existing population.

However, to achieve the RES objectives, additional employment growth would also be needed, in particular to support the Region's key economic sectors and clusters. Much of this growth is forecast to be concentrated mainly where these sectors and clusters already exist, i.e. Hertfordshire, the Cambridge sub-region and parts of west Essex.

This concentration remains true whether the target is to achieve the Enhanced Growth by 2010 scenario required by RES or by 2021. The additional employment growth implies higher rates of population and housing growth than currently planned for in existing RSS.

The economic forecasting research essentially provided a statistical assessment of the means of achieving the RES aspirations for the region, and were not specifically driven by spatial policy. When comparing the relationship between the forecast and the emerging RSS spatial strategy, it became clear that it could not fit with policy. For example, it did not fit with a number of policy-led priorities:

- Thames Gateway regeneration priority;
- Milton Keynes South Midlands growth priority;
- Stansted/M11 growth priority (Sustainable Communities Plan).

The effect of this was that while the forecast indicated the required rates of employment creation/replacement needed to meet the RES target, it did not give a workable spatial distribution, with some areas under-allocated. Hence the figures in Policy E2 of this chapter represent an 'EG2021 plus' policy-led approach.

Policy E1: Human Resource Development

Local development plan documents will include policies that ensure sufficient and accessible premises are available (taking into account the availability of services/facilities in more rural areas) for training and education purposes to suit the requirements identified through the relevant strategies, including the Regional Economic Strategy, the Framework for Regional Employment and Skills Action (FRESA) and those drawn up by Learning and Skills Councils and Lifelong Learning Partnerships.

Supporting Text

Human resource development is central to harnessing and promoting future economic success and social opportunities in the Region, in enhancing access to jobs, and providing opportunities for those currently disadvantaged in the labour market.

Skills are a key driver of productivity. The rise of the knowledge economy is causing increased demand for skills, particularly higher-level skills. The East of England is in line with England's NVQ average at level 2 but falls behind at levels 3 and 4.

The current supply of higher-level skills amongst the East of England work force will be inadequate to meet the future needs of the region's economy. FRESA identifies key priorities for action to secure the necessary skills. Top priorities include increasing participation rates in higher education, response to redundancies, skills for employability, work force development and young people and career choices.

The Learning and Skills Councils, local learning partnerships and local employers play an important role in enhancing skills and opportunities in the Region. Further and higher educational establishments are also vital to the success of training and education strategies.

Local authorities and other partners will support similar measures to those already employed by the best universities and colleges in establishing effective links with knowledge based industries. The scope for provision of training and childcare facilities in association with development should also be explored through the use of planning obligations, in order to assist access to job opportunities.

The requirement for "accessible" premises is intended to allow innovative solutions to access to reflect the Region's diversity. For example, in rural areas this might mean mobile facilities. Accessibility also encompasses the mode of travel to facilities, as dealt with in the policies in the Regional Transport Strategy.

Several of the sub-regions in Chapter 5 set out specific aspirations and policies for the improvement of Higher Education, particularly as a catalyst for regeneration.

Policy E2: Job Growth

Supporting Text

Policy SS10 sets out the overall strategic approach to the regional economy. This Policy E2 sets out the distribution of economic growth.

The distribution of projected job growth targets across the Region is based upon an analysis by Bone Wells Associates (BWA) of what is required to achieve the RES Enhanced Growth scenario by 2021 and adjusted by reference to a number of subsequent policy initiatives and research studies.

The key influencing factors are:

- the Government's Sustainable Communities Plan and its requirements for the Region's 'Growth Areas', namely Milton Keynes South Midlands (Luton and Bedford in the East of England), London-Stansted-Cambridge-Peterborough and the Thames Gateway;
- the potential for indirect and catalytic impacts of airport expansion, particularly associated with Stansted and Luton Airports, and port expansion, particularly at Tilbury, London Gateway (Shellhaven), and

Haven Gateway;

- the regeneration needs and opportunities across the Region;
- the provision of land to meet the needs of emerging and maturing key sectors and clusters in situ, as well enabling growth to occur along development corridors;
- the potential of key cities and towns to support economic development in a sustainable way (the agglomeration approach); and
- the potential of transport interchange centres and other strategic centres to act as focus points for sustainable mixed-use economic development.

Policy E2, together with policies E3 and E4, aim to secure an appropriate and effective distribution of job growth, particularly in the Sustainable Communities Plan Growth Areas. At the regional level, the employment growth figures are broadly aligned with the housing provisions in Policy H1, and create a more sustainable relationship between workers and jobs. It is more difficult to assess alignment at the sub-regional level, because of the nature of the data involved and local commuting across boundaries. In some cases a deliberate 'misalignment' is proposed to address existing deficits (e.g. provision of additional jobs in regeneration areas).

Given the dynamics of economic growth, the varying assumptions about density, vacancy rates and 'churn' in the market (take up of employment sites in the market place), policies must allow some flexibility and not be prescriptive. Proposals in local development plan documents for employment land supply need to be indicative and allow some 'spaceless growth' (job growth without the need for land allocations). Such flexibility needs to be accompanied by clear monitoring procedures and targets.Within this context EERA will work with EEDA and local partners to produce guidance on the production of 'indicative' district-level targets for job growth, and will also apply the 'plan, monitor and manage' approach to identify any required changes in policy or targets.

Further work is also to be carried out to look at the delivery of job growth in Norfolk, in particular to disaggregate the figures for the Norwich and Great Yarmouth/Lowestoft sub-regions. This may have implications for the Norwich sub-region boundary.

It is important to note that Policy E2 provides only for the net increase in employment growth. It does not take account of the need to provide supply to allow for 'churn' in the employment land market and maintaining a vacancy or availability rate to allow choice and flexibility. It is important to promote a range of sites to meet employment and investment opportunities particularly in areas of high economic pressure, and provide an improved offer in regeneration areas, contribute to dispersal of pressure, accord with agglomeration principles and provide for expansion and employment churn, within the overall urban renaissance strategy.

The delivery of employment is influenced by the delivery of infrastructure and housing. EERA will closely monitor job creation, infrastructure delivery and housing completions through its annual monitoring arrangements as describe.

Policy E3 – Approach To Employment Land Allocation

Local development plan documents will allocate employment land to provide a range of sites and premises to meet the quantitative and qualitative needs of business within the sequential approach of the core spatial strategy, and job growth targets of Policy E2, enabling urban renaissance, economic regeneration, social inclusion and rural diversification.

Where development proposals and issues cross local authority boundaries this approach will be developed and applied across the whole urban or development area.

Efficient use will be made of existing employment land resources. Sites for industry and commerce will be provided in:

- urban areas and key market towns;
- locations that minimise commuting, and promote more sustainable communities, and a closer relationship between jobs and existing *or* proposed labour supply;
- locations where the maximum use of sustainable (public) transport can be made;
- locations and ways that minimise loss or damage to environmental and social capital, and so far as possible substitute for losses and secure positive enhancements. This will often mean giving precedence to the re- use of previously developed land and, wherever possible, the intensification of use on existing sites over the release of greenfield land;
- locations which meet the needs of the region's significant clusters as set out in the Regional Economic Strategy.

Land in employment use will be considered for alternative uses only where a completed employment land assessment demonstrates that sufficient land is available, of an appropriate type, range, quality and quantity, to ensure that the Regional Economic Strategy's objectives are achievable.

Supporting Text

The availability of sites or premises is only one influence on business locations. Other factors, such as the availability and skills of the labour force, supply chain issues, the availability of funding support and housing and lifestyle choices all play a part in making location decisions. The quality of land to meet the needs of business is critical to ensuring success and attracting inward investment. Local development plan documents will ensure that there is a high quality offer of employment land, taking account of the contribution that can be made by strategic and sub-regional employment sites and ability to meet the levels of job growth identified in Policy E2. Phasing and review of policy to accommodate economic potential and demand over the plan period, will also be considered. Allocations can help to promote more sustainable communities directly by redressing an imbalance between the availability of local workers and local jobs (and hence helping to reduce the need to travel) or more indirectly such as town centre office development supporting town centre shops and leisure economy, or through townscape improvements that contribute to perceptions of local quality of life.

Policy E4: Provision of Strategic Employment Sites

Local development plan documents will provide strategic employment sites of the appropriate quality and quantity are required, particularly in the following locations, to meet the needs of business:

Harlow, development linked to the expansion of Stansted, Thames Gateway (linked to the Basildon, Southend-on-Sea and Thurrock Zones of Change), Cambridge Sub-region, Peterborough, Norwich, Ipswich, Great Yarmouth, Harwich and sites in Hertfordshire supporting key clusters and regeneration needs.

Local development plan documents will identify further sites to take account of opportunities in other areas in accordance with the core spatial strategy.

Supporting Text

Research has been carried out on the quality and quantity of sub-regional and strategic sites within the East of England and the categorisation of strategic and sub-regional employment sites (the strategic sites study).

The research highlights the changing role of strategic sites and suggests site- specific criteria against which to assess the market suitability of sites. Within each of the sub-regions, local development plan documents should provide for at least one readily available serviced strategic employment site and two sub-regional employment sites for general employment land use (B Class). Local development plan documents will propose serviced strategic employment sites solely for 'high technology' users in parts of the East of England where there is an identified need to develop significant clusters and sectors, including the Cambridge Sub-region. Where a need is identified, readily available serviced strategic employment sites solely for warehousing and distribution will also be proposed.

Strategic sites are needed for the following reasons:

- Harlow – to achieve regeneration needs, ensure growth in key sectors and clusters, and ensure a balance to housing growth;
- Harlow and Stansted-development linked to the expansion of Stansted;
- Thames Gateway – to support the role of Thurrock as a sustainable European Logistics Hub, to support the role of Basildon as a business hub and strategic centre and to promote sustainable economic regeneration in Southend-on-Sea and its role as a strategic cultural and intellectual centre;
- Cambridge Sub-region – to secure its full potential as a centre for world- class research and development;
- Peterborough – to achieve regeneration, attract business activities and key sectors and clusters including environmental services;
- Norwich – to support regeneration and its role in bio technology; • Ipswich – to support regeneration and its role in ICT as exemplified by Suffolk Innovation Park and Adastral Park;
- Harwich, Great Yarmouth and Felixstowe-development associated with port expansion; and
- Hertfordshire-at locations that support strong, continued growth of mature and emerging clusters and sectors and to support regeneration in the Lee Valley corridor and at Stevenage.

Policy E5: Supporting Economic Diversity and Business Development

Economic diversity and business development will be encouraged to facilitate small and medium enterprises, together with local economic strengths, support the growth of a variety of economic sectors, urban regeneration and growth, and to address rural isolation and rural diversification.

Local development plan documents will assess the requirements of the various sectors of the local economy, including tourism and culture, and formulate policies and proposals to support their sustainable development. Local development plan documents will ensure that sufficient range, quantity and quality of land to meet the needs of business, including the provision of smaller units, is provided and safeguarded for a balanced economy in both urban and rural areas.

Supporting Text

It is important to encourage all aspects of the economy and ensure it is broadly based. This will increase its resilience to external changes and pressures, including geo-political changes to the global economy and the impact of climate change. A balanced economy requires a range of types of employment space in terms of size, location and cost. Tourism and culture are significant elements of the region's economy and are likely to be major growth sectors. In addition to the growth sectors, it is important to retain sectors such as manufacturing which are not expected to provide large-scale additional employment.

Assessing the requirements of the local economy is likely to also involve an assessment of the availability of local labour and potential skills fit with new jobs (refer also to Policy E1).

Policy E6: Information Communications Technology (ICT)

Local authorities and EEDA will work with telecommunication companies and private sector bodies to:

- improve the regional coverage of broadband infrastructure, particularly in rural areas;
- improve the level of service from existing broadband infrastructure; and

- promote the use of information communications technologies by businesses and the public and voluntary sector.

Local development plan documents seek to ensure that acceptable provision can be made for information communications technology, taking into account environmental constraints.

Supporting Text

6.24 Information and communication technology (ICT) is an essential component and feature of a world-class economy and an inclusive society. It can overcome obstacles to access in rural and peripheral areas, enable businesses to participate in e-commerce and operate in a global market, reduce the need to travel through the encouragement of flexible and remote working, encourage flexibility in business location decisions and encourage business start-ups in areas of need of regeneration, deliver training and learning opportunities and promote social inclusion by enabling internet access for all.

6.25 But current access to this technology varies across the East of England with private sector investment in broadband so far focused on the major centres of population. The Government's target is for all communities to have access to broadband by the end of 2005. Local authorities will work with private sector providers to ensure that the benefits of ICT are spread wider.

Policy E7: Supporting Cluster Development

Clusters are an important feature of regional economic growth and prosperity. Local development plan document will support those regionally significantly clusters identified by the East of England Development Agency (EEDA) and locally significant clusters defined by local economic partnerships in collaboration with local authorities and EEDA. Local development plan documents will:

- support the sustainable and dynamic growth of inter-regional and intra- regional business clusters identified by the above process;
- ensure there is sufficient quantity, quality, choice of range of sites including provision for incubator units, grow on

space and larger facilities for established business clusters;

- address the need for accommodation and allocation of sites immediately adjacent to or close to key institutions including higher education and university facilities; and
- address the need for user restrictions to secure land use for specific activities.

Supporting Text

Clusters are defined as 'concentrations of companies in related activities, specialised suppliers, service providers and institutions, which are co- operating, competing and collaborating to build competitive advantage, often across traditional sector boundaries'. Such concentrations often depend on access to specialist skills and infrastructure within a specific area. The Government's competitiveness white paper and the DTI's 'biotechnology clusters' report (DTI August 1999) emphasises that the clustering of businesses operating in the same or complementary sectors can benefit the local, regional and national economy.

The Regional Economic Strategy states that business growth is likely to be concentrated in the key sectors and clusters. Several of these, such as biotechnology and research and development, are based upon the strengths of the Cambridge Sub-region. This will be supported and enhanced and, where possible, harnessed to benefit other parts of the region. For example the interaction between London and Cambridge is stimulating activity in the biotechnology sector at intervening locations, especially along the M11 and A1 corridors. There is potential for economic links to be strengthened between Cambridge and Ipswich and westwards through Bedfordshire to Milton Keynes and Oxford (Oxford to Cambridge Arc). Other opportunities within the region also merit further analysis, for example linking Cambridge to Norwich, Stevenage and Peterborough.

A study of economic sub-regions and clusters in the East of England identifies the land use and other requirements of each of the regionally significant clusters. Cluster development requirements include quality infrastructure, availability of land and premises, access to housing and appropriate social facilities and a suitably qualified labour force. Infrastructure requirements include freedom from of congestion, fast and reliable public transport and broadband communications. In some cases there is a need for specialist property (e.g. laboratory space for bio tech firms), while in others the requirement is related to quantity and location. If a cluster is to flourish, the institutions and resources which underpin it must be protected or supported. This will mean that sites need to be close to research establishments, research hospitals, institutes and campus.

Access to housing is a particular issue in the East of England, and inevitably tends to be more problematic for the lower value support activities within a cluster rather than the high value core.

There are opportunities to develop 'green business' clusters based on environmental industries (for example those specialising in recycling or exchange of materials) that will support the RES and other regional strategies. As an example, the Greater Peterborough sub-region has specific policies to build upon its environmental business sector.

Local development plan documents will consider the opportunity to provide specific guidance for strategic and locally important clusters. Where a key resource is critical to a cluster/ sector reaching its full potential, specific sites will be identified.

There are areas where intense development pressures are focussed on a single location and where capacity and environmental constraints require the selective management of uses. Guidance on high technology clusters and the management of the economy in the Cambridge sub-region is set out in the sub-regions chapter. Local authorities will work together to ensure that existing businesses or new investment displaced by this policy are assisted to find alternative suitable sites within the region.

Policy E8: Simplified Planning Zones

Local development plan documents may propose simplified planning zones where such proposals will complement the regional or sub-regional economic strategy, particularly to assist areas for regeneration by means of an accelerated rate of inward investment, and support regionally or subregionally important clusters and sectors while protecting local environmental, heritage and cultural interests from adverse development impacts.

Supporting Text

Simplified planning zones (SPZ), if adopted through statute, should be of high quality and should be of low environmental impact, and will set the parameters of development tightly to ensure that high quality environments are created. This is not only for the protection of those in the vicinity of the new SPZs but to enable companies operating within the zones to be guaranteed that they will have good neighbours. An environmental impact assessment will be required before a SPZ can be designated. SPZs offer a speedier development control process whilst maintaining sufficient overall control to provide necessary security for potential investors.

Policy E9: Regional Structure of Retail Centres

The regional structure of retail centres is:

- major regional centres: Basildon, Cambridge, Colchester, Chelmsford, Ipswich, Norwich, Peterborough, Southend, and Watford;
- regional centres: Bedford, Bury St. Edmunds, Great Yarmouth, Harlow, Hemel Hempstead, King's Lynn, Lowestoft, Luton, St Albans, Stevenage and Welwyn Garden City;
- other towns and market towns. Local development plan documents will define the towns and market towns that comprise the structure of main retail centres within their area; and
- villages and local centres. Local development plan documents will define the villages and local centres that complete the structure of retail provision within their area.

Supporting Text

The retail sector is an important driver of the regional economy. Policy SS4 'town centres' in the core spatial strategy chapter sets the wider context for town centres, whilst Policy E10 considers the role of retail centres (not all of which are located in town centres) based on a national ranking of retail centres. The East of England has an established structure of retail centres ranging from major regional centres to smaller market towns and villages, all of which play a key role in meeting the needs of their catchment areas. In the north of the Region retail centres tend to be more widely dispersed with relatively discrete catchments, while in the south the larger centres are closer with more complex, overlapping catchments. The south of the Region is also more strongly influenced by London.

The region is not dominated by any one retail centre although Thurrock Lakeside has the largest concentration of retail floorspace. Lakeside is not listed in Policy E9; it is a regional out of town retail centre and does not have the range of functions of a town centre.

For retail, leisure and some other services the East of England competes with surrounding national centres, particularly in London, but also with Milton Keynes, the Bluewater shopping centre and, to a more limited degree, Nottingham and Leicester in the East Midlands. During the plan period Milton Keynes is likely to continue to grow in significance and town centres in Bedfordshire will need to respond to this impact by raising and upgrading their offer.

Policy E10: Retail Strategy

In accordance with the regional structure in Policy E9:

- new retail development will be located in existing centres and will be consistent in scale with the size and character of the centre and its role in the regional structure;
- local development plan documents will propose higher order provision only where a need is clearly established, it would result in a more sustainable pattern of development and movement, including a reduction in the need to travel, there would be no significant detrimental impact on other centres or the transport network, and there is environmental capacity. Any new regional centres will be subject to similar considerations, and will be brought forward only as part of a review of this RSS;

- in the Sustainable Communities Plan Growth Areas, local development plan documents will propose development of retail and services in new and existing centres in accordance with sub-regional strategies and policies; and
- local development plan documents will consider the role of retail within Priority Areas for Regeneration and propose development and enhancement to implement regeneration strategies.

Supporting Text

Research undertaken within the region did not identify any need for major change to the retail structure to meet existing need. However, where there is significant growth within the region's Sustainable Community Plan Growth Areas and Priority Areas for Regeneration retail growth will be essential to meet new needs. The advancement of Harlow to the status of a sub-regional centre will be sought, while expansion of Stevenage's retail and services offer should also be sought in association with its regeneration. EERA and local authorities need to plan more positively for retail in order to:

- maintain and enhance the viability and vitality of retail centres; and
- make proper provision for new forms of retail distribution.

All local development plan documents will address retail needs and present an analysis of their area designed to produce a coherent retail strategy in relation to their existing town centres, edge-of-town centre and out-of-town centre retail sites, and E-tailing growth. These strategies should be prepared from robust data and analysis and make provision for new retail development whilst ensuring the viability and vitality of existing centres.

Generally new development needs to be of a scale appropriate for the centre to promote internal competition and linked trips and to ensure consistency with transport networks.

Retail centres should aim to support and enhance their existing functions and absorb expenditure growth through higher quality development without changing the centre's position in the regional structure. However, major retail development can be a driver of growth and regeneration, so in the Sustainable Communities Plan Growth Areas and the regional growth areas significant planned retail and associated services growth will be needed to deliver sustainable communities. The implications of this growth will need to be carefully considered at the sub-regional level and planned for through the development plan process.

Policy E11: Retail Distribution

Strategic retail distribution centres will only be permitted in locations with good rail and road access and, where available, waterway access. Local development plan documents will consider the needs of distribution arising from increased use of internet retailing and will implement policies to ensure that development is in accordance with the sequential test, and with good public transport, rail and road access.

Local development plan documents will consider how development supporting the local sourcing of products can be encouraged.

Supporting Text

There is potential for radical change in retail technology in the plan period as evidenced by increased use of internet retailing. The key impact of this is likely to be on the need for distribution centres and on existing town centre retailing functions. Policy needs to provide for strategic development in sustainable locations and to focus new development on existing town centres wherever possible in accordance with the sequential test.

The local sourcing of products can help to reduce 'food-miles' or distance travelled by products. Whilst it is recognised that in many cases local availability is not feasible, local development plan documents should consider how this can be encouraged for those products that are.

Policy E12: Out- of-town Retail

It is considered that there is no need for any additional regional out-of-town shopping centres in the plan period.

Local development plan documents will define the current and future role of existing out of town centre retail sites in relation to existing town centres, in particular to determine whether:

- out-of-town centre sites should remain purely retail centres; or
- they should be developed into town centres with a full range of service provision.

Out-of-town centres will only be developed into town centres where it will:

- improve social, environmental and economic sustainability; and
- deliver improved sustainable transport accessibility, particularly improved public transport access.

Supporting Text

There are some significant out of town centre retail sites within the East of England most notably Thurrock Lakeside, but also the Brookfield Centre in Broxbourne, Hatfield Gallerias, and London Colney. Local development plan documents will set policy for such centres, to indicate the role they should fulfil within the retail structure.

Policy E13: Tourism

Local planning authorities, in liaison with the East of England Tourist Board, will ensure that local development plan documents:

- include policies to encourage investment in the maintenance, improvement and appropriate diversification of the region's tourist industry. This investment should be based on maximising the benefits to, and minimising negative effects on, the natural and built environment, local distinctiveness and host communities;
- integrate with the range of tools in use for managing tourism, particularly local and regional tourism strategies and visitor management plans, and secure policy compatibility with neighbouring authorities. In drafting locational policies authorities must recognise that some forms of tourism development are not footloose;

- promote development that encourages more sustainable tourism including: the coordination of activities and accommodation to minimise the need to travel; enhancing existing facilities and/or re-using existing buildings; the regeneration of seaside resorts; extending employment outside the normal tourist season; regeneration (rural and urban); or urban renaissance; and
- encourage new development where it would add to the tourist product being offered, attract additional visitors and be based on realistic projections of demand.

Supporting Text

Tourism is one of the East of England's key economic sectors and, with leisure and heritage, is projected to make among the highest contributions to absolute increase in the Region's Gross Domestic Product. A Regional Tourism Strategy is in preparation and will assist the preparation of local development plan documents and development proposals.

Careful management and sustainable development of tourism can create opportunities to boost local economies, enhance the natural and built environment and contribute to the social well-being of an area. Tourism can be a catalyst to stimulate investment, revitalise deprived areas and encourage growth in other employment sectors. Particular attention should be given to tourism development in environmentally sensitive areas, e.g. Areas of Outstanding Natural Beauty (AONBs), Sites of Special Scientific Interest (SSSIs) and conservation sites.

These may include some 'honeypot' tourist areas. Such areas often attract large numbers of visitors due to their unique appeal as visitor destinations and it is important that these qualities are protected for future generations to enjoy. Significant growth in visitor numbers in such areas can have lasting effects on the natural and historic environment and it is in the interests of tourism developers to conserve the environment upon which they rely.

This can be particularly important in locations such as the Heritage Coast and the Broads. Measures to disperse visitors away from sensitive tourist hotspots to areas that have the capacity to cope with larger visitor numbers can often be used as an effective tool for sustainable visitor management. It is also important to consider the impact of tourism on areas that do not have the capacity or suitable infrastructure to accommodate large numbers of visitors such as some popular historic towns and villages and coastal resorts. Effective visitor management strategies are crucial to their sustainability.

Tourism has traditionally been focused on a limited season leading to potential for excessive pressures on the environment, host communities and seasonal employment. Reducing seasonality through the development of off- peak tourism can help to provide year-round employment, provide businesses with an incentive for retaining staff and spread visitor numbers.

Improved facilities to cope with increased visitor numbers at existing highly utilised tourist sites, concentration of visitors in special areas to make better use of visitor management resources and enhancing host community relationships should be encouraged. Proposals for strategic tourism facilities will need to comply with the requirements of Policy C2.

Tourism development can contribute to finding new uses for existing buildings whether in rural or urban locations, and so can help stimulate regeneration and investment. Sensitive adaptation of historic or locally distinctive buildings can capitalise on the region's unique qualities. Although new development is required to extend the tourism infrastructure, priority should also be given to investment by existing businesses to ensure that the quality of tourism products is maintained.

Regional flagship tourism projects have the potential to both boost the profile of the region in terms of attracting new visitors and to stimulate further growth and investment in tourism and related sectors. Thorough commercial assessments should be required for such projects, particularly where projects are dependent on public grant aid.

A sustainable approach to tourism development needs to reflect not only the physical impact of tourism on an area but also its potential economic and social value. Integration of tourism planning policies is vital between neighbouring authorities as destination areas and visitor movements rarely follow administrative boundaries.

The East of England Tourist Board (EETB) identifies five key principles of development: Partnership, Quality, Sustainability, Competitiveness and Accessibility and Inclusion. It is important to ensure that new tourism development meets the broad objectives of EETB along with the specific requirements of strategic and local planning policies. Effective tourism development should not focus solely on destinations but should exploit opportunities from a range of tourism initiatives, including events, specialist activities, food and drink, shopping, leisure and recreation, not necessarily linked to places of interest.

Policy E14 Regional Airports

Airports have an important and strategic role as drivers in the regional economy and local economy as well as having significant potential to contribute to meeting regeneration needs. Airport growth is supported to the maximum capacity of the existing runways in the case of Luton and Stansted and modest expansion to meet local market demand in the case of Norwich and Southend.

It is vital that the future growth of airports in the region achieves an acceptable balance between economic, employment and other benefits and environmental and other considerations. The support of the Regional Assembly for appropriate growth at each regional airport is subject to:

- a surface access strategy for each airport being prepared, agreed and implemented;
- effective and timely implementation of other necessary infrastructure requirements;
- safeguarding of the amenity, character and appearance of the environment and communities in proximity to and affected by airport operations;
- minimising noise and air pollution. Levels must be monitored against national and local targets. Energy and resource conservation measures need to be introduced as appropriate to achieve pollution reduction;
- ensuring best practice in air and ground safety provision;
- airport development not leading to consequential pressures to exceed levels of planned growth,

infrastructure and service provision beyond that provided for in local development plan documents; and

- the completion and regular review by airport operators of their airport master plans (5 yearly) and review no less frequently of their operating procedures.

Supporting Text

Studies of Stansted and Luton Airports have highlighted the important role that airports perform in their local and in the regional economy. They provide a range of employment opportunities with a significant proportion of jobs that do not rely on high skill and educational attainment levels and can attract firms that value proximity to airport services. Airports can provide a useful catalyst for economic regeneration, which is likely to be a positive outcome for local communities resulting from the growth of Luton, Norwich and Southend Airports. Local planning authorities will need to make appropriate provision to meet the employment needs of airports operating in their area or nearby.

Airports give rise to serious environmental impacts on surrounding areas and overall increases in air transport usage contribute to global warming. EERA has weighed economic and employment benefits with environmental and other consequences and, in consequence, supports growth at Stansted and Luton Airports being restricted to the existing runways as built (2160 metres long in the case of Luton). It also supports modest expansion of Norwich and Southend airports to meet local market demand.

Airport operators are required to update or prepare master plans for their airports by 2005, to review these five yearly thereafter, and to engage the local community in their preparation. They will be a valuable informative for local development plan documents.

This policy lists areas that require special consideration by airport operators. These need to be addressed satisfactorily if airport growth is to occur without undue adverse consequences for the local and wider community.

Transport choice and adequate provision are essential to airport growth and to minimising congestion and related problems for local communities so a surface access strategy will need to be prepared by each airport operator, agreed by the relevant local planning and highway authority(ies) and implemented within an agreed timescale. Progress will need to be monitored and reviewed. The strategy will include proposed measures to achieve a progressive increase in the proportion of employees and passengers travelling to an airport by modes other than the car and to minimise congestion, particularly at peak times. The strategy will also need to cover car parking both on and off airport and its management.

It is imperative that airport operators ensure adequate and timely provision of all essential infrastructure in advance of need, in particular the implementation of key items of infrastructure, including enhanced public transport service provision, by key date(s) including schemes listed in the Regional Transportation Strategy and/or as required by local development plan documents.

A major objective of strategic planning policy is safeguarding the amenity, character and appearance of the environment and communities in proximity to and affected by airport operations. This includes minimising noise and air pollution. Both day and night noise cause concern but night noise is particularly problematic. Levels must be monitored against national and local targets with energy and resource conservation measures introduced whenever appropriate. At all times best practicable means should be used to achieve pollution reduction.

3

Trends in Medical Hospitality

Medical tourism (also called medical travel, health tourism or global healthcare) is a term initially coined by travel agencies and the mass media to describe the rapidly-growing practice of travelling across international borders to obtain health care. It also refers pejoratively to the practice of healthcare providers travelling internationally to deliver healthcare.

Services typically sought by travellers include elective procedures as well as complex specialized surgeries such as joint replacement (knee/hip), cardiac surgery, dental surgery, and cosmetic surgeries. However, virtually every type of health care, including psychiatry, alternative treatments, convalescent care and even burial services are available. As a practical matter, providers and customers commonly use informal channels of communication-connection-contract, and in such cases this tends to mean less regulatory or legal oversight to assure quality and less formal recourse to reimbursement or redress, if needed.

Over 50 countries have identified medical tourism as a national industry. However, accreditation and other measures of quality vary widely across the globe, and there are risks and ethical issues that make this method of accessing medical care controversial. Also, some destinations may become hazardous or even dangerous for medical tourists to contemplate.

In the context of global health, "medical tourism" is a pejorative because during such trips health care providers often practice outside of their areas of expertise or hold different standards of care. Greater numbers than ever before of student volunteers, health professions trainees, and researchers from resource-rich countries are working temporarily and anticipating future work in resource-starved areas. This emphasizes the importance of understanding this other definition.

History

The concept of medical tourism is not a new one. The first recorded instance of medical tourism dates back thousands of years to when Greek pilgrims travelled from all over the Mediterranean to the small territory in the Saronic Gulf called Epidauria. This territory was the sanctuary of the healing god Asklepios. Epidauria became the original travel destination for medical tourism.

Spa towns and sanitariums may be considered an early form of medical tourism. In eighteenth century England, for example, patients visited spas because they were places with supposedly health-giving mineral waters, treating diseases from gout to liver disorders and bronchitis.

Description

Factors that have led to the increasing popularity of medical travel include the high cost of health care, long wait times for certain procedures, the ease and affordability of international travel, and improvements in both technology and standards of care in many countries.

Medical tourists can come from anywhere in the First World, including Europe, the Middle East, Japan, the United States, and Canada. This is because of their large populations, comparatively high wealth, the high expense of health care or lack of health care options locally, and increasingly high expectations of their populations with respect to health care. An authority at the Harvard Business School recently stated that "medical tourism is promoted much more heavily in the United Kingdom than in the United States".

A forecast by Deloitte Consulting published in August 2008 projected that medical tourism originating in the US could jump by a factor of ten over the next decade. An estimated 750,000 Americans went abroad for health care in 2007, and the report estimated that a million and a half would seek health care outside the US in 2008. The growth in medical tourism has the potential to cost US health care providers billions of dollars in lost revenue.

A large draw to medical travel is convenience and speed. Countries that operate public healthcare systems are often so taxed that it can take considerable time to get non-urgent medical care. Using Canada as an example, an estimated 782,936 Canadians spent time on medical waiting lists in 2005, waiting an average of 9.4 weeks. Canada has set waiting-time benchmarks, e.g. 26 weeks for a hip replacement and 16 weeks for cataract surgery, for non-urgent medical procedures.

Additionally, patients are finding that insurance either does not cover orthopedic surgery (such as knee/hip replacement) or imposes unreasonable restrictions on the choice of the facility, surgeon, or prosthetics to be used. Medical tourism for knee/hip replacements has emerged as one of the more widely accepted procedures because of the lower cost and minimal difficulties associated with the travelling to/from the surgery. Colombia provides a knee replacement for about $5,000 USD, including all associated fees, such as FDA-approved prosthetics and hospital stay-over expenses. However, many clinics quote prices that are not all inclusive and include only the surgeon fees associated with the procedure.

According to an article by the University of Delaware publication, U Daily:

> *"The cost of surgery in India, Thailand or South Africa can be one-tenth of what it is in the United States or Western Europe, and sometimes even less. A heart-valve replacement that would cost $200,000 or more in the US, for example, goes for $10,000 in India—and that includes round-trip airfare and a brief vacation package. Similarly, a metal-free dental bridge worth $5,500 in the US costs $500 in India, a knee replacement in Thailand with six days of physical therapy costs about one-fifth of what it would in the States, and Lasik eye surgery worth $3,700 in the US is available in many other countries for only $730. Cosmetic surgery savings are even greater: A full facelift that would cost $20,000 in the US runs about $1,250 in South Africa.*

Popular medical travel worldwide destinations include: Argentina, Brunei, Cuba, Colombia, Costa Rica, Hong Kong, Hungary, India, Jordan, Lithuania, Malaysia, The Philippines,

Singapore, South Africa, Thailand, and recently, Saudi Arabia, UAE, South Korea, Tunisia and New Zealand.

Popular cosmetic surgery travel destinations include: Argentina, Bolivia, Brazil, Colombia, Costa Rica, Cuba, Mexico and Turkey. In South America, countries such as Argentina, Bolivia, Brazil and Colombia lead on plastic surgery medical skills relying on their experienced plastic surgeons. In Bolivia and Colombia, plastic surgery has also become quite common. According to the "Sociedad Boliviana de Cirugia Plastica Reconstructiva", more than 70% of middle and upper class women in the country have had some form of plastic surgery. Colombia also provides advanced care in cardiovascular and transplant surgery.

In Europe Belgium, Poland and Slovakia are also breaking into the business. South Africa is taking the term "medical tourism" very literally by promoting their "medical safaris".

A specialized subset of medical tourism is reproductive tourism and reproductive outsourcing, which is the practice of travelling abroad to undergo in-vitro fertilization, surrogate pregnancy and other assisted reproductive technology treatments including freezing embryos for retro-production.

However, perceptions of medical tourism are not always positive. In places like the US, which has high standards of quality, medical tourism is viewed as risky. In some parts of the world, wider political issues can influence where medical tourists will choose to seek out health care.

Health tourism providers have developed as intermediaries to unite potential medical tourists with provider hospitals and other organisations. Companies are beginning to offer global health care options that will enable North American and European patients to access world health care at a fraction of the cost of domestic care. Companies that focus on medical value travel typically provide nurse case managers to assist patients with pre- and post-travel medical issues. They also help provide resources for follow-up care upon the patient's return.

Process

The typical process is as follows: the person seeking medical treatment abroad contacts a medical tourism provider. The provider usually requires the patient to provide a medical report, including the nature of ailment, local doctor's opinion, medical history, and diagnosis, and may request additional information. Certified medical doctors or consultants then advise on the medical treatment. The approximate expenditure, choice of hospitals and tourist destinations, and duration of stay, etc., is discussed.

After signing consent bonds and agreements, the patient is given recommendation letters for a medical visa, to be procured from the concerned embassy. The patient travels to the destination country, where the medical tourism provider assigns a case executive, who takes care of the patient's accommodation, treatment and any other form of care. Once the treatment is done, the patient can remain in the tourist destination or return home.

International Healthcare Accreditation

Because standards are important when it comes to health care, there are parallel issues around medical tourism, international healthcare accreditation, evidence-based medicine and quality assurance. In the United States, the best known accreditation group is the Joint Commission International (JCI). They have been inspecting and accrediting health care facilities and hospitals outside of the United States since 1999. Many international hospitals today see obtaining JCI accreditation as a way to attract American patients.

Joint Commission International is a relative of the Joint Commission in the United States. Both are independent private sector not-for-profit organizations that develop nationally and internationally recognized procedures and standards to help improve patient care and safety. They work with hospitals to help them meet Joint Commission standards for patient care and then accredit those hospitals meeting the standards. In the UK and Hong Kong, the Trent International Accreditation Scheme is a key player. The different international healthcare accreditation schemes vary in quality, size, cost, intent and the skill and intensity of their marketing. They also vary in terms of cost to hospitals and healthcare institutions making use of them. A forecast by Deloitte Consulting regarding medical tourism published in August 2008 noted the value of accreditation in ensuring quality of healthcare and specifically mentioned JCI, ISQUA and Trent.

Increasingly, some hospitals are looking towards dual international accreditation, perhaps having both JCI to cover potential US clientele and Trent for potential British and European clientele. As a result of competition between clinics for American medical tourists, there have been initiatives to rank hospitals based on patient-reported metrics. Other organizations providing contributions to quality practices include:

- The Society for International Healthcare Accreditation (SOFIHA), a free-to-join group providing a forum for discussion and for the sharing of ideas and good practice by providers of international healthcare accreditation and users of the same. The primary role of this organisation is to promote a safe hospital environment for patients.
- Healthcare Tourism International, the first US-based non-profit to accredit the non-clinical aspects of health tourism, such as language issues, business practices, and false or misleading advertising prevention. The group provides accreditation for all major groups involved in the health tourism industry including hotels, recovery facilities, and medical tourism booking agencies.
- The United Kingdom Accreditation Forum (UKAF) is an established network of accreditation organisations with the intention of sharing experience good practice and new ideas around the methodology for accreditation programmes, covering issues such as developing healthcare quality standards, implementation of standards within healthcare organisations, assessment by peer review and exploration of the peer review techniques to include the recruitment, training, monitoring and evaluation of peer reviewers and the mechanisms for awards of accredited status to organisations.
- The International Medical Travel Association, (IMTA, based in Singapore), is a non-profit association formed to help address quality standards, liability issues, continuity of care, and other issues.

Risks

Medical tourism carries some risks that locally-provided medical care does not. Some countries, such as India, Malaysia, or Thailand have very different infectious disease-related epidemiology to Europe and North America. Exposure to diseases without having built up natural immunity can be a hazard for weakened individuals, specifically with respect to gastrointestinal diseases (e.g. Hepatitis A, amoebic dysentery, paratyphoid) which could weaken progress, mosquito-transmitted diseases, influenza, and tuberculosis. However, because in poor tropical nations diseases run the gamut, doctors seem to be more open to the possibility of considering any infectious disease, including HIV, TB, and typhoid, while there are cases in the West where patients were consistently misdiagnosed for years because such diseases are perceived to be "rare" in the West.

The quality of post-operative care can also vary dramatically, depending on the hospital and country, and may be different from US or European standards. However, JCI and Trent fulfil the role of accreditation by assessing the standards in the healthcare in the countries like India, China and Thailand. Also, travelling long distances soon after surgery can increase the risk of complications. Long flights and decreased mobility in a cramped airline cabin are a known risk factor for developing blood clots in the legs such as venous thrombosis or pulmonary embolus economy class syndrome. Other vacation activities can be problematic as well — for example, scars may become darker and more noticeable if they sunburn while healing. To minimise these problems, medical tourism patients often combine their medical trips with vacation time set aside for rest and recovery in the destination country.

Also, health facilities treating medical tourists may lack an adequate complaints policy to deal appropriately and fairly with complaints made by dissatisfied patients.

Differences in healthcare provider standards around the world have been recognised by the World Health Organization, and in 2004 it launched the World Alliance for Patient Safety. This body assists hospitals and government around the world in setting patient safety policy and practices that can become particularly relevant when providing medical tourism services.

Legal Issues

Receiving medical care abroad may subject medical tourists to unfamiliar legal issues. The limited nature of litigation in various countries is one reason for the lower cost of care overseas. While some countries currently presenting themselves as attractive medical tourism destinations provide some form of legal remedies for medical malpractice, these legal avenues may be unappealing to the medical tourist. Should problems arise, patients might not be covered by adequate personal insurance or might be unable to seek compensation via malpractice lawsuits. Hospitals and/or doctors in some countries may be unable to pay the financial damages awarded by a court to a patient who has sued them, owing to the hospital and/or the doctor not possessing appropriate insurance cover and/or medical indemnity.

Ethical Issues

There can be major ethical issues around medical tourism. For example, the illegal purchase of organs and tissues for transplantation has been alleged in countries such as India and China prior to 2007.

Medical tourism may raise broader ethical issues for the countries in which it is promoted. For example in India, some argue that a "policy of 'medical tourism for the classes and health missions for the masses' will lead to a deepening of the inequities" already embedded in the health care system. In Thailand, in 2008 it was stated that, "Doctors in Thailand have become so busy with foreigners that Thai patients are having trouble getting care". Medical tourism centred on new technologies, such as stem cell treatments, is often criticized on grounds of fraud, blatant lack of scientific rationale and patient safety. However, when pioneering advanced technologies, such as providing 'unproven' therapies to patients outside of regular clinical trials, it is often challenging to differentiate between acceptable medical innovation and unacceptable patient exploitation.

Medical Tourism Poised for Growth in Middle East

The Middle East has a number of advantages that make it well positioned to emerge as a leader in the medical tourism sector, but it needs to do more to change perceptions about the quality of care that is offered in the region, according to an expert in the industry.

Unlike other tourism sectors, medical tourism has grown during the economic downturn as countries around the world have struggled to control health care costs and ensure medical procedures are available when needed, said Dr. Prem Jagyasi, a medical tourism consultant and CEO of ExHealth in Dubai Healthcare City.

'Healthcare in the developed world is in serious crisis, and each country has a different problem,' he noted. 'For example, in the US, there are 50 million people uninsured, 250 million underinsured, and 150 million without dental insurance. So if they need medical services they cannot go to the local hospital because of the high cost.'

But cost is just one of just several factors driving growth in the industry. In countries such as Canada and the UK, a major complaint is not the price but the wait times for many elective procedures. 'In some cases you need to wait three-to-six months for a surgical procedure, and sometimes even a consultation takes two-to-three months,' he noted.

Another key driver is the availability of certain medical procedures, which is a problem in underdeveloped countries and some Middle East states.

These factors have helped boost the value of the medical tourism industry to about $50bn a year, with over 50 countries actively seeking a slice of the pie.

Growth Opportunity

The rise of medical tourism provides an opportunity for the Middle East, which so far has made few inroads in the sector. 'Until a few years ago, a top priority for medical providers around the world was to attract medical tourists from the Middle East,' Jagyasi told AME Info.com. 'Now the trend has reversed as the Middle East is seeking to attract medical tourists from places such as the US and Europe where the cost of health care and delays in getting treatment have risen sharply.'

Around 20% of people in the UAE used to visit the US prior to 9/11 for medical treatment, but now that has decreased to less than 5%, he noted. Instead, locals from the UAE and other countries in the region are going to Singapore, India, and Malaysia for medical procedures.

Many hospitals in these countries have received international accreditation, which gives tourists some assurance that these facilities are high quality. 'This is lacking in the Middle East,' he noted.

The lack of trust in the quality of care in the Gulf is evidenced by the fact that large numbers of locals travel outside the region for medical services, including simple check-ups.

Key Considerations

However, the Middle East still has a good opportunity to capture a larger slice of the international market, but to do so it needs to recognize the most critical factors that medical tourists consider in choosing a medical tourism destination, Jagyasi said. The first is the quality of care offered at the destination, and the Middle East is making headway in this area through its development of GCC-wide medical accreditation standards.

The second is the perception of the destination, including safety or quality of facilities and infrastructure. In this regard the GCC is also making strides through its investment in its medical facilities, while crime the region is perceived to be relatively low.

The final consideration is whether the destination offers leisure or cultural attractions, as medical tourists will often combine medical and leisure tourism. Again, the Middle East can compete in this category with its rich cultural heritage and high-quality resorts.

Looking ahead, the Middle East should initially focus on capturing medical tourists from within the region, which is a huge market and perhaps the easiest to attract because of the shared cultural beliefs, Jagyasi said.

The region also must establish legal protections and guidelines, which are lacking at present and could create problems down the road as more medical tourists arrive from places like the US and Europe where patients' rights are taken for granted.

With this in mind, another major priority must be to develop a board of key stakeholders from within and outside of the healthcare industry to establish common standards and promote the medical tourism industry in the region, Jagyasi added.

Employer-sponsored Health Care in the US

Some US employers have begun exploring medical travel programs as a way to cut employee health care costs. Such proposals have raised stormy debates between employers and trade unions representing workers, with one union stating that it deplored the "shocking new approach" of offering employees overseas treatment in return for a share of the company's savings. The unions also raise the issues of legal liability should something go wrong, and potential job losses in the US health care industry if treatment is outsourced.

Employers may offer incentives such as paying for air travel and waiving out-of-pocket expenses for care outside of the US. For example, in January 2008, Hannaford Bros., a supermarket chain based in Maine, began paying the entire medical bill for employees to travel to Singapore for hip and knee replacements, including travel for the patient and companion. Medical travel packages can integrate with all types of health insurance, including limited benefit plans, preferred provider organizations and high deductible health plans. Insurers are beginning to establish partnerships with overseas health providers to treat their insureds as well. A 2008 article in *Fast Company* discusses the globalization of healthcare and describes how various players in the US healthcare market have begun to explore it.

Subfields

Dental involves individuals seeking dental care outside of their local healthcare systems.

Fertility

Fertility tourism is the practice of travelling to another country for fertility treatments. The main reasons for fertility tourism are legal regulation of the sought procedure in the home country, or lower price. In-vitro fertilization, donor insemination and surrogacy are major procedures involved.

Destinations in Africa and Middle East

Countries in this region involved in medical tourism include Saudi Arabia, South Africa, and Tunisia.

Israel

Israel is emerging as a popular destination for medical tourists. In 2006, 15,000 foreigners travelled to the country for medical procedures, bringing in $40 million of revenue. Medical tourists choose Israel for several reasons. Some come from European nations such as Romania where certain procedures are not available.

Others come to Israel, perhaps most commonly from the US, because they can receive quality health care at a fraction of the cost it would be at home, for both surgeries and in-vitro fertilization treatments. Other medical tourists come to Israel to visit the Dead Sea, a world-famous therapeutic resort. The Israel Ministry of Tourism and several professional medical services providers have set out to generate awareness of Israel's medical capabilities.

Jordan

Jordan is an emerging medical tourism destination, with related revenues exceeding one billion dollars in 2007. More than 250,000 patients from other countries sought treatment in Jordan that year. This included an estimated 45,000 Iraqis and approximately 25,000 patients each from Palestine and Sudan. An estimated 1,800 US citizens, 1,200 UK citizens, and 400 Canadians also sought treatment in Jordan that year. Treatment costs can be as low as 25 percent of costs in the US. The kingdom was rated as number one in the region and fifth in the world as a medical tourism hub in a study by the World Bank.

UAE

Hospitals in Dubai and other emirates have expressed an intent to develop in medical tourism. Some have American-sourced international healthcare accreditation, while others are looking towards the UK, Australia and Canada for accreditation services.

The Americas

Countries in the Americas that are treating foreign patients include Argentina, Bolivia, Brazil, Colombia, Costa Rica, Cuba, Dominican Republic, Guatemala, Mexico, Panama, Peru and Uruguay.

Brazil

Brazil has long been known as a destination for cosmetic surgery. For non-cosmetic procedures, Brazil is only now entering the global market. However, Albert Einstein Jewish Hospital in Sao Paulo was the first JCI-accredited facility outside of the US, and more than a dozen Brazilian medical facilities have since been similarly accredited. Brazil requires visas for US citizens based on a reciprocal arrangement since Brazilians are required to obtain a visa to visit the US.

Canada

Canada has entered the medical tourism field. In comparison to US health costs, medical tourism patients can save 30 to 60 percent on health costs in Canada. Canada's quality of healthcare is cited by the World Health Organization as equal to if not better than that of the US in most categories.

Cuba

Cuba has been a popular medical tourism destination for more than 40 years. Thousands of patients travel to Cuba, particularly from Latin America and Europe, attracted by the "fine reputation of Cuban doctors, the low prices and nearby beaches on which to recuperate." In 2006, Cuba attracted nearly 20,000 health tourists. Medical treatments included joint replacement, cancer treatment, eye surgery, cosmetic surgery and addictions rehabilitation. Costs are about 60 to 80 percent less than US costs.

Cuba has hospitals for Cuban residents and others that focus on serving foreigners and diplomats. In the 2007 American documentary film, *Sicko,* which criticizes the US healthcare system, producer Michael Moore leads a group of uninsured American patients to Cuba to obtain more affordable medical treatment. *Sicko* has greatly increased foreigners' interest in Cuban healthcare. A recent Miami Herald story focused on the high quality of health care that Canadian and American medical tourism patients receive in Cuba.

The Cuban government has developed Cuban medical tourism to generate income for the country. Residents of Canada, the UK and most other countries can travel to Cuba without any difficulty a tourist visa is generally required. For Americans, however, because of the US trade policy towards Cuba, travellers must either obtain US government approval, or, more frequently, travel to Cuba from Canada, Mexico, the Bahamas, Jamaica or the Dominican Republic. Cuban immigration authorities do not stamp the passports of US visitors so that Americans can keep their travels a private matter. To date no Cuban facility has achieved JCI Accreditation.

Mexico

Americans, particularly those living near the Mexican border, now routinely cross to Mexico for medical care. Popular specialities include dentistry and plastic surgery. Mexican dentists often charge one-fifth to one-fourth of US prices, while other procedures typically cost a third what they would in the US.

This trend has alarmed American healthcare providers who, fearing a loss of business, warn patients away from Mexico. "The phenomenon has unsettled US-based dentists who tell horror stories of rampant infections, undetected cases of oral cancer and shoddy work south of the border", claims hotly disputed by Mexican dentists. "In Texas, legislators explored the possibility of allowing health maintenance organizations to operate on both sides of the border. However, physicians in south Texas lobbied against the changes, arguing that local doctors could not compete with the lower costs in Mexico". US doctors point out that the Mexican legal system makes it almost impossible to sue Mexican doctors for malpractice. However, many who travel to Mexico for care report that they are satisfied. According to a report commissioned by Families U.S.A., a Washington advocacy group for healthcare issues, "About 90 percent the care they had received in Mexico had been good or excellent. About 80 percent rated the care they had received in the United States as good or excellent".

Indeed "some U.S. dentists... have conceded to the competition and begun a 'reverse migration' opening offices in Mexico to take advantage of lower costs". More American insurers are providing coverage for travellers, as the out-of-pocket costs to them are much lower. "With healthcare costs in the United States continuing to rise, many employers in Southern California are turning to insurance plans that send their workers to Mexico for routine care, plans that are growing by nearly 3,000 people a year."

In addition to dental and plastic surgery, Mexican hospitals are popular for bariatric surgery for weight loss, considered an elective procedure that is not covered by some US insurers. A popular bariatric procedure, lap band surgery, which was approved by the FDA in the US in 2001, has been performed for longer by Mexican surgeons.

Panama

In Panama, health and medical tourism is growing rapidly. Factors drawing medical tourists include Panama's tourist appeal, position as a hub for international travel, and use of the American dollar as the official currency. Many of Panama's doctors are bilingual, board certified, and accustomed to working with the same medical equipment and technology used in the United States and Europe. On most procedures, Panama offers savings of more than 50% compared to the US and Europe. No Panamanian hospitals currently have international healthcare accreditation, whether through US, British, Australian or Canadian sources.

United States

Although much attention has been given to the growing trend of uninsured Americans travelling to foreign countries, a report from 2008 found that a plurality of an estimated 60,000 to 85,000 medical tourists were travelling to the United States for the purpose of receiving in-patient medical care. The availability of advanced medical technology and sophisticated training of physicians are cited as driving motivators for growth in foreigners travelling to the U.S. for medical care. Also, it has been noted that the decline in value of the U.S. dollar is offering additional incentive for foreign travel to the U.S. However, costs differences between the US and many locations in Asia far outweigh any currency fluctuations. Several major medical centres and teaching hospitals offer international patient centres that cater to patients from foreign countries who seek medical treatment in the U.S. Many of these organizations offer service coordinators to assist international patients with arrangements for medical care, accommodations, finances and transportation including air ambulance services. It should be noted that many locations in the US that offer medical care comparable in price to foreign medi . l facilities are not Joint Commission Accredited.

Uruguay

Uruguay recently entered the medical tourism market. A private medical tourism initiative, Uruhealth, has been created with support from the Ministries of Tourism and Public Health. The initiative involves the infrastructure, human resources and experience of two healthcare companies: MP Personalized Medicine (Montevideo) and SEMM-Mautone Hospital.

Asia/Pacific

Many Asian Pacific countries are medical tourism destinations.

China

China is fast emerging as a desirable destination for individuals seeking medical care in a wide range of medical specialities, including cardiology, neurology, orthopedics and others. A number of private and government hospitals in major cities have established international departments. Many leading hospitals provide treatments integrating Traditional Chinese Medicine with Western medical technology and techniques. China is home to leading stem cell research and treatment hospitals that offer Westerners who want to take advantage of stem cell treatments that are still considered experimental or have yet to be approved in their home country..

Hong Kong

As of 2006, Hong Kong had 12 private hospitals and 39 public hospitals, providing 3,124 and 27,755 beds respectively. A wide range of health care services are offered. All 12 of Hong Kong's private hospitals have been surveyed and accredited by the UK's Trent Accreditation Scheme since early 2001. This has been a major factor in the ascent of standards in Hong Kong's private hospitals. The Trent scheme works closely with the hospitals it assesses to generate standards appropriate to the locality (with respect to culture, geography, public health, primary care interfaces etc.), and always uses combinations of UK-sourced and Hong Kong-sourced surveyors. Some of Hong Kong's private hospitals have now gone on to obtain dual international accreditation, with both Trent and JCI (and have therefore attained a standard surpassing some of the best hospitals in Thailand and Singapore). Others are looking towards dual international accreditation with Trent and the Australian group. Hong Kong public hospitals have yet to commit to external accreditation.

India

India's medical tourism sector is expected to experience an annual growth rate of 30%, making it a Rs. 9,500-crore industry by 2015. Estimates of the value of medical tourism to India go as high as $2 billion a year by 2012. Advantages for medical tourists include reduced costs, the availability of latest medical technologies and a growing compliance on international quality standards, as well as the fact that foreigners are less likely to face a language barrier in India. The Indian government is taking steps to address infrastructure issues that hinder the country's growth in medical tourism.

Most estimates claim treatment costs in India start at around a tenth of the price of comparable treatment in America or Britain. The most popular treatments sought in India by medical tourists are alternative medicine, bone-marrow transplant, cardiac bypass surgery, eye surgery and orthopedic surgery. India is known in particular for heart surgery, hip resurfacing and other areas of advanced medicine.

Ministry of Tourism India(MoT) is planning to extend its Market Development Assistance (MDA) scheme to cover Joint Commission International (JCI) and National Accreditation Board of Hospitals (NABH) certified hospitals. A policy announcement of this effect is likely soon.

The south Indian city of Chennai has been declared India's Health Capital, as it nets in 45% of health tourists from abroad and 30-40% of domestic health tourists. Other major cities where medical tourists are catered to include New Delhi, Bangalore and Mumbai.

Korea, Republic of

Listed on CNN.com as one of the "hot destinations" for medical tourism, Korea is quickly establishing itself in the field of medical tourism. Korea is especially popular with Japanese cosmetic surgery patients due to the cheap costs and high standards of care practiced by Korean medical facilities. In 2008, Korea had 27,480 foreign-based patients and the Korean health ministry expects that number to increase to 140,000 by 2015. Due to legislation passed in May 2009, state-licensed clinics and hospitals are now allowed to directly seek out foreign patients through various promotional activities. Korean hospitals and clinics provide a variety of medical services for medical tourists including comprehensive health screening, cancer treatment, organ transplantation, joint/rheumatism care, spinal treatment, ophthalmology, dental care, infertility treatment, otorhinolaryngology, and Korean traditional medicine. Currently, the most popular treatments for medical tourists are cosmetic procedures such as eyelid surgery, nose jobs, face-lifts, and skin lightening. Over 30 Korean hospitals and clinics are member providers under the Council for Korea Medicine Overseas Promotion (CKMOP). Among these facilities are the "Big Four" – Seoul National University Hospital, Samsung Medical Centre, Asan Medical Centre, and Yonsei Severance Hospital. Severance Hospital is Korea's only JCI accredited hospital and with over 2,000 beds, is also the world's largest JCI accredited hospital.

Malaysia

Malaysia is well on its way to develop itself as a medical tourism hub. The country has excellent hospitals, English is widely spoken, and many staff have been trained to a high level in the UK or in the US. There is a highly active Association for Private Hospitals of Malaysia working to develop medical tourism. However, while Malaysia has a national accreditation healthcare scheme (MSQH) and many Malaysia's hospitals are currently firmly on the way to achieve international healthcare accreditation. Malaysian hospitals International Specialist Eye Centre, Penang Adventist Hospital and many others such as Gleneagles Hospital Kuala Lumpur have or are going to be JCI accredited. The Ministry of Health has launched a medical tourism page with medical tourism portals such as Wellness Visit.

New Zealand

New Zealand is a relatively new destination to medical travel. It has all the hallmarks of a very successful destination especially for North American based patients. This includes being a first world, developed economy with a sophisticated and comprehensive medical system. It is first and foremost English speaking with a rich heritage of producing world class doctors and medical research. Many of its private hospitals are internationally accredited, state of the art and offer an integrated package of care. The surgeons in New Zealand are trained both in New Zealand and abroad, usually spending years of their training in either North America or Western Europe. While New Zealand is aligned medically and culturally to North America, the cost of the surgical care is significantly cheaper. On average it is considered that New Zealand's surgical costs are around 15 to 20% the cost of the same surgical procedure in the USA. One patient who had his prosthetic hip replaced in New Zealand said the total cost including travel, lodging and the surgery at a private hospital was $20,000, as opposed to the $80,000-$140,000 he was told the operation would have cost at home. Added to this the personalized level of medical care, the world renown natural beauty and tranquility, the fact that New Zealand is one of the safest places in the world and only 12 hours direct flight from the west coast of North America, then New Zealand as a medical travel destination looks set to develop.

Philippines

The Philippines has been growing as a destination for medical tourism. The US Medical Tourism Association magazine reported that this services sub-sector grew 8.0% in 2007. The Philippines is one of a few countries that sends qualified physicians and dentists to the US, a testament to its quality of medical education. Procedures can be performed at a fraction of the amount that a patient would spend on the same procedure in the US or Europe. Some medical centres are accredited by the American accreditation group Joint Commission International (JCI).

Singapore

Singapore has a dozen hospitals and health centres with JCI accreditation. In 1997, the World Health Organization ranked Singapore's health care system sixth best in the world and the highest ranked system in Asia. "Singapore Medicine" is a multi-agency government-industry partnership committed to strengthening Singapore's position as a medical hub and promoting Singapore as a destination for advanced patient care. Patients come from neighbouring countries, such as Indonesia and Malaysia, and patient numbers from Indochina, South Asia, the Middle East and Greater China are growing. Patients from developed countries such as the United States and the UK are also beginning to choose Singapore as their medical travel destination for relatively affordable health care services in a clean cosmopolitan city.

Taiwan

The Taiwanese government has declared its determination for the country to become a medical tourism centre. It is estimated that the government will contribute NT$44.4 million to construct a platform for the collaboration of the government and the medical sector in promoting medical tourism. Costs for procedures remain comparatively low. Taiwan is known for liver transplants, joint replacement surgery, bone marrow transplants, and reconstructive and plastic surgery.

Thailand

Medical tourism has been a growing segment of Thailand's tourism and healthcare sectors. In 2005, one Bangkok hospital took in 150,000 treatment seekers from abroad. In 2006, medical tourism was projected to earn the country 36.4 billion baht. Treatments for medical tourists in Thailand range from cosmetic, organ transplants, cardiac, and orthopaedic treatments to dental and cardiac surgeries. Treatments also include spa, physical and mental therapies. One patient who had coronary artery bypass surgery at Bumrungrad International hospital in Bangkok said the operation cost him US$12,000 (8,200 euros), as opposed to the $100,000 (68,000 euros) he estimated the operation would have cost him at home. Bumrungrad treated approximately 55,000 American patients in 2005 alone, a 30% increase from the previous year.

Hospitals in Thailand are a popular destination for other Asians. Bangkok Hospital, which caters to medical tourists, has a Japanese wing, and Phyathai Hospitals Group has interpreters for over 22 languages, besides the English-speaking medical staff. When Nepal Prime Minister Girija Prasad Koirala needed medical care in 2006, he went to Bangkok.. Many Thai physicians hold US or UK professional certification. Bumrungrad International hospital states that many of its doctors and staff are trained in the UK, Europe and the US. Bumrungrad International was accredited most recently in 2005 by the Joint Commission. Some of the country's major hospitals have also achieved certification by the International Organization for Standardization's ISO 9001:2000. However, ISO 2000 is not an accreditation scheme.

The US consular information sheet gives the Thai health care system high marks for quality, particularly facilities in Bangkok.. The World Health Organization's 2000 ranking put the Thai healthcare system at number 47, below the USA's ranking at 37 and the United Kingdom's ranking at 18. The UK's Foreign and Commonwealth Office web site states "There are excellent international hospitals in Bangkok but they can be expensive".

Serious political problems during late 2008, including mass demonstrations and the complete closure of major airports, have made travel to Thailand less appealing than in the past, and the US State Department has issued a travel alert for the country.

Europe

Countries in Europe that have active medical tourism sectors include Cyprus, Germany, Hungary, Lithuania, Malta, Poland, Portugal, Czech Republic, Slovakia, Spain, and Ukraine.

Czech Republic

Czech Republic has built its medical tourism on spas and medical care equalling the world standards.

Germany

Germany is a destination for patients seeking advanced medical technology, high standards, safety, and quick treatment. All German citizens have health coverage, resulting in a high hospital density, with twice as many hospitals per capita as the United States. The high hospital density results in shorter waitlists for treatment. Costs for medical treatment compete well with other developed European countries and are commonly 50% of those in the USA.

Germany is an attractive destination for patients from the Middle East since travelling to the USA has become more difficult for them since the September 11 attacks. US citizens sometimes travel to Germany to seek treatments such as artificial cervical disc replacement that are not US Food and Drug Administration (FDA) approved.

Poland

Since 2004, when Poland joined the European Union, it has become another locale for people seeking cheaper medical treatments. The quality of care in Poland must comply with EU standards. One well-known medical centre in Poland is "medical-poland.com" with The Clinical Hospital No. 10 and Polyclinic in Bydgoszcz.

Turkey

Turkey has since many years attracted medical tourists from Europe, the United States and the Middle East as the country combines quality healthcare, the newest medical technologies (Cyberknife) and low-cost. Many tourists come to Turkey for medical or cosmetic surgery but the country is also seeking to build on its geothermal resources for an expansion of therapeutic spas. The German Hospital in Istanbul operates the country's first ISO-certified IVF centre, while Memorial Hospital was the first private hospital to receive American JCI accreditation. Since then, over 34 hospitals and medical institutions have achieved Joint Commission International accreditation.

4

Modern Sustainable Health Hospitality

Sustainable tourism is an industry committed to making a low impact on the environment and local culture, while helping to generate income and employment for local people.The aim of sustainable tourism is to ensure that development is a positive experience for local people; tourism companies; and tourists themselves. But sustainable tourism is not the same as 'ecotourism'. Global economists forecast continuing international tourism growth, ranging between three and six percent annually, depending on the location. As one of the world's largest and fastest growing industries, this continuous growth will place great stress on remaining biologically diverse habitats and indigenous cultures, which are often used to support mass tourism. Tourists who promote sustainable tourism are sensitive to these dangers and seek to protect tourist destinations, and to protect tourism as an industry. Sustainable tourists can reduce the impact of tourism in many ways, including:

- informing themselves of the culture, politics, and economy of the communities visited
- anticipating and respecting local cultures' expectations and assumptions
- contributing to intercultural understanding and tolerance
- supporting the integrity of local cultures by favouring businesses which conserve cultural heritage and traditional values

- supporting local economies by purchasing local goods and participating with small, local businesses
- conserving resources by seeking out businesses that are environmentally conscious, and by using the least possible amount of non-renewable resources

Increasingly, destinations and tourism operations are endorsing and following "responsible tourism" as a pathway towards sustainable tourism. Responsible tourism and sustainable tourism have an identical goal, that of sustainable development. The pillars of responsible tourism are therefore the same as those of sustainable tourism – environmental integrity, social justice and economic development. The major difference between the two is that, in responsible tourism, individuals, organisations and businesses are asked to take responsibility for their actions and the impacts of their actions. This shift in emphasis has taken place because some stakeholders feel that insufficient progress towards realising sustainable tourism has been made since the Earth Summit in Rio. This is partly because everyone has been expecting others to behave in a sustainable manner. The emphasis on responsibility in responsible tourism means that everyone involved in tourism – government, product owners and operators, transport operators, community services, NGO's and CBO's, tourists, local communities, industry associations – are responsible for achieving the goals of responsible tourism.

Responsible Tourism

Responsible Tourism can be regarded as a movement. It is more than a form of tourism as it represents an approach to engaging with tourism, be that as a tourist, a business, locals at a destination or any other tourism stakeholder. It emphasises that all stakeholders are responsible for the kind of tourism they develop or engage in. Whilst different groups will see responsibility in different ways, the shared understanding is that responsible tourism should entail an improvement in tourism. Tourism should become 'better' as a result of the responsible tourism approach.

Within the notion of betterment resides the acknowledgement that conflicting interests need to be balanced. However, the objective is to create better places for people to live in and to visit. Importantly, there is no blueprint for responsible tourism: what is deemed responsible may differ depending on places and cultures. Responsible Tourism is an aspiration that can be realised in different ways in different originating markets and in the diverse destinations of the world.

Focusing in particular on businesses, according to the Cape Town Declaration on Responsible Tourism, it will have the following characteristics:

- minimises negative economic, environmental, and social impacts
- generates greater economic benefits for local people and enhances the well-being of host communities, improves working conditions and access to the industry
- involves local people in decisions that affect their lives and life chances
- makes positive contributions to the conservation of natural and cultural heritage, to the maintenance of the world's diversity
- provides more enjoyable experiences for tourists through more meaningful connections with local people, and a greater understanding of local cultural, social and environmental issues
- provides access for physically challenged people and
- is culturally sensitive, engenders respect between tourists and hosts, and builds local pride and confidence.

Sustainable tourism is where tourists can enjoy their holiday and at the same time respect the culture of people and also respect the environment. It also means that local people (such as the Masaai) get a fair say about tourism and also receive some money from the profit which the game reserve make. The environment is being damaged quite a lot by tourists and part of Sustainable tourism is to make sure that the damaging does not carry on.

There are many private companies who are working into embracing the principles and aspects of Responsible Tourism, some for the purpose of Corporate Social Responsibility activities, and others such WorldHotel-Link, which was originally a project of the International Finance Corporation, have built their entire business model around responsible tourism, local capacity building and increasing market access for small and medium tourism enterprises.

Responsible Hospitality

As with the view of Responsible Tourism, Responsible Hospitality is essentially about creating better places for people to live in, and better places for people to visit. This does not mean all forms of hospitality are also forms of tourism although hospitality is the largest sector of the tourism industry. As such we should not be surprised at overlaps between Responsible Hospitality and Responsible Tourism. In the instance where place of permanent residence is also the place where the hospitality service is consumed, if for example a meal is consumed in a local restaurant, this does not obviate the requirement to improve the place of residence. As such, the essence of Responsible Hospitality is not contingent upon touristic forms of hospitality.

While Frideman (1962) famously argued that, admittedly within legal parameters, the sole responsibility of business was to generate profit for shareholders the idea that businesses' responsibility extends beyond this has existed for decades and is most frequently encountered in the concept of corporate social responsibility.

There are numerous ways businesses can and do engage in activities that are not intended to benefit shareholders and management, at least not in the short term. However, often acts of corporate social responsibility are undertaken because of the perceived benefit to business. Usually in hospitality this relates to the cost reductions associated with improved energy efficiency but may also relate to, for example, the rise in ethical consumerism and the view that being seen to be a responsible business is beneficial to revenue growth.

As per the Capetown Declaration on Responsible Tourism, Responsible Hospitality is culturally sensitive. Instead of then calling for the unachievable, Responsible Hospitality simply makes the case for more responsible forms of hospitality, hospitality that benefits locals first, and visitors second. Certainly, all forms of hospitality can be improved and managed so that negative impacts are minimised whilst striving for a maximisation of positive impacts.

Coastal Tourism

Many coastal areas are experiencing particular pressure from growth in lifestyles and growing numbers of tourists. Coastal environments are limited in extent consisting of only a narrow strip along the edge of the ocean. Coastal areas are often the first environments to experience the detrimental impacts of tourism. A detailed study of the impact on coastal areas, with reference to western India can be an example.

The inevitable change is on the horizon as holiday destinations put more effort into sustainable tourism. Planning and management controls can reduce the impact on coastal environments and ensure that investment into tourism products supports sustainable coastal tourism.

Some Conceptual Models in Coastal Tourism

Some of the recent studies have led to some interesting conceptual models applicable for coastal tourism. The 'inverted funnel model' and the 'embedded model' can be good metaphors for understanding the interplay of different stake-holders like government, local community, tourists and business community in developing tourist destinations.

Community-based Management

There has been the promotion of sustainable tourism practices surrounding the management of tourist locations by locals or more concisely, the community.

This form of tourism is based on the premise that the people living next to a resource are the ones best suited to protecting it. This means that the tourism activities and businesses are developed and operated by local community members, and certainly with their consent and support.

Sustainable tourism typically involves the conservation of resources that are capitalized upon for tourism purposes, such as coral reefs and pristine forests. Locals run the businesses and are responsible for promoting the conservation messages to protect their environment.

Community-based sustainable tourism (CBST) associates the success of the sustainability of the ecotourism location to the management practices of the communities who are directly or indirectly dependent on the location for their livelihoods.

A salient feature of CBST is that local knowledge is usually utilised alongside wide general frameworks of ecotourism business models. This allows the participation of locals at the management level and typically allows a more intimate understanding of the environment. The use of local knowledge also means an easier entry level into a tourism industry for locals whose jobs or livelihoods are affected by the use of their environment as tourism locations. The involvement of locals restores the ownership of the environment to the local community and allows an alternative sustainable form of development for communities and their environments that are typically unable to support other forms of development.

Stakeholders

Stakeholders of sustainable tourism play a role in continuing this form of tourism. This can include organizations as well as individuals.

Non-governmental Organizations

Non-governmental organizations are one of the stakeholders in advocating sustainable tourism. Their roles can range from spearheading sustainable tourism practices to simply doing research. University research teams and scientists can be tapped to aid in the process of planning. Such solicitation of research can be observed in the planning of Cat Ba National Park in Vietnam.

Dive resort operators in Bunaken National Park, Indonesia, play a crucial role but developing exclusive zones for diving and fishing respectively, such that both tourists and locals can benefit from the venture

Large conventions, meetings and other major organized events drive the travel, tourism and hospitality industry. Cities and convention centres compete to attract such commerce, commerce which has heavy impacts on resource use and the environment. Major sporting events, such as the Olympic Games, present special problems regarding environmental burdens and degradation. But burdens imposed by the regular convention industry can be vastly more significant.

Green conventions and events are a new but growing sector and marketing point within the convention and hospitality industry. More environmentally aware organizations, corporations and government agencies are now seeking more sustainable event practices, greener hotels, restaurants and convention venues, and more energy efficient or climate neutral travel and ground transportation.

Additionally, some convention centres have begun to take direct action in reducing the impact of the conventions they host. One example is the Moscone Centre in San Francisco, California, which has a very aggressive recycling program, a large solar power system, and other programs aimed at reducing impact and increasing efficiency.

Tourists

With the advent of the internet, some traditional conventions are being replaced with virtual conventions, where the attendees remain in their home physical location and "attend" the convention by use of a web-based interface programmed for the task. This sort of "virtual" meeting eliminates all of the impacts associated with travel, accommodation, food wastage, and other necessary impacts of traditional, physical conventions.

Travel over long distances requires a large amount of time and/or energy. Generally this involves burning fossil fuels, a largely unsustainable practice and one that contributes to climate change, via CO_2 emissions. Air travel is perhaps the worst offender in this regard, contributing to between 2 and 3% of global carbon emissions. Given a business-as-usual approach, this could be expected to rise to 5% by 2015 and 10% by 2050. Car travel is the next worst offender.

Mass transport is the most climate friendly method of travel, and generally the rule is "the bigger the better"- compared to cars, buses are relatively more sustainable, and trains and ships are even more so. Human energy and renewable energy are the most efficient, and hence, sustainable. Travel by bicycle, solar powered car, or sailing boat produces no carbon emissions (although the embodied energy in these vehicles generally comes at the expense of carbon emission).

Introduction Of Sustainable Tourism

There are a myriad of definitions for Sustainable Tourism, including eco-tourism, green travel, environmentally and culturally responsible tourism, fair trade and ethical travel. The most widely accepted definition is that of the World Tourism Organisation. They define sustainable tourism as "*tourism which leads to management of all resources in such a way that* economic, social and aesthetic needs can be fulfilled while maintaining cultural integrity, essential *ecological processes, biological diversity and life support systems.*" In addition they describe the development of sustainable tourism as a process which meets the needs of present tourists and host communities whilst protecting and enhancing needs in the future.

Tourism is one of the world's largest industries. For developing countries it is also one of the biggest income generators. But the huge infrastructural and resource demands of tourism can have severe impacts upon local communities and the environment if it is not properly managed.

To reach this current state, we have witnessed an exponential growth in global tourism over the past half century. 25 million international visitors in 1950 grew to an estimated 650 million people by the year 2000. Several factors have contributed to this rise in consumer demand in recent decades. This includes an increase in the standard of living in the developed countries, greater allowances for holiday entitlements and declining costs of travel. Tourism is an important export for a large number of developing countries, and the principal export for about a third of these. Statistics for domestic tourism are not so easily available. However it is certain that domestic tourism is also growing rapidly in many Asian and Latin American countries.

World Travel and Tourism Council (WTTC) estimates show that in 2002 travel, tourism and related activities will contribute 11% to the world's GDP, rising to 12% by 2010. The industry is currently estimated to generate 1 in every 12.8 jobs or 7.8% of the total work force. This percentage is expected to rise to 8.6% by 2012. Tourism is also the world's largest employer, accounting for more than 255 million jobs, or 10.7% of the global labour force (WTTC 2002).

It is clear that ecotourism, in the strictest sense of the word, still only accounts for a small proportion of the total tourism market. Current estimates are between 3-7% of the market (WTTC, WTO, Earth Council 1996). Taking the WTO's full definition of tourism, there's a risk that ecotourism alone will fail to fully realise the potential to support more sustainable development across the entire sector – suggesting that there may be real benefits trying to make all of the Travel and Tourism industry more sustainable.

Current Global and Regional Trends

Tourism and Travel Statistics and Trends

The magnitude of the tourism industry can be clearly seen from the World Travel and Tourism Council (WTTC) statistics. The WTTC estimates that in the year 2002, travel, tourism and related activities will contribute to approximately 10% of the world's GDP, growing to 10.6% by 2012. The industry is currently estimated to help generate 1 in every 12.8 jobs, 7.8% of total employment. This will rise to 8.6% by 2012 (WTTC 2002). Tourism has helped to create millions of jobs in developing countries. For example official estimates for 2002 suggest China has 51.1 million jobs associated to tourism and India 23.7 million jobs. In terms of the relative importance of different sectors for job creation, the largest contributors in travel and tourism employment are found in island states and destinations- ranging from 76.3% of the total number of people employed in Curacao, to 34.6% employment in Antigua and Barbuda. The top ten countries with greatest expected relative growth in employment over the next ten years are all developing countries. Vanuatu is predicted an annual growth rate of 8.8% in employment and tops the list. The balance of bene- fits begins to tilt toward the developed countries in terms of visitor exports and capital investments, in absolute terms.

The top ten list for visitor exports is led by the US. The rest are all European countries, except for China.

On capital investments, US receives an estimated investment of US$ 205.2 million- far ahead of all other countries. Japan with an investment of US$ 42.7 million and China with US$ 42.5 million follow. The expected growth rates for capital investments over the next ten years are significant for developing countries. Turkey has an annualised growth rate of 10.4% (WTTC 2002). Whilst it can be argued that tourism creates an incentive for environmental conservation, tourism is also responsible for damage to the environment. The phenomenal growth of the sector has been accompanied by severe environmental and cultural damage. The projected growth for the industry frequently occurs in destinations that are close to or have exceeded their natural carrying-capacity limits. The consequences are that short term economic gain clearly incurs long term environmental and social costs. Beyond these environmental aspects, other issues of a more social, cultural and rights-based nature have gained increased attention since the mid- 1990's. These include financial leakages, disruptive impacts to local livelihoods and culture, gender bias, sexual exploitation, formal vs. informal sector, domestic vs. international tourism, the growth of "all-inclusive" package tours. Some of the key issues and challenges related to these problems are outlined in the sections below.

Issues: Progress and Challenges

Tourism and the Environment

The natural environment is an important resource for tourism. With increasing urbanisation, destinations in both industrialised and developing countries with significant natural features, scenery, cultural heritage or biodiversity are becoming increasingly popular sites for tourist destinations. Efforts to preserve and enhance the natural environment should therefore be a high priority for the industry and for governments.

But the reality is not quite as clear cut. Environments where past human interaction has been minimal are often fragile. Small islands, coastal areas, wetlands, mountains and deserts, all now popular as tourist destinations, are five of the six 'fragile ecosystems' as identified by Agenda 21 that require specific action by governments and international donors. The biophysical characteristics of these habitats often render them particularly susceptible to damage from human activities. As the scale of tourism grows, the resource use threatens to become unsustainable. With a degraded physical environment, the destination is in danger of losing its original attraction, increasing the levels of cheaper mass tourism and forcing more "nature-based" tourism to move on to new destinations, which are likely to be even more inaccessible and fragile. Mainstream "ecotourism", as promoted after the Rio Earth Summit, hasn't always enjoyed a good reputation. Tour operators have used the concept merely as a "greenwash" marketing tool. In reality it often meant introducing unsustainable levels of tourism into fragile areas, having scant regard for either the environment or for the residents of the destination areas. As the International Council for Local Environmental Initiatives (ICLEI) pointed out:

"Tourism in natural areas, euphemistically called "eco-tourism," can be a major source of degradation of local ecological, economic and social systems. The intrusion of large numbers of foreigners with high-consumption and high-waste habits into natural areas, or into towns with inadequate waste management infrastructure, can produce changes to those natural areas at a rate that is far greater than imposed by local residents. These tourism-related changes are particularly deleterious when local residents rely on those natural areas for their sustenance. Resulting economic losses can encourage *socially deleterious economic activities such as prostitution, crime, and migrant and child labour"* (ICLEI 1999).

Some of the different kinds of impacts that tourism development and operational activities can have include:

* Threats to ecosystems and biodiversity – e.g loss of wildlife and rare species, habitat loss and degradation,
* Disruption of coasts – e.g shoreline erosion and pollution, impact to coral reefs and fish spawning grounds,
* Deforestation – loss of forests for fuel wood and timber by the tourist industry also impact on soil and water quality, bio-diversity integrity, reducing the collection of forest products by local communities,
* Water overuse – as a result of tourism/recreational activities e.g. golf courses, swimming pools, and tourist consumption in hotels,
* Urban problems- Congestion and overcrowding, increased vehicle traffic and resultant environmental impacts, including air and noise pollution, and health impacts,
* Exacerbate climate change – from fossil fuel energy consumption for travel, hotel and recreational requirements,
* Unsustainable and inequitable resource use- Energy and water over consumption, excessive production of wastes, litter and garbage are all common impacts.

Further study could be carried out regarding the negative relationship between tourism and environment, however the many examples across the globe indicate this scenario is quite typical and widely recognised, emphasising the need to identify more mutually beneficial approaches in tourism development.

Tourism and Economics

Economic gains have been a major driving force for the growth of tourism in developing countries. The initial period of growth happened in the late 1960's and 1970's, when tourism was perceived as a key activity for generating foreign ex- and employment by both development institutions, such as the World Bank, as well as by governments. Despite the negative economic impacts of tourism (such as inflation; dominance by outsiders in land and property markets; inward-migration eroding economic opportunities for domestic industry including the poor) the demand for travel and tourism continues to grow. The WTTC has estimated there was an approximate 40% cumulative growth in tourism demand between 1990 and 2000. This demand was largely driven by economic gains at all levels, including in the communities in remote, and hitherto relatively isolated, destinations. There is significant scope for enhancing the possible gains through addressing a number of issues that can help improve opportunities for entrepreneurs and the communities in the destinations, for the poorer sections within these communities, as well as at the macro level for the national economy. Some of these are options are discussed below.

Financial leakages: Powerful trans-national corporations (TNCs) continue to dominate the international tourism market. Estimates suggest that about 80% of international mass tourism is controlled by TNCs. These companies have an almost unhindered access to markets and use this to drive down the cost of supplies. The result is high levels of financial leakage, and limited levels of revenue retention in the destination or host countries. Financial leakages tend to occur due to various factors, including importation of foreign building material, skilled labour and luxury products, and packaged travel arranged with TNCs. This is as opposed to locally sourcing the necessary resources. It has been estimated that, on average, at least 55% of tourism expenditure flows back out of the destination country, rising to

75% in certain cases e.g. the Gambia and Commonwealth Caribbean.

During the seventh UN Commission on Sustainable Development (CSD) meeting (1999), financial leakages was identified as a key area for stakeholders to take action and work together in order to try and assess the situation, as well as seek solutions to better support local communities in host/developing countries. The CSD called upon the UN and the World Tourism Organization, in consultation with major groups, as well as other relevant international organizations, to jointly facilitate the establishment of an ad-hoc informal open-ended working group on tourism to:

* Assess financial leakages and determine how to maximize benefits for indigenous and local communities,
* Prepare a joint initiative to improve information availability and capacity-building for participation, and address other matters relevant to the implementation of the international work programme on sustainable tourism development (UN CSD 1999).

Impacts on livelihoods in destination communities: In most tourist destinations of developing countries, the livelihood impacts of tourism, takes various forms. Jobs and wages are only a part of livelihood gains and often not the most significant ones. Tourism can generate four different types of local cash income, involving four distinct categories of people:

* Wages from formal employment.
* Earnings from selling goods, services, or casual labour.
* Dividends and profits arising from locally-owned enterprises.
* Collective income: this may include profits from a community-run enterprise, dividends from a private sector partnership and land rental paid by an investor.

Waged employment can be sufficient to lift a household from an insecure to a secure footing, but it may only be available to a minority of people, and not the poor. Casual earnings may be very small, but more widely spread, and may be enough, for instance, to cover school fees for one or more children. Local participation in the industry can be categorised into three different categories; the formal sector (such as hotels), the informal sector (such as vending) and secondary enterprises that are linked to tourism (such as food retail and telecommunications). Experience from Asia suggests that:

* As a destination is developing, accommodation for tourists can be as simple as offering home stays at the early stage, with lodges, guest houses and hotels replacing more basic options as tourism grows, and some of these may include foreign companies. Once luxury resorts start to develop, the scenario becomes more complex with international investors beginning to play a much more dominant role.
* Transport tends to fall into a grey area between formal and informal sectors. Most destinations have taxis, jeeps or other motorised forms of transport, often driven by the owners. As things expand organised associations of owners, operating on a rota system become more common.
* Data about employment in the formal sector is scattered and collection is often not very systematic. There are references of cases where high-status jobs in resorts typically go to non-locals, expatriate staff or foreign-trained nationals. However, there is almost no analysis of who is employed in middle and lower ranking jobs. The potential for employment of local staff seems to improve as one moves away from the luxury resorts into less established areas.
* The informal sector includes activities such as vending, running stalls and collecting fuel wood for the tourist industry. The informal sector often provides an easy entry into the industry for the poor, especially for women. The incomes can be substantial but unreliable as it is often a seasonal activity. However it can still provide a substantial boost to the income of the poor. Towards Earth Summit 2002 Economic Briefing No. 4· The informal sector tends to get the least attention when interventions are planned, and interventions such as planning permissions are frequently detrimental to this sector. However, there are cases where initiatives such as flexible

licensing systems and cooperatives and associations have helped the sector.

* Causal labour and self-employment provide major opportunities for local communities to enhance their livelihood opportunities from tourism. Unlike formal employment, self-employment tends to highlight the entrepreneurial spirit of village communities. Villagers are used to stringing together a livelihood from a diverse variety of sources, often giving them a knack for enterprise. Causal labour includes porters, cooks, guides, launderers, cleaners, caterer and entertainers. Nepal, for instance, has a well- organised labour market to employ porters, cooks and guides on a seasonal basis. An estimate made in 1989 showed that trekking alone generated 0.5 to 1 million person days of employment in a year in Nepal.
* Significant gains also accrue from economic linkages between tourism and other economic sectors such as agriculture, horticulture, animal husbandry and handicrafts.

There continues to be fairly poor quantitative data available regarding the economic gains that can be generated from travel and tourism, particularly data that quantifies the impacts to formal, informal and indirect activities as touched upon above. There is a need for a standardised framework and guidelines for the collection and analysis of comparative data sets, to better identify the possible economic impacts for different segments of the market, as well as to develop policies which better reflect the needs of the informal as well as formal tourism ventures. Another gap in research about tourism relates to understanding how domestic tourism benefits formal and informal segments in a country and the degree to which the extreme poor gain at all from the industry.

* Domestic or regional tourists are particularly important clients for self-employed sellers and owners of small establishments (the skilled poor and not-so-poor). Studies in Yogyakarta (Indonesia) and elsewhere in South East Asia show that domestic and other Asian tourists tend to buy more from local vendors than Western tourists.

* Budget and independent tourists, particularly back packers are also more likely than luxury tourists to use the cheaper guest houses, home-stays, transport and eating services provided by local people. They tend to stay longer at a destination than groups of tourists and interact more with the local economy, but also spend less per day, often bargaining over prices.
* Nature-based tourism (including 'eco-tourism') does not necessarily provide more opportunities for the poor than 'mass tourism'. Nature tourism does offer some potential advantages however. It takes place in less developed areas, often involves smaller operators with more local commitment. It involves a higher proportion of independent travellers, and if marketed as 'eco-tourism' can stimulate consumer pressure for ensuring domestic socio-economic benefits. But it remains a niche in the market, can be heavily dependent on imports, and can spread disruption to less developed areas.
* Mass tourism is highly competitive, and usually dominated by large suppliers who have little commitment to a destination. They are less likely to use local suppliers. However the segment does generate jobs and negative impacts are not always spread beyond immediate localities. Further knowledge is needed about how local economic opportunities can be expanded under such circumstances, as well as to identify how the negative impacts can be minimised in the mass tourism segment.
* Cruises and 'all-inclusives' are rapidly growing segments of the market, but by their nature are unlikely to generate few economic linkages. Some governments are trying to actively reduce this, for example the Gambian Government has recently decided to ban 'all-inclusives' in response to local demands.
* The informal sector is where opportunities for small-scale enterprise or labour by the poor are maximised. For example, at Bai Chay, Ha Long Bay in Vietnam, almost a dozen local families run private hotels, but local involvement in tourism spreads far beyond this, to

an estimated 70–80% of the population. Apart from those with jobs in the hotels and restaurants, local women share the running of noodle stalls, many women and children are walking vendors, and anyone with a boat or motorbike hires them out to tourists. However, the informal sector is often neglected by planners.

Tourism and Society Culture

Tourism developments often stop people from having the right of access to land, water and natural resources. NGO's such as Tourism Concern and Rethinking Tourism have reported on examples worldwide where the articles in the UN Declaration of Human Rights are flouted, and where indigenous rights are lost or exploited. Adverse social impacts also include poor working conditions, low wages, child labour and sex tourism. The International Labour Organisation and International Confederation Free Trade Unions (ICFTU) note that some parts of the tourist industry still degrades labour and drives workers to the lowest levels, exhibiting the worst side of unsustainable production.

Cultural transformation: Fears of tourism threatening local cultures can be misplaced and many cultures have proved resilient enough to be able to take rapid changes required by tourism in their stride. However it is true that popular destinations are typically transformed at a very rapid pace. Buzzing small towns can replace sleepy one lane bazaars. Areas where once only officials rode in motorised vehicles become a familiar site for traffic jams, and dealing with unknown faces can become a daily occurrence for people whose previous focus had been confined to a few score square kilometres to their home and work.

Communities visited by tourists can (or have to!) adapt surprisingly quickly. For example, they rapidly adopt businesslike attitudes to maximise profits. They are creative in inventing and staging events to entertain and provide information on their culture. These attractions, while usually not explicitly developed to protect back regions (i.e. areas of a host society reserved only for local residents, where tourists are not welcome), can function to deflect the tourist gaze from private space and activities. Host communities take specific, active measures to protect their values and customs. This can either be covert action such as private communal functions, fencing off of domesticities but also overt action such as organised protests and even aggression to protect their interests. Tourism development in remote areas can be positive however, bringing with it infrastructure, health services and education facilities. It could be a by-product, or a result of increased incomes, or as is happening increasingly, a result of corporate and customer social responsibility.

Nevertheless, rapid tourism development can come at a price and often creates its own unique problems. Tourism activities can degrade the social and natural wealth of a community. The intrusion of large numbers of uninformed foreigners into local social systems can undermine pre-existing social relationships and values. This is particularly a problem where tourism business is centred in traditional social systems, such as isolated communities or indigenous peoples (ICLEI 1999). There are also examples in ecotourism segment, of communities becoming marginalised and forced out of traditional lands as protected areas and destinations become established. Involving host and particularly local communities in all stages of tourism development, from planning right through operations, will help to alleviate some of these issues- if their needs and perspectives are properly taken into account. There is growing amount of work in this area and an expanding body of good practice examples but such approaches need to extended. In addition, programmes which aim to train and assist communities adversely affected by tourism development i.e. providing a social safety net need to be openly assessed for their suitability, and promoted where appropriate.

Tourism and Child Prostitution: On the darker side to global tourism, the sex trade and drug tourism remain areas that are poorly reported or regulated, especially where it concerns children. The root causes behind these growing problems may not wholly lie with growth in tourism, but it is significant and should be a real cause for concern throughout the sector. In recent years the industry has started to try and tackle such problems. In 1998 it collaborated with ECPAT (End Child Prostitution and Trafficking in Children for Sexual Purposes) to draw up a Code of Conduct for tour operators in relation to child prostitution and tourism. Signatories to ECPAT's Code of Conduct commit themselves to:

* working against child exploitation in their policy documents;
* training staff on how to combat child exploitation;
* provision of information to customers;
* putting pressure on suppliers by including a clause against the commercial sexual exploitation of children in the contract (with hotels, for example);
* provision of information to key local people and organizations by creating a network in destinations to raise awareness amongst local people.

The Fritidresor Group (FRG), a subsidiary of Thomson Travel Group, has risen to the challenge by following up on this initiative in a systematic manner. Since 1999 it has designed and conducted workshops, developed an elaborate customer information programme and initiated pilot programmes in five destinations where child abuse is common (Brazil, Cuba, Dominican Republic, India and Thailand). Feedback from ECPAT from one of the pilots has been positive, e.g. the number of paedophiles in Thailand is decreasing. There are concerns, however, that this is happening at the expense of other countries, especially in Central America, where ECPAT has a weaker presence (Tour Operators Initiatives for Sustainable Tourism Development).

Gender: Gender dis-aggregated data for the tourism sector are not easily available. Using the data for restaurant, catering and hotels as proxy, the Gender and Tourism Report prepared by Stakeholder Forum for the CSD in 1999, reached some tentative conclusions. The general picture suggests that the formal tourism industry seems to be a particularly important sector for women (46% of the work force are women, compared to 34-40% in other general labour markets). However the proportion of women in the tourism work force varies greatly – from as low as 2% in some countries and up to over 80% in others, depending upon the maturity of the tourism industry. For example, in countries where there is a mature industry, women generally accounted for around 50% of those employed in the industry. Using data from 39 countries, the proportion of women's working hours compared to men's working hours was 89%. Whilst the proportion of women's wages to men's wages is 79% (based on data available from 31 countries). This suggests that women continue to receive disproportionately lower wages than their male counterparts – often in equivalent positions of status in an organisation. Furthermore the statistics, typically do not include the contribution of women employed in the informal sector. Several studies have indicated, whilst this area is frequently ignored, it also tends to be a significant contributor, particularly in developing countries.

Solutions and Partnerships –Towards Sustainable Tourism

Tourism was only specifically mentioned in a few sections of 1992 Rio Agenda 21, despite its huge economic significance. Agenda 21 for the Travel and Tourism Industry was written in 1996 by the World Trade Organisation, the World Travel and Tourism Council and Earth Council to try and fill this gap. It noted that with a growing standing in the world economy the tourism industry has "a moral responsibility in making the transition to sustainable development. It also has a vested interest in doing so.". The document highlights the vital importance of the environment as the main base upon which the market relies.

These and other activities have supported a growing awareness of the positive and negative impacts of tourism, including a growing realisation of the impact that a degrading environment has on the livelihoods of communities living in destination areas. This has contributed towards the initiation of positive actions for mitigating and minimising the more negative aspects. Various different approaches have been explored, especially in the last couple of decades. Emerging from these efforts is a better recognition of the importance of the role of local communities, their valuable knowledge base and understanding of local circumstances, as well as their strong vested interest in preserving a sustainable system. Establishing partnerships with local communities is being increasingly recognised as necessary for sustainable tourism. The trend now is moving towards more integrated approaches, which include communities working with governments. Some broad proposals and responses for moving towards more sustainable tourism, from various stakeholders, are outlined below.

International Institutions, Agreements and Action Plans

International institutions such as UNEP are working in a number of ways (often in partnership) to promote sustainable tourism. This includes a proposal by UN Economic and Social Council to the UN General Assembly to designate 2002 the "UN International Year of Ecotourism". Though facing some controversy regarding the definition and breadth of the term "ecotourism", the idea was that the year would aim to recognise tourism's potential benefit as both a tool for environmental protection and development. For ecotourism, it is particularly seen as a means to advance three basic goals of the UN Convention on Biological Diversity: To conserve biological diversity; 2. To promote sustainable use of biodiversity to generate income, jobs and business opportunities in ecotourism etc.; 3. To share the benefits of ecotourism developments equitably with local communities & indigenous peoples). Other groups like the World Tourism Organisation do work to try and encourage good practice in the sector. For example the World Tourism Organisation has produced a "Global Code of Ethics for Tourism in 1999 (an extension of the WTO "Manila Declaration on the Social Impacts of Tourism" 1997), as well as a "Compilation of good practices in sustainable tourism", and a practical guide for the development and application of indicators of sustainable tourism, "What Tourism Managers Need to Know".

Business Activities and Tourism

The Rio Earth Summit 1992 was a major turning point for the tourism industry. Environmental issues subsequently became an important part of the agenda for the industry. However, the approach has not yet generally been an integrating one. Instead the focus has been on minimising environmental impacts that the industry is directly responsible for.

There is growing support by lead companies throughout the private sector to implement principles of Corporate Social Responsibility (CSR), Environmental Management and Auditing Systems (EMAS), "Triple Bottom Line" accounting procedures (Environment, Society and Economics) and Sustainability Reporting. Measures are predominately based on adopting a voluntary approach to tackling impacts rather than having regulations/legislation imposed on business by governments.

The action plan for the industry, "Agenda 21 for the Travel & Tourism Industry: Towards Environmentally Sustainable Development" contains a number of priority areas for action and suggested steps to achieve them. The importance of partnerships between government, industry and NGOs is stressed, along with the enormous benefits that will be obtained by making the tourism industry more sustainable. The document warns the industry not to under-estimate the challenge which requires "fundamental reorientation". However it also makes it clear that the long-term costs of inaction will far outweigh those for starting to act now. Companies are encouraged to set up systems and procedures to incorporate sustainable development issues into core management functions and to identify actions needed to bring sustainable tourism into being. A long-term communications programme was initiated after the document launch to increase awareness and promote regional implementation (WTTC). The 10 priority areas for action are:

* Waste minimization, re-use and recycling
* Energy efficiency, conservation and management
* Management of freshwater resources
* Waste water treatment
* Hazardous substances
* Transport
* Land-use planning and management
* Involving staff, customers and communities in environmental issues
* Design for sustainability
* Partnerships for sustainability.

Another major voluntary activity highlighted by many companies is the use of codes of conduct and certification. However, even the voluntary codes lag far behind activities for environmental performance in the area of social responsibility (UNED 1999). The World Tourism Organisation recently produced a study "Voluntary Initiatives for Sustainable Tourism" examining 104 schemes worldwide and gives recommendations to improve the conditions for voluntary initiatives and achieve better effectiveness in the operation and support of voluntary initiatives. In addition it gives a checklist for the planning and assessing of your own voluntary initiatives and makes recommendations for eco-labelling. The report states that voluntary practice has not yet had a significant impact on the mass market. The report recognises that "their current impact has been minimal across the sector as a whole". It finds that 78% of tourism certificates focus on tourism within Europe and not further afield. However the report also says that

> *"they are revealing tremendous potential to move the industry towards sustainability, but not without careful nurturing and support from key industry partners" (WTO 2000).*

When it comes to building more mainstream corporate responsibility, the vast majority of tourist companies state that whilst they would like to do something they feel they are unable to do so because of being faced with 'cut throat' business competition. They argue that the costs involved in acting more responsibly would drive them out of the market, especially if they take unilateral action without wider industry support. Industry surveys have identified the need for establishing mandatory regulations, making it compulsory for everyone to meet the same standards and thereby incur similar costs. Legal and fiscal regulation of corporate sector includes market-based tools such as carbon trading, as supported through the Kyoto Protocol of the UN Framework Convention for Climate Change. Also environmental standards legislated by governments on water quality and waste management, labelling standards, are growing but need to be more widely implemented and effectively enforced.

NGOs are increasingly engaging with the travel sector. They have been playing an active role in addressing problems such as financial leakages and in trying to encourage greater corporate responsibility. Key activities involve consumer education about the potential impacts of tourism and about how local communities might benefit more from the industry.

They actively lobby policy-makers on associated issues of trade liberalisation, fair trade and globalisation. There has also been a concerted effort to set up common certification standards, independent of the industry, along the lines of Fair Trade certification or eco-labelling. Initiatives include the International Fair Trade in Tourism Network, established by Tourism Concern in 1999 and a feasibility study for setting up a Sustainable Tourism Stewardship Council being conducted by the Rainforest Alliance, New York.

Initiatives for Assisting Local Communities to Realise Tourism Opportunities

During the 1990's a number of initiatives emerged which aimed to help communities in destination countries make the most from opportunities provided by tourism. Many have been self initiated, locally and have continued to expand under their own steam, sometimes attracting external technical and/or financial assistance on their own terms. In others, external agents have acted as catalysts. The nature of the activities have been broad, ranging from small one-village initiatives for organising handicrafts production to building powerful networks of small accommodation providers and creating a marketing network for them. Over time, and by learning from experience and sharing knowledge, these initiatives have tended to become more complex and inclusive. Effective multi-stakeholder processes have evolved from the ground. Backed with success and experience at the ground level and on a significant scale, lessons learnt here have the potential for wide and rapid replication. This also requires support from the international community for creating space and resources to assist the players who have been the active leaders of these processes so far to take the lead in formulating a strategy.

Local Authorities: A World Tourism Organisation report on the role of local authorities noted that local authorities have a key role to play in many aspects of tourism development and operations. As countries becomes more decentralised, they are taking on more in this area and realising that the sector may assist local areas in achieving development. Community involvement is referred to as a key part of this process – ensuring participation in planning and development, therefore increasing the possibility of achieving more local benefits from tourism e.g. employment, income, establishing tourism related enterprises.

The report notes that many local authorities lack in experience for planning, nurturing and developing tourism however. This can result in wasted resources and opportunities. The report states that proper planning, efficient implementation and effective management are all essential to optimise the benefits of tourism (WTO 1998). The statement by the International Council for Local Environmental Initiatives (ICLEI) during the seventh session of the CSD said that *"in addition to their direct roles in the development process, perhaps the most important role that local authorities* can play in a global economy is that of facilitator among the diverse interests seeking to influence the direction *of local development"*. ICLEI also stated that *"solutions to adverse tourism impacts are to be found in the shared interest* of local communities, tourism businesses, and tourism consumers to maintain the natural wealth and social heritage of *the tourist destination"*. Thus a major challenge for "sustainable tourism" will be the creation of tangible and working local partnerships. One way to approach this will be through the principles espoused in Local Agenda 21. These principles should be applied, through partnerships, to evaluate and improve efforts to address sensitive tourism development issues, including:

* Inequitable distribution of tourism revenues and "financial leakages"
* Displacement of pre-existing local settlements by tourism developments
* Equal access to local coastal and recreational resources
* Conflict over use and long-term protection of those areas
* Concerns related to lack of foreign tourist sensitivity to cultural traditions and sites

Governments: It is fairly disappointing to say that many Governments have been slow to take the lead in ensuring the progress of sustainable tourism and much more work could be done by them to engage more pro-actively with this sector than in the past. Further engagement includes action at all levels, from international forums and negotiations, down to development of tourism plans and policy, and the enforcement of key regulation at national and local levels. A study for the European Union made some useful recommendations for governments to take action in support of sustainable tourism.

In addition, it recommends production of regional and national tourism strategies, as well as the development and exchange of knowledge through regional networks on sustainable tourism, engaging stakeholders as well as government ministries. PPT is an approach that gaining recognition by national governments and local authorities.

Although PPT is still relatively new and has not been widely applied in practice, existing case studies reveal a number of lessons. These include:

* Diverse activities- beyond community tourism it includes product development, marketing, planning, policy, and investment.
* A lead advocate for PPT is useful, but involving other stakeholders is critical. PPT can be incorporated into the tourism development strategies of government or business.
* Location: PPT works best where the wider destination is developing well.
* PPT strategies often involve development of new products, particularly products linked to local culture. These products should be integrated with mainstream markets where possible.
* Ensuring commercial viability is a priority. This requires understanding demand, product quality, marketing, investment in business skills, and involving the private sector.
* Economic measures should expand both formal and casual earning opportunities.
* Non-financial benefits (e.g. increased community participation, access to assets) can reduce market vulnerability.
* PPT is a long-term investment. Expectations must be prudent and opportunities for short-term benefits investigated.
* External funding may be necessary to cover substantial transaction costs of establishing partnerships, developing skills, and revising policies.

Opportunities for Mutual Gain and Partnership

Conserving and documenting biodiversity: The scientific community has played a role in promoting conservation and research on biodiversity through tourism. One example is Earthwatch, an organisation that supports scientific research through volunteer tourists and funding. In the UK, Earthwatch has a programme which sponsors teachers to be volunteers, and as a result has encouraged greater environmental education in schools in the UK. Another example is the Monteverde Cloud Forest Preserve (MCFR) in Costa Rica, a unique case of what private initiative and a spirit of internationalism can do.

Community Based Wildlife Tourism: In Africa, Community Based Wildlife Tourism (CBWT) has succeeded in conserving the environment as well as empowering communities. The principle behind CBWT is simple- the benefits to wildlife must exceed the costs. In reality this is not so straight forward. A number of the caveats and complexities necessary for success have been identified through experiences on the ground:

* The link between tourism resource and wildlife conservation is not always obvious. It has to be emphasised through education, dialogue and negotiations. Financial incentives will be ineffective in the absence of institutions and capacity for sustainable management. Hence, responsibility for wildlife management and institutional capacity should take precedence over the benefits.
* Equitable distribution of local earnings from tourism is critical and they should be widely shared within the community managing tourism resources.
* Even if tourism creates incentives for wildlife conservation, wider impacts on ecosystems or bio-diversity maintenance should also be considered.

ICT and alternative technologies: The growing use of Information Communication Technology has been cited as a way to cut down on "unnecessary travel", particularly for work-related travel e.g. through using video conferencing instead of travelling to meetings all the time (IIIEE 2002). However for recreational tourism, the main focus of this paper, the link is less obvious. There are, however, numerous examples of web-based guides and tools, aiming to support sustainable tourism, that are springing up all over the place, a few of which have been cited in this paper. A recent study, for the Global Information Society International Research Programme, identified a number of ways that ICT can support tourism as well as protection of biodiversity:

* Helping to establish global tourism/biodiversity databases to enable more effective planning and monitoring in an inter-related and comprehensive way,
* Encouraging global exchange of information and expertise among professionals and stakeholders,
* Allowing small operators and others to be included in discussion and to gain greater access to data,
* Encouraging direct dialogue, including that of marketing and promotion, between sites and tourists, and between tourist providers and tourists;
* Generally improving consumer and operator awareness of impacts and outcomes of tourism.

The study indicated that it is the immediacy of ICT, its capacity to retain and distribute information and its flexibility that are some of its strongest benefits. Another is that ICT can assist the creation of new connections and networks between practitioners, operators and tourists across the globe. Such groups are important to help learn and exchange good practice in sustainable tourism.

Alternative technologies are another important area. Organisations which combine alternative technology with "learning by living" holidays are growing in number. They include activities like agro-ecotourism, which link tourism, education and promoting traditional conservation and sustainable use practices. Tourists are taught new skills for sustainable living, such as organic farming, using alternative renewable energies, through visiting eco-villages, alternative technology centres and traditional communities (ITDG 2002).

Education, Capacity Building and Participation

Education is the key to changing tourist behaviour. Some examples, such as marketing and publicity campaigns by tour operators, have already been cited. Other opportunities also exist, such as learning about sustainability in tourism through job training. These activities should be a shared responsibility between government, private sector operators and trade associations, as well as local tourist organisations, formal training institutions, unions and representative bodies (ICFTU 1999). "*Responsible tourism is the job of everyone involved* – governments, local authorities, the tourist *industry and tourists themselves*" (UNEP 2001) Recognising the substantial impacts of tourism yet also its potential to help implementation of Sustainable Development, the CSD addressed sustainable tourism for the first time in 1999. Many of the issues raised are already considered within this paper but a direct result was the designation of 2002 as UN 2002 UN International Year of Ecotourism (IYE). IYE has not been without its critics (e.g. Third World Network, Rethinking Tourism) who expressed real concerns about assuming that Ecotourism was already a "success", when even the World Bank (who has been supporting ecotourism for over a decade) suggests that few projects have actually generated substantial income for local communities. The Quebec Declaration on Ecotourism is expected to become a major point of reference for future discussion about eco-tourism but "much work remains to be done, notably in the fight against poverty" (WTO 2002). Promoting a broader and more inclusive approach towards seeking sustainable tourism development and capacity building will be key. According to UNEP some of the conditions for a successful transition towards sustainable tourism include:

* Involvement of stakeholders: Increase the long-term success of tourism projects by involving key stakeholders in the development and implementation of tourism plans,
* Information exchange: Raise awareness of sustainable tourism and its implementation by promoting exchange of information, between governments and stakeholders, on best practice for sustainable tourism, and establishing networks for dialogue on implementation of Sustainable Tourism Principles,
* Promote understanding and awareness: to strengthen attitudes, values and actions compatible with sustainable development.
* Capacity Building: Ensure effective implementation of sustainable tourism, through capacity building

programmes to develop and strengthen human resources and institutional capacities in government at national and local levels, and amongst local communities; and to integrate environmental and human ecological considerations at all levels.

Monitoring and Measuring Progress through Indicators

The effectiveness of sustainable tourism initiatives requires effective monitoring of progress, through collecting data around key sustainability indicators for the tourism sector. During CSD 7 participants proposed that the CSD should encourage international agencies to develop indicators to measure the environmental, cultural and social impacts of coastal tourism. The World Tourism Organisation has also done some work in this area. Their Agenda 21 for the Travel and Tourism Industry noted that indicators were a relatively new area for the industry although a number of National Tourism Authorities (including Argentina, Canada, France, Malta, Mexico, Netherlands, Spain, Turkey and the USA) had participated in the World Tourism Organization ongoing programme to develop a key set of indicators for use by national and local authorities. Also UNESCO and UNEP's Tour Operators Initiative recently signed a Memo of Understanding with the Global Reporting Initiative (GRI) to develop Sustainability Reporting Guidelines specially targeted at tour operators.

As we've seen ecotourism is just one approach towards seeking sustainable tourism. Responsible and pro-poor tourism are emerging as new specialist approaches. And new initiatives which aim to push the mainstream tourism industry are building. One example is a new alliance between the World Tourism Organisation and UNCTAD aimed at "poverty alleviation through tourism". The initiative was announced in July 2002 and it will be presented at the Johannesburg Summit in an attempt to gain wider support. Model projects and successful multi-stakeholder initiatives, albeit on a small-scale, are also beginning to grow. Even these few examples perhaps prove that tourism has the potential to meet many of the objectives of sustainable development – to revitalize economies, support local communities, protect the environment and even generate cost savings and efficiency gains for tourism companies.

Promotion of sustainable tourism, through the development of policy tools, capacity building and awareness-raising programmes, local involvement, guidelines for good practice and actual implementation remain essential goals. Sustainable tourism should aim to directly support poverty eradication and sustainable production and consumption – in line with the general aims of Agenda 21. Making progress on a larger scale will be a fine balancing act and will require a massive "sea-change" in approach from the entire Travel and Tourism industry but it is an approach that is clearly worthy of support from all stakeholders interested and involved in the industry.

With more than 900 million people travelling each year, the tourism industry wields tremendous economic importance, especially in areas rich in biological and cultural diversity. But unless tourism is practiced responsibly and in harmony with the environment, it can lead to unchecked development, cultural exploitation, habitat destruction, waste and pollution.

The Rainforest Alliance is working to help tourism entrepreneurs conserve their environments and contribute to local livelihoods, while improving their own bottom line. We do this by:

- Training tourism businesses to adopt more sustainable practices and encourage them to pursue voluntary certification with one of the numerous existing programs.
- Providing marketing support to certified tourism businesses, and those in the process of becoming certified.
- Working with tour operators who motivate the hotels they work with to adopt sustainable practices.
- Educating travellers to seek out certified operations as a means to differentiate legitimate eco-friendly operations from those that might make misleading claims.
- Promoting sustainability certification as a strategic conservation and business development tool within the industry and to the public.
- Supporting the efforts of the Sustainable Tourism Certification Network of the Americas and the proposed accreditation body, the Sustainable Tourism Stewardship Council, to help certification programs

worldwide to develop internationally sound standards for certification programs.

- Establishing regional networks of certification programs to share resources and information

Sustainable Tourism: Tourism, the Big Picture

Tourism is big business. According to the World Tourism Organization (WTO) tourism has grown at an amazing rate in the last 30 years. Currently, the business of travel (comprising everything from airlines to resorts to boutique organizations like Context) represents 6% of the entire global GDP and nearly 30% of the entire service economy. Total tourism receipts in 2004 were $622 billion. According to the WTO, tourism is on track to eclipse oil as the single largest industry on the planet by 2010.

Like all big industries tourism has an impact on the environment, local economies, and the social and cultural fabric of the places where it operates. If not managed properly a tourism program can easily become extractive, over time reducing the value of a destination rather than enhancing it. This is obvious in places like Rome, Paris, Venice, and Florence—European cities that are among the most touristed places on the planet and where the presence of huge crowds diminishes the meaning of monuments; tour buses emit huge amounts of air pollution; and small businesses lose out to tourist-friendly chains able to serve the lowest common denominator. Over time, mass tourism strips a place of its character and turns entire quarters of a city into mere "tourist zones."?

Context, the Small Picture

Though we didn't articulate it at the time, Context was founded on principles of sustainable tourism; that is, it was designed to tread lightly on the places where we operate. We organize only small groups of people and design our itineraries to venture off the beaten path. We've always encouraged our clients to visit local businesses and eat in authentic restaurants. And we've always considered that the soul of the traveller is important to the city: If an American comes to Rome or Paris, say, and is moved on a fundamental level by the cultural heritage here, then he or she will become a defender of that cultural heritage. An educated, impassioned tourist can be a powerful advocate. After the National Geographic Society asked Context founder Paul Bennett to join their panel on geotourism and evaluate the sustainability of cities and tourism destinations, we began to get a lot more interested in the international "sustainable tourism"? movement. Eventually, we started honing our general philosophy into something more articulate and coherent, a vision to make our business truly sustainable, so that we can protect the places that we love while enhancing the experience of the people we serve.

Our sustainable program has three main components:

1. Reducing and mitigating the environmental footprint of our office and our programs.
2. Controlling the social and economic impact of our programs.
3. Giving back to the cities where we operate.

Environmental Impact

Greening Context involves two separate initiatives. The first concerns our offices and the daily operations of our staff. This has been pretty simple, since our offices are quite small, comprising a mere 480 square feet of space between three locations in the U.S., Rome and Paris.

In each place we recycle waste, use recycled goods, and bike or use mass transit to commute. (This last is made easier by the fact that no one, including founders Lani and Paul, owns a car.) Next, we look at our programs. The majority of our seminars are organized as walking tours. When forced to go farther afield on an excursion we usually use the train system, partly because they are more efficient than the highways in Italy and France.

Beyond this, we participate in a carbon-offset program. Using carbon calculators developed by Terrapass and The Conservation Fund, we estimate that our offices produce about 11.78 tons of carbon each year, including plane travel for our staff moving between our offices in Paris and Rome and the United States. We offset this with an annual contribution to a carbon-offset program overseen by Sustainable Tourism International (STI), a non-profit organization that coordinates research and projects in sustainable tourism (and of which Context is a member).

We also measure how much carbon any of our car-assisted itineraries and car transfers produce, and offset these twice yearly. The cost of this offset is included in our prices.

Social & Economic Impact

In order to manage our impact on the social and economic fabric of our cities, we generally follow the guidelines of the Sustainable Tourism Initiative and the National Geographic Society's Geotourism Charter. Specifically, we approach this issue from two directions.

Firstly, we look for ways that we can shape our programs so that they have a minimal footprint on the city. This includes dividing large groups into smaller subgroups and avoiding overcrowded spaces like the Eiffel Tower or Colosseum, except when absolutely necessary. Thus, we find ourselves in intimate groups in intimate settings, whether it's strolling through a hidden quarter of Paris or sitting down for a salad at a mom-and-pop trattoria in Naples. This has an obvious economic effect: Instead of directing the spending power of our clients towards touristy chains that have a negative effect on the city, we help them to invest in the health of small enterprises and the living fabric of the place. We also believe that this fosters a great rapport between the host (the local business owner) and the visitor, instead of alienating the one from the other as so often happens in crowded tourist zones. (For a clear example of the enervating effect of tourism economics on a place, spend some time watching the fake gladiators extorting tourists outside of the Colosseum.) The second tack we take is to include some amount of discussion about the traveller's role in the social and economic life of the host city into every itinerary we run. This is an uneven and haphazard element of what we do. Since our docents don't follow a script and work independently to develop their own narrative experience of these cities, the amount of time spent talking about preserving the social fabric of Paris or encouraging our clients to venture outside the Centre Storico in Florence can vary a lot. We distribute copies of the National Geographic Society's Geotourism Principles to our clients along with a copy of our own, in-house "Six Steps to Being a Responsible Visitor" document as part of our orientation guidebooks.

Investment in Cultural Heritage

The last component of our sustainable tourism program involves donating part of our profits to the Context Foundation for Sustainable Travel, a U.S.-based 501 c.3 charity that invests projects that mitigate the impact of tourism on the seven cities where Context Travel operates. We also encourage our clients to donate to the Foundation as part of their travel experience.

The Context Foundation looks at both the negative and positive aspects of travel, aiming to mitigate the former in enhance the latter. Projects that mitigate the negative effects of travel fall into three project areas: research on tourism and its effects, cultural preservation projects, and economic development to offset the impact of tourism. The Foundation also invests in projects that seek to broaden and enhance the transformative and educational impact of travel by making it available to populations, such as inner-city youths. In 2007-8, the Context Foundation earmarked five projects for support:

- An apprenticeship program for the artisans of the Oltrarno neighbourhood of Florence. Economic changes in Florence fuelled by the tremendous rise of mass tourism have put serious pressure on the silversmiths, wood-workers, paper makers, and other traditional craftsmen who have defined the Oltrarno as a centre of Italian artisanship for more than a century. In conversations with many of these artisans, with whom Context Travel works as part of their walking seminars there, we discovered that the artisans are facing tremendous difficulties in keeping their businesses viable; and there is a very real threat that in a couple of years few traditional crafts-men will continue to practice in Florence. A major problem for these artisans is their ability to attract and retain apprentices who can learn these crafts and eventually become masters in their own right. The artisans simply can't compete with global companies, including the tour companies, as employers in Florence. The Context Foundation, in response, has set up a fund to help offset the cost of employing these apprentices. We will begin with a single shop—the Bini Brothers woodworkers, who have resided in Piazza Santo Spirito for more than 100 years. We hope to grow and develop this support for more artisans over the coming years, though it is a race against time.

- Study of the effects of tourism on Venice. As any traveller to Venice knows, tourism has a major impact there, both on the environment and on its social fabric. To the first point, wake from cruise ships, daunting garbage management issues, and pollution of various types have had a serious impact on a city that is already in a fragile state. To the second point, as tourists and tourism-focused enterprises crowd out the Venetian population, the city is losing population at a tremendous rate. Venice as we know it—as it's been known for 1000 years—is facing serious challenges. Teaming up with the UK charity Venice in Peril, we are financing a major study of the effect of tourism on Venice by noted ecologist, Venice resident, and Context Travel docent Jane da Mosto, which promises to bring into full relief the challenges facing this city and chart a roadmap for its preservation.
- Study and promotion of Ostia Antica, outside of Rome. The ancient Roman town of Ostia is often overshadowed by Pompeii. However, for travellers to Rome it really makes better sense to visit this equally important site in-stead of making such a long (and fossil-fuel consuming) trip to Naples. Working with the Rome-based American Institute for Roman Culture, we are supporting a series of projects in Ostia, including measured drawings of its buildings and promotion of it as a more sustainable destination for Rome travellers than Pompeii.
- Restoration of La Chapelle des Petits-Augustins, Paris. La Chapelle des Petits-Augustins at the Ecole des Beaux Arts is important to the study of French art, for it was here (at the Ecole) that most of France's greatest painters studied, and the chapel became a kind of repository for their studies–mostly of Italian art, of which it is filled with scale copies. The chapel stands in great need of restoration, which the Foundation helps fund through special visits.
- Travel fellowship for economically disadvantaged youths Working with the innovative St. HOPE, which has

transformed the inner-city community of Oak Park, Sacramento and established a new standard for public education and economic revitalization of urban communities in the U.S., we sponsor a yearly travel fellowship for a high-achieving student. The fellowship includes travel and accommodations in Europe, plus a week-long study trip with the scholars in the Context network. The program is intensive and includes six days of seminars, classes, workshops, and other programs, capped by a writing project. The first student for 2008 has been selected and will arrive in Rome in August.

In 2008, the Foundation will continue to investigate new projects that fit its mission in other cities–namely, London, New York, and Naples.

Resources & Notes

The World Tourism Organization (WTO) is the UN agency for tourism. They produce some of the best reports on tourism economics and also advocate for tourism as a tool for economic development. The numbers cited here are drawn from their published statistics.

Sustainable Tourism International is an American non-profit that provides education and outreach services that will lessen the toll that travel and tourism takes on the environment and local cultures. STI's blend of environmental and cultural sustainability was very influential in our thinking.

National Geographic's Geotourism program was also quite important to us and serves an important blueprint for travellers and travel businesses alike.

Treehugger, a great resource for environmental sustainability, published a good report on carbon offset programs, which influenced the course of our program.

National Geographic Society's Geotourism Program

Context has modelled its Sustainable Travel Program in part on the National Geographic Society's Geotourism program. Context founder Paul Bennett sits on the Society's panel for sustainable tourism and is a contributor to both National Geographic and National Geographic Adventure. The following is taken from NGS's geotourism website:

About Geotourism: Geotourism is defined as tourism that sustains or enhances the geographical character of a place—its environment, culture, aesthetics, heritage, and the well-being of its residents. Geotourism incorporates the concept of sustainable tourism—that destinations should remain unspoiled for future generations—while allowing for enhancement that protects the character of the locale. Geotourism also adopts a principle from its cousin, ecotourism, that tourism revenue can promote conservation, and extends that principle beyond nature travel to encompass culture and history as well: all distinctive assets of a place.

What is Sustainable Tourism?: Sustainable tourism, like a doctor's code of ethics, means "First, do no harm." It is basic to good destination stewardship.

Sustainable tourism does not abuse its product—the destination. It seeks to avoid the "loved to death" syndrome. Businesses and other stakeholders anticipate development pressures and apply limits and management techniques that sustain natural habitats, heritage sites, scenic appeal, and local culture.

It conserves resources. Environmentally aware travellers favour businesses that minimize pollution, waste, energy consumption, water usage, landscaping chemicals, and excessive nighttime lighting.

It respects local culture and tradition. Foreign visitors learn about and observe local etiquette, including using at least a few courtesy words in the local language. Residents learn how to deal with foreign expectations that may differ from their own. It aims for quality, not quantity. Communities measure tourism success not by sheer numbers of visitors, but by length of stay, distribution of money spent, and quality of experience.

What is Geotourism?: Geotourism adds to sustainability principles by building on geographical character—"sense of place"—to create a type of tourism that emphasizes the distinctiveness of its locale, and that benefits visitor and resident alike.

Geotourism is synergistic: All the elements of geographical character together create a tourist experience that is richer than the sum of its parts, appealing to visitors with diverse interests.

It involves the community. Local businesses and civic groups work together to promote and provide a distinctive, authentic visitor experience.

It informs both visitors and hosts. Residents discover their own heritage and how the ordinary and familiar may be of interest to outsiders. As local people develop pride and skill in showing off their locale, tourists get more out of their visit. It benefits residents economically. Travel businesses do their best to use the local work force, services, and products and supplies. When the community understands the beneficial role of geotourism, it becomes an incentive for wise destination stewardship.

It supports integrity of place. Destination-savvy travellers seek out businesses that emphasize the character of the locale. Tourism revenues in turn raise local perceived value of those assets. It means great trips. Enthusiastic visitors bring new knowledge home, telling stories that send friends and relatives off to experience the same thing—a continuing business for the destination.

What is Sustainable Tourism?

Sustainable tourism is tourism development that avoids damage to the environment, economy and cultures of the locations where it takes place. The aim of sustainable tourism is to ensure that development is a positive experience for local people; tourism companies; and tourists themselves. Under sustainable tourism, it may be unlikely to experience the kind of 'boom and bust' that led to the rapid growth, and then despoliation of locations such as the east coast of Spain in the 1970s.

But despite this optimistic objective, sustainable tourism is still not widely understood. For a start, 'sustainable tourism' is not necessarily 'ecotourism'. Ecotourism became popular in the 1980s as a form of tourism that focused exclusively on wildlife, nature, or exotic cultures. Recent research, however, has indicated that such tourism may not actually be good for environment, or for the people who experience this attention. Safaris in Kenya, for example, are undoubtedly 'ecotourism'. But Kenya is full of cases where lions have been forced into erratic behaviour because of excessive tourists, or where the local Masai people have failed to benefit from this kind of development. More importantly, 'ecotourism' does not involve more mainstream beach-or city-based tourism, where impacts are much greater than any nature-based tourism. Sustainable tourism, therefore, is an attempt to improve the impacts of all types of tourism, and this implies seeking ways to build partnerships between tourism companies and local governments or managers of resorts.

But how can sustainable tourism be achieved? Evidence suggests that it requires co-operation between concerned companies and the managers of destinations. It does not, however, require a marked interest from consumers. Some companies have suggested that they will only take steps to achieve sustainable tourism if they recognize a clear 'market demand' for holidays that are overtly 'green' or 'environmentally friendly'. Research, however, has indicated that few tourists want holidays that are 'green' within the mass tourism market; and that holidays that are 'green' may repeat the pitfalls of ecotourism. It may not be profitable or sustainable to encourage market demand for 'green' tourism as this demand may not occur, and also may not lead to sustainable tourism.

Instead, evidence has suggested that sustainable tourism does not have to be advertised as environmentally or culturally sensitive in order to succeed. Research has indicated that profits may be increased simply by adopting some general environmental principles, such as recycling waste, planning for long-term sustainability, and seeking local partnerships for resort management. If these actions result in cleaner, less crowded, holiday resorts, then they are in effect sustainable tourism without being labelled so.

But how can companies and resort managers achieve this kind of success? This question is more controversial. One proposal has been to increase the vertical integration of tourism companies, so that individual companies have greater control over the marketing of holidays, transportation of tourists, and then management of resorts. Such integration may help avoid the disappointment and despoliation of resorts that occurs when tourists interested in conventional mass tourism are sent to sites perhaps better suited to bird watchers or hill walkers, as has occurred in Corfu. But this suggestion, however, is occasionally opposed as it may imply that smaller tourism companies cannot enter the market. Furthermore, reducing competition from smaller companies may result in reducing the pressure for lower prices of holidays. Since the 1980s, the British tourism industry has experienced rapid cuts in prices as a result of deep competition between major companies such as Airtours, First Choice, and Thompson. But it is generally the presence of competition from smaller, less regulated, companies that leads to the rapid over-development of resorts, or the reluctance of large companies to increase their costs by attending to the long-term sustainability of locations.

Thinking Point

Do you Think the Distinction Between Sustainable Tourism and Ecotourism is Useful? Why?

The achievement of sustainable tourism, therefore depends in part on providing the right incentives for companies and resort managers to reduce the negative impacts of tourism, and then a variety of local practical steps (such as limiting numbers, or zoning land use) to reduce these impacts.

But in the long term, the ultimate achievement of sustainable tourism also requires tourists and companies to think more about how tourism may impact on other people's homes and livelihoods. Marcel Proust once wrote that most tourists seem to want to travel through one hundred countries with one pair of eyes, whereas the best journey would be to travel through one country with a hundred pair of eyes. By seeking more diversity and depth in holiday destinations, tourists may help avoid the impacts of tourism on destinations, and also achieve a more satisfying experience.

What is Sustainable Tourism?

* Its informative. Travellers not only learn about the destination, they learn how to help sustain its character while deepening their own travel experiences. Residents learn that the ordinary and familiar may be of interest and value to outsiders.
* It supports integrity of place. Destination-savvy travellers seek out businesses that emphasize the character of the locale in terms of architecture, cuisine,

heritage, aesthetics, and ecology. Tourism revenues in turn raise local perceived value of those assets.

* It benefits residents. Travel businesses do their best to employ and train local people, buy local supplies, and use local services.
* It conserves resources. Environmentally aware travellers favour businesses that minimize pollution, waste, energy consumption, water usage, landscaping chemicals, and unnecessary nighttime lighting.
* It respects local culture and tradition. Foreign visitors learn about and observe local etiquette, including using at least a few courtesy words in the local language. Residents learn how to deal with foreign expectations that may differ from their own.
* It does not abuse its product. Stakeholders anticipate development pressures and apply limits and management techniques to prevent the "loved to death" syndrome. Businesses cooperate to sustain natural habitats, heritage sites, scenic appeal, and local culture.
* It strives for quality, not quantity. Communities measure tourism success not by sheer numbers of visitors, but by length of stay, money spent, and quality of experience.
* It means great trips. Satisfied, excited visitors bring new knowledge home and send friends off to experience the same thing- which provides continuing business for the destination.

Environmental Protection and Natural Resource Management

Introduction: Recent and Future Trends in Tourism

Tourism can be considered one of the most remarkable socio-economic phenomena of the twentieth century. From an activity "enjoyed by only a small group of relatively well-off people" during the first half of the last century, it gradually became a mass phenomenon during the post- World War II period, particularly from the 1970s onwards. It now reaches larger and larger numbers of people throughout the world, and is a source of employment for a significant segment of the labour force.

Although domestic tourism currently accounts for approximately 80 per cent of all tourist activity, many countries tend to give priority to international tourism because, while the former basically involves a regional redistribution of national income, the latter has now become the world's largest source of foreign exchange receipts. According to the latest figures compiled by the World Tourism Organization (WTO), foreign exchange earnings from international tourism reached a peak of US$ 476 billion in 2000, which was larger than the export value of petroleum products, motor vehicles, telecommunications equipment or any other single category of product or service.

International tourist arrivals grew at an annual average rate of 43 per cent during the 1990s, despite major international political and economic crises, such as the Gulf War and the Asian financial crisis. According to the latest WTO figures, compiled with data received up to August 2001, the turn of the millennium recorded one of the most impressive annual growth rates in international tourism. All regions of the world recorded significant growth in international tourism in 2000, during which the number of international arrivals grew at an extraordinary rate of 7 per cent to reach almost 700 million arrivals. The September 2001 terrorist attacks in the United States, however, appear to have had a more serious impact on the tourist sector than any other major international crisis in recent decades.

The attacks had a particularly severe impact on air transport, business travel and long-haul travel. Worldwide travel reservations were estimated to have dropped by 15 per cent at the end of October 2001, although not every destination nor every part of the tourism sector was badly affected. For example, while air transport and luxury hotels have suffered from considerable fall in demand, travel within the same country or region, as well as travel by rail and road, appear to have weathered the worst effects of the crisis, or even benefited from it. Nevertheless, initial forecasts of 3-4 per cent rise in international tourist arrivals for 2001, made before the September 2001 attacks, were subsequently revised downwards to around a 1 per cent increase over the 2000 figures.

The latest data, released by WTO in January 2002, show that there was a sharp decline of 1.3 per cent in international arrivals, to a total of less than 690 million, in 2001.7 Given that the northern hemisphere summer holiday season was coming to end by the time the attacks took place, this significant drop confirms that the short-term impacts of the attacks were devastating to international tourism as a whole. The last four months of 2001, in fact, recorded a drop of almost 11 per cent in arrivals worldwide and substantial decreases in all regions of the world.

It is worth noting, however, that this considerable fall in international arrivals was caused not only by a widespread fear of travelling generated by the attacks– particularly in airplanes and to certain destinations – but also by a downturn in the world economy. The economic downturn that began in the United States during the first half of 2001 had already been affecting the tourism sector before the terrorist attacks were carried out. The attacks merely aggravated the economic slowdown already under way.

According to the most recent United Nations economic forecasts, growth of only 1.5 per cent in gross world product (GWP) is expected in 2002, as compared to 1.3 per cent last year. Such a modest improvement is linked to a number of economic uncertainties, notably the high dependency of the global economy on the recovery of the United States. Higher rates of population growth would thus make 2002 the second consecutive year with no real growth in per capita GWP.

This, in turn, is also likely to undermine the short-term prospects for a recovery in international tourism, at least until mid-2002, when the summer holiday season begins in the northern hemisphere, and probably until the end of the year. Although much will depend on the evolution of the world economy during this year, it is also likely that some destinations will experience a prolonged decline in tourism revenues regardless of any world economic improvements. In the medium and long term, however, international tourism is expected to resume its rapid growth, in view of rising living standards and discretionary incomes, falling real costs of travel, expansion and improvement of various transport modes, increasing amounts of free time and other factors. The World Tourism Organization has recently reiterated its long-term forecasts, made before the September 2001 attacks, of an average annual growth rate in international arrivals of over 4 per cent in the period up to 2020. The number of international arrivals is thus expected to reach the striking mark of 1 billion by 2010 and 1.6 billion by 2020.

Main Economic Benefits of Tourism

Tourism, as a sector that comprises an extensive range of economic activities, can be considered the largest industry in the world. International tourism is also one of the fastest growing and most ramified sectors of the global economy, covering a broad range of enterprises, sectors and stakeholders. During the 1990s, when the globalization of tourism reached unprecedented proportions, international tourism receipts had a much higher average annual growth rate (7.3 per cent) than that of gross world product. By 1999, international tourism receipts accounted for more than 8 per cent of the worldwide export value of goods and services, overtaking the export value of other leading world industries such as automotive products, chemicals, and computer and office equipment.

Tourism is also the only major service sector in which developing countries have consistently recorded trade surpluses relative to the rest of the world. Between 1980 and 1996, for instance, their travel account surplus increased from $4.6 billion to $65.9 billion, due primarily to the impressive growth of inbound tourism to countries in Africa, the Caribbean, and the Asia and Pacific regions. The 1990s also experienced a significant growth of international tourism receipts in the 49 poorest developing countries: total tourism receipts in these countries more than doubled from US$ 1 billion in 1992 to over US$ 2.2 billion in 1998. Tourism is now the second largest source of foreign exchange earnings in the 49 least developed countries (LDCs) as a whole, after the oil industry, which is concentrated in only three of these countries. Tourism has become the main source of income for the economies of an increasing number of small island developing States (SIDS) – as well as less developed regions of large countries– with a natural environment appealing to tourists. Foreign exchange earnings can, however, vary significantly among these tourism-driven economies because of 'leakages' arising from imports of equipment for construction and consumer goods required by tourists, repatriation of profits earned by foreign investors and amortization of foreign debt incurred in tourist development. Besides export earnings, international tourism also generates an increasingly significant share of government (national and local) tax revenues throughout the world. In addition, the development of tourism as a whole is usually accompanied by considerable investments in infrastructure, such as airports, roads, water and sewerage facilities, telecommunications and other public utilities. Such infrastructural improvements not only generate benefits to tourists but can also contribute to improving the living conditions of local populations. This increase in social overhead capital can also help attract other industries to a disadvantaged area and thus be crucial to regional economic development.

The tourism sector is an increasingly important source of employment – including in tourism-related sectors, such as construction and agriculture – primarily for unskilled labour, migrants from poor rural areas, people who prefer to work part-time, and notably women. Because the sector is relatively labour-intensive, investments in tourism tend to generate a larger and more rapid increase in employment than equal investment in other economic activities. Furthermore, given that the sector provides a considerable amount of jobs for women and unskilled workers, tourism can significantly contribute to empowering women and alleviating poverty. At the same time, available data suggests that most workers in the tourism sector, notably in hotels and catering, tend to earn less than workers in socially comparable occupations in both developed and developing countries. In addition, the differential tends to be larger in less developed countries and regions, particularly those with high rates of unemployment amongst unskilled labour. Informal employment relations in small and medium-sized enterprises, which employ about half of the labour force in the hotel and catering sub-sectors worldwide, also contribute to a relatively high proportion of child labour and non-remunerated employment in these sub-sectors in many countries.

The increasing reliance of less diversified economies on tourism also increases their vulnerability to international shocks, such as, natural disasters, regional wars and other unexpected events. The recent crisis generated by fear of international terrorism, for example, caused devastating immediate effects on tourism-dependent economies, including regional economies in large countries. In addition, sudden changes in consumer tastes and sharp economic downturns pose significant risks to such economies, given that demand for mass tourism tends to be relatively income-elastic and can produce drastic negative responses to economic recession in source markets. Nonetheless, it is now generally recognized that tourism can make a vital contribution to employment, export receipts and national income in most countries and regions. Furthermore, tourism is often identified as the most promising driving force for the economic development of less developed countries and regions endowed with areas of natural beauty – including small island developing States – because it offers them a valuable opportunity for economic diversification.

Environmental Impacts of Tourism

While tourism provides considerable economic benefits for many countries, regions and communities, its rapid expansion can also be responsible for adverse environmental (and sociocultural) impacts. Natural resource depletion and environmental degradation associated with tourism activities are sometimes serious problems in tourism-rich regions. The management of natural resources to reverse this trend is thus one of the most difficult challenges for governments at different levels. The fact that most tourists chose to maintain their relatively high patterns of consumption (and waste generation) when they reach their destinations can be a particularly serious problem for developing countries and regions without the appropriate means for protecting their natural resources and local ecosystems from the pressures of mass tourism. The main environmental impacts of tourism are (a) pressure on natural resources, (b) pollution and waste generation and (c) damage to ecosystems. Furthermore, it is now widely recognized that not only uncontrolled tourism expansion is likely to lead to environmental degradation, but also that environmental degradation, in turn, poses a serious threat to tourism.

Pressure on Natural Resources

In addition to pressure on the availability and prices of resources consumed by local residents – such as energy, food and basic raw materials – the main natural resources at risk from tourism development are land, freshwater and marine resources. Without careful land-use planning, for instance, rapid tourism development can intensify competition for land resources with other uses and lead to rising land prices and increased pressure to build on agricultural land. Intensive tourism development can also threaten natural landscapes, notably though deforestation, loss of wetlands and soil erosion. Tourism development in coastal areas – including hotel, airport and road construction – is a matter for increasing concern worldwide as it can lead to sand mining, beach erosion and land degradation.

Freshwater availability for competing agricultural, industrial, household and other uses is rapidly becoming one of the most critical natural resource issues in many countries and regions. Rapid expansion of the tourism industry, which tends to be extremely water-intensive, can exacerbate this problem by placing considerable pressure on scarce water supply in many destinations. Water scarcity can pose a serious limitation to future tourism development in many low-lying coastal areas and small islands that have limited possibility for surface water use and storage, and whose ground-water may be contaminated by saltwater intrusion.

Over-consumption by many tourist facilities – notably large hotel resorts and golf courses – can limit current supplies available to farmers and local populations in water-scarce regions and thus lead to serious shortages and price rises. In addition, pollution of available freshwater sources, some of which may be associated with tourism-related activities, can exacerbate local shortages.

Rapid expansion of coastal and ocean tourism activities, such as snorkelling, scuba diving and sport fishing, can threaten coral reefs and other marine resources. Disturbance to marine aquatic life can also be caused by the intensive use of thrill craft, such as jet skis, frequent boat tours and boat anchors. Anchor damage is now regarded as one of the most serious threats to coral reefs in the Caribbean Sea, in view of the growing number of both small boats and large cruise ships sailing in the region. Severe damage to coral reefs and other marine resources may, in turn, not only discourage further tourism and threaten the future of local tourist industries, but also damage local fisheries.

Pollution and Waste Generation

Besides the consumption of large amounts of natural and other local resources, the tourism industry also generates considerable waste and pollution. Improper disposal of liquid and solid waste generated by the tourism industry has become a particular problem for many developing countries and regions that lack the capacity to treat these waste materials properly. Disposal of such untreated waste has, in turn, contributed to reducing availability of the above-mentioned resources at the local level. Apart from the contamination of freshwater from pollution by untreated sewage, tourist activities can also lead to land contamination from solid waste and the contamination of marine waters and coastal areas from pollution generated by hotels and marinas, as well as cruise ships. It is estimated that cruise ships in the Caribbean Sea alone produced more than 70,000 tons of liquid and solid waste a year during the mid-1990s. The fast growth of the cruise sector in the region may have exacerbated this problem in recent years. Furthermore, a particular cause of concern for coastal areas and small islands is the illegal disposal of sewage, solid waste and cargo residues by merchant ships, which cause marine and beach pollution.

In addition, relatively high levels of energy consumption in hotels – including energy for airconditioning, heating and cooking – as well as fuel used by tourism-related transportation can also contribute significantly to local air pollution in many host countries and regions. Local air and noise pollution linked to exhaustive tourism development or urban congestion can sometimes even discourage tourists from visiting some destinations.

Damage to Ecosystems

Intensive tourism activity in natural areas can interfere with fragile vegetation and wildlife and cause irreversible damage to ecosystems, particularly if the infrastructure in those areas is not adequately prepared to absorb mass tourism. Uncontrolled tourism activities can lead to the severe disruption of wildlife habitats and increased pressure on endangered species. As it has been widely documented, it can also disrupt wildlife behaviour, such as, tourist vehicles in Africa's national parks that approach wild cats and thus distract them from hunting and breeding; tour boat operators in the Caribbean Sea that feed sharks to ensure that they remain in tourist areas; and whale-watching boat crews around the world that pursue whales and dolphins and even encourage petting, which tends to alter the animals' feeding and behaviour.

Tourism can also lead to the indiscriminate clearance of native vegetation for the development of new facilities, increased demand for fuelwood and even forest fires. Ecologically fragile areas, such as rain forests, wetlands and mangroves, are also threatened by intensive or irresponsible tourist activity. Moreover, as will be discussed below, it is increasingly recognized that, the rapid expansion of nature tourism (or 'ecotourism') may also pose a threat to ecologically fragile areas, including natural world heritage sites, if not properly managed and monitored. In many countries, coastlines are becoming overbuilt due to tourism development until the damage caused by environmental degradation – and the eventual loss of revenues arising from a collapse in tourism arrivals – becomes irreversible. As mentioned above, intensive tourism development and recreational activities in coastal areas can not only lead to beach destruction and coastal degradation, but can also threaten coral reefs and other marine ecosystems. The delicate ecosystems of most small islands, together with their increasing reliance on tourism as a main tool of socio-economic development, means that these environmental impacts can be particularly damaging since the success of the sector in these islands often depends on the quality of their natural environment. In addition, pollution of coastal waters – in particular by sewage, solid waste, sediments and untreated chemicals – often leads to the deterioration of coastal ecosystems, notably coral reefs, and thus harms their value for tourism. The equally fragile ecosystems of mountain regions are also threatened by increasing popular tourist activities such as skiing, snowboarding and trekking. One of the most serious environmental problems in mountainous developing countries without appropriate energy supply is deforestation arising from increasing consumption of fuelwood by the tourism industry. This often results not only in the destruction of local habitats and ecosystems, but also in accelerating processes of erosion and landslides. Other major problems arising from tourist activities in mountain regions include disruption of animal migration by road and tourist facilities, sewage pollution of rivers, excessive water withdrawals from streams to supply resorts and accumulation of solid waste on trails.

Environmental Threats to Tourism

In many mountain regions, small islands, coastal areas and other ecologically fragile places visited by tourists, there is an increasing concern that the negative impacts of tourism on the natural environment can ultimately hurt the tourism industry itself. There is now plenty of evidence of the 'life-cycle' of a tourist destination, that is, "its evolution from discovery, to development, to eventual decline, ... attributed to a site's overuse and the subsequent deterioration of key attractions or facilities." In other words, the negative impacts of intensive tourism activities on the environmental quality of beaches, mountains, rivers, forests and other ecosystems also compromise the viability of the tourism industry in these places.

In addition, tourism in many destinations could be particularly threatened by global environmental problems, notably the potential threat of 'global warming'. There is increasing scientific evidence that human activity has begun to change the average temperature on the Earth's surface. According to the authoritative United Nations Intergovernmental Panel on Climate Change (IPCC), this process of global warming has been caused by several factors associated with the intensification of economic activities, including the emissions of 'greenhouse gases', such as carbon dioxide produced by burning fossil fuels and forests. According to the Third Assessment Report of IPCC, it is expected that the globally averaged surface air temperature will have warmed between 1.4 and 5.8 degrees Celsius by 2100 relative to 1990. One of the main consequences of global warming will be sea-level rise: according to IPCC, it is projected that the globally averaged sea level will have risen between 9 and almost 90 centimetres by 2100. Global warming is also expected to increase climate variability and to provoke changes in the frequency and intensity of extreme climate events, such as tropical windstorms and associated storm surges and coastal flooding.

Significant rises in sea level could cause serious problems to tourism activities, particularly in low-lying coastal areas and small islands. According to IPCC, because of their high degree of environmental vulnerability, small island States are likely to be among the countries most seriously affected by global warming. The likely impacts of sea-level rise and coastal flooding on small islands and in some coastal areas would include: (a) increased coastal erosion, (b) loss of land and property, including tourist facilities, (c) dislocation of people, (d) increased risk from storm surges, (d) saltwater intrusion into scarce freshwater resources and (e) high financial costs associated with attempts to respond and adapt to these changes. Severe negative impacts on coastal ecosystems, such as bleaching of coral reefs and deterioration of mangroves, are also expected to threaten tourism in many destinations around the world. In fact, global warming is expected to severely disrupt tourism activities not only in coastal areas and small islands, but also in mountain regions because snow conditions in ski resorts are likely to become less reliable.

Sustainable Tourism: The Way Forward

Countries and regions where the economy is driven by the tourism industry are becoming increasingly concerned with the environmental, as well as the socio-cultural problems associated with unsustainable tourism. As a result, there is now increasing agreement on the need to promote sustainable tourism development to minimize its environmental impacts and to ensure more sustainable management of natural resources. The concept of sustainable tourism, as developed in the United Nations sustainable development process, refers to tourist activities "leading to management of all resources in such a way that economic, social and aesthetic needs can be fulfilled while maintaining cultural integrity, essential ecological processes, biological diversity and life support systems." These sustainability concerns are, therefore, beginning to be addressed by governments at national, regional and local, as well as international, levels. In addition, given the leading role of the private sector in the tourism industry in most countries, many initiatives have also been taken by this sector. Broadly speaking, the main policy areas regarding sustainable tourism are: (a) the promotion of national strategies for sustainable tourism development, including the decentralization of environmental management to regional and local levels, (b) the use of both regulatory mechanisms and economic instruments, (c) the support for voluntary initiatives by the industry itself, and (d) the promotion of sustainable tourism at the international level.

National and Regional Strategies for Sustainable Tourism Development

Generally speaking, the main priority for national and regional governments is to incorporate tourism planning and development effectively into overall sustainable development strategies. For example, regional development strategies for areas containing water resources that are potentially attractive to tourism, should carefully consider the availability of those resources in an integrated manner that considers all potential water users. Government policies to promote the domestic tourism industry and to attract foreign direct investment should also ensure that tourism is properly planned and managed so as to minimize adverse environmental impacts and its use of natural resources.

Since the environmental impacts of tourism development are primarily felt at the local and regional levels, national Governments need to promote decentralization of public environment management to the regional and municipal levels. Given that in many countries, local and regional governments already have important responsibilities for tourism development, central Governments should also support capacity building programmes at lower levels in order to enable local and regional authorities to better respond to the challenges of sustainable tourism development in the areas under their jurisdiction. National and local governments also need to develop clear strategies to monitor progress towards sustainable tourism.

Last but far from least, governments at all levels can greatly benefit from working in partnership with all major stakeholders, including local communities, to ensure their active participation in tourism planning, development and management, as well as in the sharing of benefits. Participation of local communities in decision-making and sharing of benefits also helps to generate better awareness of the environmental costs of tourism and thus provides strong incentives to conserve natural resources and protect local environmental assets. Governments, together with the tourism industry and other stakeholders, should also promote or support various efforts to raise public awareness about the impact of tourists on destinations, to promote respect for local communities and their cultures and to protect the environment. Such public awareness campaigns often succeed in promoting positive behavioural changes not only in tourists, but also in tourism workers and host communities as a whole.

Regulatory Mechanisms and Economic Instruments

Sustainable tourism can also be promoted by a careful mix of government policies comprising both direct regulation and market-based instruments, although financial incentives that encourage environmentally damaging activities, such as energy subsidies, should be reduced or removed. The major challenge for governments is, therefore, to formulate and effectively apply an appropriate mix of regulatory and economic instruments for both sustainable natural resources management and environmental protection. The most direct tool for promoting sustainable tourism involves the use of regulatory mechanisms, such as, integrated land-use planning and coastal zone management. In many cases, it may be necessary to protect coastlines through rigid building restrictions, such as, existing legislation in several Mediterranean countries that bans any buildings within a defined distance from the coast. It is also essential that environmental regulations be applied transparently throughout the tourism sector, regardless of business size, type of tourism activity concerned or location.

Mass tourism, in particular, should be carefully monitored, regulated and sometimes even prohibited in ecologically fragile areas. In protected areas, such as national parks and natural world heritage sites, tourism activities should be strictly subject to the preservation of biological diversity and ecosystems, not stressing their limited capacity to absorb human presence without becoming damaged or degraded. In addition to regulation, governments should also consider the use of economic instruments to promote sustainable tourism, including in remote regions where institutional capacity for environmental regulation may be limited. In fact, it can be argued that market-based mechanisms, which apply monetary values to environmental assets, are more efficient for environmental management than government regulation, even at the global level. Since the tourism industry consumes significant amounts of natural resources, economic pricing of scarce local resources – together with the phasing-out of existing subsidies that encourage wasteful consumption – will help to ensure that the true costs of these resources are adequately incorporated into tourist activities. Prices that reflect the economic value of water and energy, for example, will promote their efficient use and conservation, and provide additional revenue that can be used to improve the management of those resources. Pollution taxes can also be applied on the amounts of liquid and solid waste generated, as a means to reduce discharges and to generate funds for proper treatment and disposal. Similarly, market-based instruments can also be used effectively for the sustainable use of marine natural resources.

Economic instruments, such as user fees and tourist taxes, can actually be used to better internalise environmental costs and thus to promote broader environmental protection objectives. As it is well known, one of the main reasons why markets fail is that important environmental costs, such as pollution, are not reflected in the prices of goods and services. In a free-market economy, individual economic agents will only attempt to maximize their own utility or profit; external costs will thus not be reflected in prices. If total production costs do not incorporate full environmental costs, resources will be allocated inefficiently, both within countries and globally. One way to deal with externalities is thus to internalize them through taxes so that the full costs of production are reflected in prices.

One well-known example of charging user fees to support environmental conservation is the Bonaire protected marine areas in the Netherlands Antilles. This was one of the first protected marine parks in the Caribbean to become entirely self-financing through the levying of admission fees on scuba divers. The (private) diving industry in Bonaire was initially opposed to the levy because of its potential negative impacts on future demand and revenues, against the background of intense competition offered by many Caribbean diving destinations. The system, however, has been an unqualified success since it was introduced in January 1992 because many divers (and an increasing number of tourists in general) are willing and able to pay higher prices to support environmental protection. Fees from this scheme also support the active management of the park's coral reef and mangrove ecosystems, as well as educational activities and orientation sessions for divers.

Voluntary Industry Initiatives

As noted above, tourism services in most countries are provided primarily by the private sector, which tends to oppose greater government regulation and taxation of the industry on the grounds that they are ultimately detrimental to efficiency, competitiveness and profits. The predominantly private tourism industry has thus developed several self-regulation and voluntary initiatives to promote greater environmental sustainability. These include waste and pollution reduction schemes, voluntary codes of conduct, industry awards and eco-labels for sustainable tourism. In addition, environmental management schemes to encourage responsible practices have been promoted in various sub-sectors, including hotel and catering, recreation and entertainment, transportation, travel agencies and tour operators.

For example, the World Travel and Tourism Council (WTTC), the main international industry association, has developed an environmental management programme (Green Globe), for both travel and tourism companies and tourism destinations, aimed to raise the level of environmental awareness and to provide a low-cost practical means for improving the environmental performance of the industry. It is also responsible for ECoNETT, an internet-based tool that provides an extensive information resource on all tourism and environmental issues. Another innovative global programme is the International Hotel Environment Initiative (IHEI), led by a council of leading international hotel chains, aimed to promote environmental management in the hotel industry, which is one of the main consumers of resources and sources of waste. Such initiatives are particularly important not only because they can lead to significant reductions of water and energy consumption, as well as liquid and solid waste, but also because they promote positive behavioural changes in both tourists and employees. In addition, they can lead to improved economic efficiency and increased profitability. At the regional level, it is worth noting the successful implementation of the Blue Flag Programme, which now extends to 18 countries in Europe, in providing an incentive to protect and improve the quality of beaches and coasts. Under this programme, environmental standards at individual beaches in Europe are assessed by measuring compliance with acceptable concentrations of a range of pollutants to ensure clean bathing water. Beaches are also judged by their compliance with guidelines dealing with litter management, the availability of sanitary and beach safety facilities, and environmental education. Beaches that meet these stringent criteria receive Blue Flag awards, which also serve as a marketing tool to attract tourists. Despite these helpful initiatives of the tourism industry to improve its standards of environmental management and protection, the very proliferation of such voluntary codes of conduct and eco-label awards at global, regional and local levels – which are not, in any case, adopted or recognized by all industry enterprises – can sometimes lead to confusion and difficulty to evaluate and compare them. While national and regional governments should fully support these voluntary initiatives and encourage the dissemination of the best practices in the private tourism industry, there is also a role for independent supervision, monitoring and comparative assessment by relevant government agencies. In addition, trustworthy codes of conduct, transparent eco-label awards and internationally agreed programmes of action for sustainable tourism are required at the international level. The international community has a particularly crucial role to play in developing a set of internationally recognized accreditation and monitoring systems for assessing the sustainability of tourism services around the world.

International Activities in Support of Sustainable Tourism

Although tourism was not specifically addressed in Agenda 21 – the international programme of action on sustainable development agreed on at the 1992 Earth Summit in Rio de Janeiro (Brazil) – its growing economic importance, significant use of natural resources and environmental impact all contributed to its gradual introduction into the international sustainable development agenda over the past ten years. One of the first concrete sectoral programmes of action arising from the increasing cooperation between the tourism industry and inter-governmental agencies was 'Agenda 21 for the Travel and

Tourism Industry,' an action plan for sustainable tourism development jointly launched by the World Tourism Organization, the above-mentioned WTTC and the Earth Council in 1996.

Among its innovative key objectives are the estimation of the economic value for resources, such as wildlife, natural areas and cultural heritage, "whose conservation would otherwise be seen as having no financial value," and the establishment of "essential infrastructure, such as water treatment plants, for residents as well as visitors ... (in order to) stimulate other economic activities." Many tourism-based communities and regions have also formulated their own 'Agenda 21s' at the local and regional levels.

In 1997, the United Nations General Assembly, at its special session to review the five-year implementation of Agenda 21, decided that there was a need to consider the importance of tourism in the context of Agenda 21 and to "develop an action-oriented international programme of work on sustainable tourism." This request was followed up during the seventh annual session of the United Nations Commission for Sustainable Development (CSD), held in New York in 1999, which discussed tourism as an economic sector and held a multi-stakeholder dialogue on the topic. The Commission adopted an international work programme on sustainable tourism development, which is due to be reviewed during the forthcoming World Summit for Sustainable Development in Johannesburg (South Africa) later this year, as part of the ten-year review of progress achieved since the Earth Summit. The CSD also invited the World Tourism Organization to seek further input from the private sector, non-governmental organizations and other stakeholders in the further development of its proposed global code of ethics that had been drafted in consultation with the industry over the previous two years. The final 'Global Code of Ethics for Tourism,' introduced by the World Tourism Organization in late 1999, sets a frame of reference for the responsible and sustainable development of international tourism. It includes nine articles outlining the basic rules for governments, tour operators, developers, travel agents, workers, as well as host communities and the tourists themselves. The tenth article deals with implementation and includes a proposed mechanism for conciliation, through the creation of a World Committee on Tourism Ethics made up of representatives of each region of the world and representatives of each group of stakeholders in the tourism sector, governments, the private sector, and labour and non-governmental organizations. The United Nations General Assembly adopted the Global Code of Ethics for Tourism at the end of 2001.

Although progress has been achieved over the past ten years, one of the key remaining challenges for the international community is to devise ways and means to assist developing countries to ensure that their tourism industries become more internationally competitive without damaging their natural resources and environmental assets base. This will require, amongst other things, greater technical and financial assistance, including human resources development, institutional capacity building and the transfer of environmentally sound technologies to many developing countries. The international community could also support the wider use of 'debt-fornature swaps', through which a portion of the foreign debt of developing countries is purchased at a discount by various international partners in exchange for the debtor's country investment of an agreed sum of local currency in environmental protection projects.

Conclusion

As stressed above, tourism is expected to resume its rapid growth in the future because of improved living standards, rising incomes and amounts of free time, the falling real cost of travel, and improved transportation around the world. This growth can be harnessed not only for the enjoyment of tourists themselves but, more importantly, for maximizing economic benefits and thus increasing the living standards of host communities and countries. At the same time, it is bound to have negative environmental and socio-cultural impact on those communities, whose involvement in tourism planning, development and management can be crucial to minimizing the impact. The major challenge for the international community is, therefore, not only to minimize the negative impact of tourism but also to ensure that the economic benefits of tourism can contribute to environmental protection and the sustainable use of natural resources. The International Year of Ecotourism – officially launched at the United Nations headquarters in New York on 28 January 200249 – offers an ideal opportunity not only to review ecotourism experiences around the world, but also to promote worldwide recognition of the important role of sustainable tourism in the broader international sustainable development agenda. Ecotourism is one of the fastest growing segments of the tourism sector and further rapid growth is expected in the future. There is, however, little agreement about its exact meaning because of the wide variety of so-called ecotourism activities provided by many different tour operators and enjoyed by an equally broad range of diverse tourists. Its main features include (a) all forms of nature tourism aimed at the appreciation of both the natural world and the traditional cultures existent in natural areas, (b) deliberate efforts to minimize the harmful human impacts on the natural and socio-cultural environment and (c) support for the protection of natural and cultural assets and the well-being of host communities.

In other words, if carried out responsibly, ecotourism can be a valuable means for promoting the socio-economic development of host communities while generating resources for the preservation of natural and cultural assets. In this way, ecologically fragile areas can be protected with the financial returns of ecotourism activities made by both the public and private sectors. In many developing countries, ecotourism has been particularly successful in attracting private investments for the establishment of privately owned natural parks and nature reserves. Many of such reserves are well-managed, self-financed and environmentally responsible, even when profit remains the main motivation behind the operation of a private reserve. In this way, the tourism industry can help to protect and even rehabilitate natural assets, and thus contribute to the preservation of biological diversity and ecological balance.

However, if not properly planned, managed and monitored, the concept of ecotourism can be distorted for purely commercial purposes and even for promoting ecologically-damaging activities by large numbers of tourists in natural areas. Given their inadequate physical infrastructure and limited capacity to absorb mass tourism, the fragile land and ocean ecosystems of many developing countries can be literally overwhelmed by large numbers of tourists. It is increasingly recognized, therefore, that unsustainable ecotourism activities may threaten the very natural environment upon which they depend. There is, in fact, a crucial distinction between ecotourism and sustainable tourism: while the former can be broadly defined as an alternative, nature-based type of tourism, the above-mentioned sustainability principles must be applied to all types of tourism activities and all segments of the tourism industry. At a campsite on the long trekking route to Concordia and K-2 base camp in northern Pakistan, there is a presumably 'politically correct' sign that says: "Take nothing but photos; Leave nothing but footprints." If tourists follow those instructions, but do so insensitively or in mass numbers, those seemingly inoffensive acts can disturb local cultural values and ecological balance, respectively. It should be clear by now that even ecotourism activities can cause adverse ecological impacts, particularly if they are not properly managed or if they involve tourist numbers beyond the local carrying capacity.

5

The Educational Origins of Hospitality

Tourism was used at key points in British history to educate people. It is possible to argue that it was filling an educational role most of the time, at least in its early stages. Virtually all forms of tourism began for educational reasons. Most currently available work under plays this fact, with the possible exception of discussions on the Grand Tour. Holloway makes a statement about "tourists and locals alike widening their horizons" almost as an afterthought to a short discussion of sociocultural problems. Cooper et. al. refer to myths surrounding tourism which "should be broken", pointing out "Tourism is not purely for the purposes of leisure. It also includes business tourism, pilgrimages and tourism for health purposes". A later chapter on "The Future of Tourism" makes only passing mention to 'new' tourists looking for "rewarding activities to fill their leisure time and to satisfy their cultural, intellectual and sporting interests", but it is only in the context of the needs of certain market segments in "multi-interest travel". Voase (1995) in an interesting and useful book touches on many aspects of tourism which relate to education, without dealing with it as a perspective. A chapter about the future discusses economics, global warming, people in tourism, sustainability, transport and fashions, but not tourism as an educative activity.

Ryan's "The Chase of a Dream, the End of a Play" refers to tourism as an educative process within the context of sociological discussion. The historical references consider tourism largely as leisure and escapism. Hollinshead's "Heritage Tourism Under

Post-modernity: Truth and the Past" in the same collection as Ryan (1997), shows how great a gap there is between the sociological critic on the one hand and the teacher of history on the other, as the scholarship of Samuel's "Theatres of Memory" (1994) illustrates. Hollinshead paints a pessimistic picture of a world in which all history teaching outside the classroom or library appears impossible since it long ago succumbed to a conspiracy by various forces of darkness. There is little illumination in this kind of writing for the history teacher working out of the classroom. History teachers know well that all interpretations-including books and academic papers-of the world take particular viewpoints, selecting, interpreting and presenting reality as they see it. Even so, a re-assessment of tourism which hopes to be accepted at a higher academic level will have to establish a credible, theoretical and practical counter-argument to the Hollinshead kind of view.

Weiler and Hall edited a collection of papers in "Special Interest Tourism" (1992) which look at a number of case studies and review some sectors. They point to the "diversity of market segments and products... encompassed within the rubric of `special interest tourism'" and "the limited amount of research that has been done". The book unfortunately suffers from being more a collection of snapshots of relevant areas, but the opening chapter does attempt an overview. Sadly, it remains only a collection of separate perspectives such as marketing, ethics and green tourism, rather than shining a well-focused new light on the whole issue.

Within the book, the paper on "Educational Travel" is particularly disappointing in its attempt to take a historical perspective. It makes only two references, the first to the Grand Tour as the originator of educational travel and second to 'Chautauqua'. "The modem-day learning vacation concept seems to have originated at Chautauqua, a residential institution in New York. Initiated in 1874 by a Methodist minister and an Ohio businessman, Chautauqua blends the concept of an outdoor recreation setting with social activities and learning opportunities". This American example is interesting and important as it led to some 12,000 similar centres within the United States, but they were largely centres where general educational activities took place, rather than centres where people discovered their (temporary) new environments through first-hand contact. As a perspective on educational tourism it is disappointing. Another look must be taken at the history of tourism forms.

The pilgrimage was an early form of informal education as it brought devotees closer to knowledge of sacred sites and introduced them to new experiences and knowledge, but not in any didactic way. Prehistoric pilgrimages took place to centres associated with magical properties and religious beliefs, and specifically Christian pilgrimages were undertaken at least from the late fourth century AD. Around 610 AD pilgrims could buy a guide to the churches of Rome-an early aid to visitor interpretation. The Canterbury Pilgrims, following a well-used route from Winchester or London to Canterbury Cathedral relied on a growing infrastructure of tracks, inns and stables in order to make their journey. In Poland, the monastery of Jasna Gora in Czestochowa, founded in 1382, received thousands of pilgrims each year to see an image of the Blessed Virgin Mary housed there: by 1682 it was around 140,000, and by the present day it sometimes welcomes a million in a single year. Historically, each visit was part of a process of communication and teaching in which what the pilgrims had seen and experienced was fed back to others in their own villages and towns.

The nature of the Grand Tour as an education for the sons of the English gentry has been well covered. Rooted in the explorations of Queen Elizabeth I's age, the Grand Tour was encouraged by her as a means of training men for government. Feifer quotes James Howell's "Instructions for Forraine Travel" (1642) comparing the stay-at-home with the traveller. "To run over and traverse the world by hearsay... other men's eyes... is but a confused and imperfect kind of speculation, which leaveth but weak and distrustful notions" said Howell of the former, and praised the first-hand view of the latter: "the eye... as through a clear and crystal casement we... in one instant comprehend half the whole universe".

Though the later Grand Tourists were more interested in pleasure than in being educated, the whole experience remained educational in the widest of senses. Even time spent in a brothel would teach the young buck about life. The part played by Grand Touring in British culture is well documented, but there was an important influence on industry and technology, too. Thomas Cook's entry into the history of travelling was made by a desire to educate. The 1841 railway excursion from Leicester to Loughborough took five hundred people to an open space where Cook, a Baptist preacher, could educate them about the evils that he saw in alcohol. However successful he might have been in his chosen aim, he was certainly successful in his method. With a combination of the excitement of open-wagon rail travel, the leisurely nature of the day, and the ambience of a different environment, the Leicester folk must have been in a receptive and tolerant mood. No consumer motivator could ask for more. Thomas Cook's contributions were all about packaging travel, an attention to detail, and the providing of quality experiences, but above all the enjoyment by his customers of discovering new places.

The growth of seaside holidays is also well documented. From them it can be seen that even the hedonism of the seaside existed alongside the wonders of discovery. In 1788 Catherine Hutton from Birmingham wrote home about the people she encountered in Blackpool: "The Boltoners are sincere, good humoured and noisy. The Manchestrians reserved and purse-proud, the Liverpoolians free and open as the ocean upon which they get their riches". And while Blackpool was a place of social encounter, it was also one with an Opera House, an Aquarium, a Menagerie, a Winter Gardens with "high class concerts", and its famous Circus. From 1910 even the Pleasure Beach had its "edutainment" in devices like the Naval Spectatorium which used 360-degree film projection and mechanical devices to present representations of the American Civil War, and later, World War I naval battles. Such devices were the norm for resorts which wanted to entertain their visitors, and indeed, Scarborough retains its "Naval Warfare" event to this day.

Presenting the wonders of the world has been a foundation for entertainment ever since the earliest bards told their stories. In due course the resorts of the industrialised world built fair grounds, theatres, museums, galleries, menageries and gardens drawing upon the culture, artefacts, flora and fauna of the world around them. Fairs like the Kursaal at Southend-on-Sea, Dreamland at Margate, and the Paradium at Great Yarmouth derived excitement from representations, however distorted, of reality. The huge Coney Island parks in New York almost became international expositions in their own right by building theatres, cinemas and other shows. They were in direct line of descent from the London, Paris, Vienna and Chicago Exhibitions long before Disney.

Visiting great houses and museums, and the educational value that related to such excursions, has been a recent subject of analysis. Ousby says that "Travel was a leading instrument of that post-Reformation spirit of enquiry which valued empirical knowledge over abstract speculation or book-learning derived merely from tradition".

It was during the middle years of the nineteenth century, and in parallel with the beginnings of formalised education for various age groups from young to old, that the practice was established of townspeople and city dwellers making day visits to the country. These were not only for what we might term 'escapist' entertainment, but for 'self-improvement'.

Local newspapers of the time are full of the accounts of annual outings by social groups from chapels or work-places. There are detailed accounts preserved of the organisation required for the bigger trips, such as the well-known railway excursions from the Bass Breweries. These show how guide books and visits of an 'improving nature' were made integral to the excursions by those who organised them. One quotation from the 40-page booklet distributed to 8,000 participants in the 1914 visit to Scarborough will give a flavour:

"The improvements made since our last visit in 1910 consist of deepening the old or West Harbour by about three to four feet, so as to accommodate and give more room for fishing craft of a larger size and to the increasing number of Steam Drifters now engaged in the Herring Fishery, in addition to the Sailing Herring Fishers. The West Pier, where the fish is landed, sold and packed, has been widened-70 feet being added-and now provides excellent curing and packing spaces for the herring curers and exporters".

A videotaped account given by a retired worker from John Crossley and Sons' carpet mills in Halifax shows in anecdote some of the cultural effects. Mrs Florence Waite took part in a long railway excursion over 30 hours to Edinburgh, Glasgow and the Isle of Bute in 1934 with Crossley's Social Club. The impact made by Edinburgh's particular historic character, and the Clyde's glorious scenery, are clear even after sixty years.

Delgado has shown how important the annual excursion was as an escape from the industrial city. In 1912 the Duchess of Sunderland foresaw "A day that is a glimpse of Paradise to the poor little mites who live in the darkness of squalid back courts and the mean streets of our cities", when raising money for a charity sending children on a countryside excursion.

Thomas Cook had religious motives (it was his son John Mason Cook who went fully commercial in tourism), believing that through his tours "man has been brought nearer to man and nearer to his Creator". It must be stressed that Cook began as an evangelist, a communicator, and not a tour operator. However unconsciously, he succeeded because he removed his audience from the stress of everyday life, induced within them a receptive and relaxed frame of mind, and then tried to persuade them to adopt a new lifestyle based on Christianity and, in particular, teetotalism. This aligns with Turner's analysis of the pilgrimage with its ideas of separation, liminality and communitas. But it also aligns with the principles of propaganda and persuasion of the use of group psychology, removing his audience to a different setting, creating a receptive mood and using crowd psychology to persuade individuals to adopt new attitudes. Cook's Loughborough excursion operated in terms of communication between people, and between people and environments, depending on the contrasts between Leicester (a city full of the stresses of everyday life), the thrills of the railway journey (excitement, empowerment, and innovation) and the Loughborough destination (comparative arcadia, relaxation, and enjoyment). Cook's aim was to educate, and educate effectively.

A similar set of motives inspired the Reverend T A Leonard. The Congregational minister preached a sermon at Dockray Street Church in Colne in August 1891 in which he criticised the habit some people had of 'laking' about-playing-saying that "the devil wields no small influence over holiday times". Holidays should be taken sensibly, sacredly indeed. Leonard's view was "Speak to the earth and it will teach thee". The idea of education within holidays was present when Leonard went on to encourage a group of thirty men to organise a holiday in Ambleside in 1891, and Caernarfon the next. By 1893 he was Secretary "of a scheme which embodies a new idea of summer holidays", inviting adult education classes and Pleasant Sunday Associations to join in visits to Ambleside and Keswick, walking by day and enjoying music and `lecturettes' in the evenings. The rambles were conducted by a University companion guide appointed by the National Home Reading Union. This was the beginning of the Co-operative Holidays Association, now the Countrywide Holidays Association and operating many holiday homes for its members.

Formal education out of doors is little covered in tourism books, yet it is one which by its variety and early encounter by students must underlie so much of their subsequent interest in travel. A very early example of this activity is that of the herbarizing organised by the Society of Apothecaries of London. This was the practical means by which apprentice apothecaries could be taught to recognise plants which would have medicinal values. The first one known took place in May of 1620, beginning at 5.00 am with a rendezvous at St Paul's in the City. The day was spent out in the country, then relatively close by. Within a short while six excursions a year were being held. After a while a paid official known as the Demonstrator of Plants was employed to lead the excursions, and in 1673 the Chelsea Physic Garden was established as a permanent demonstration area. It has since become an important tourist attraction in its own right. Herbarizings continued up to 1824 when it was decided London was too big to allow for day excursions to open countryside, and the educational practice was abandoned. By then, many botanists had received their introduction to the subject through these events.

In 1732 The Society of Dilettante was formed from a group of men who had been on the Grand Tour. The Society helped to pioneer archaeological field study. Geology field teaching was in turn developed from 1804 by Robert Jameson of Edinburgh who took formal field classes as far away as the Western Isles. Geography field teaching in the UK got off to a relatively late start and in 1938 a survey of London schools showed that "hardly a half are able to conduct outdoor field work". This was despite John Ruskin having said that "the country will become an outer and uncovered classroom, a Divine museum utilised by our teachers". Excursions were the exception, rather than the rule. One did occur in 1886, when Scott Keltie reported to the Royal Geographical society that the children of Gordon's Hospital School, Aberdeen, were "taken out into the country and in a simple, rough but effective, and to them, interesting and instructive way, are taught to draw maps of a small area for themselves". On the other hand, adult geographers made group excursions quite early. The Manchester Geographical Society went to inspect the new docks in Preston in the autumn of 1887 for example. It should be remembered that individual adult travellers were being drawn towards industrial locations to see the changed landscapes presented from at least the 1780s onwards, as has been seen above. Field Societies, Scientific and Literary Societies and Geographical Societies continued through the nineteenth and twentieth centuries to make such excursions.

The practice widened out in the twentieth as manufacturers like Cadburys and Wedgwoods, anxious to promote their methods and products, opened their doors to all kinds of groups. Lever Brothers joined with the LMS railway company to promote tourism to their factory in Port Sunlight in 1926. In the 1950s and 1960s both companies handled thousands of adult and school visitors. The present author recalls making visits to factories such as Lotus Shoes in Stone, British Rail Engineering in Crewe, a Co-op Dairy in Llangadog, the Velindre Tinplate Works and the Steel Company of Wales, Port Talbot. The steel and engineering companies used visits for general public relations purposes, the consumer goods makers used them to sell their wares. Even tiny manufacturers got involved, for example Joseph Dobson and Sons of Elland who from 1980 welcomed visitors in order to raise their profiles against their big competitors.

Indeed, Marling has recently shown how even that great icon of theme park tourism, Walt Disney, began with ideas for a "kiddies park". Disney's new Burbank studio of 1939 was laid out on production-line principles. Having seen Snow White, people were asking to see how the animation was done. Disney thought that those who did visit found the whole process boring, and in any case there was none of the fairy tale magic on the production floor. So he began to plan a special area which would show both magic and motion picture production.

Early in the twentieth century it took people like James Fairgrieve, training geography teachers in the 1920s, to foster an interest in school excursions and holidays. He suggested children in east London could begin by finding out "information about the commodities that their fathers are handling". They could look at the doors of Fleet Street to see listed the newspapers of the British Empire as a starting point for discussing its geography. They would continue by making excursions to other places. "This is a benefit not only to the understanding of other lands but to the understanding of the homeland also. In a very real sense the homeland is measured by other lands: also, unless it is seen in its world setting, it is not really understood". Factory visits were being added by progressive teachers at least from the late 1940s.

The nineteenth century was the great age of self-improving societies, often growing out of church or chapel groups who began to investigate interesting subjects. Others were specifically for self-help. The earliest-and still thriving with its private museum and lecture programme and visits-was the Spalding Gentlemen's' Society, founded in 1710. There were Mechanic's Institutes and worker's educational groups, and the subject societies for literary and scientific pursuits, from botany to geology and geography, many of which organised and ran their own excursions. In the United States similar self help groups emerged in the diverse and often isolated settlements further west, while in the east urban groups sprang up, and the Chautauqua, already mentioned, had an important effect.

The original Chautauqua started as a summer vacation and training centre for Sunday School teachers at Chautauqua Lake, near to Lake Erie, in New York State. It developed as a place for discussion and debate on classical and current topics. Scholars, actors, speakers and exhibits were arranged, plays put on, great speeches re-made and debates staged. Home-reading circles became part of the system, and for a time participants could study for a degree at a Chautauqua University.

The idea was imported to Britain largely through the work of J B Paton, who had been involved in setting up a University Extension in Nottingham. In 1887 Paton formed a small committee with John Percival, Headmaster of Rugby School, and from 1888 they organised Summer Meetings at Oxford with educational courses. This line continued as the growth in the UK of adult education.

By the late nineteenth century the ideas of Frederic Le Play and then Patrick Geddes had formed the basis for sociological field work with a strong geographical basis. Geddes' ideas has particularly interesting features in the context of the present paper. In Paris in 1878 he visited the International Exhibition and was enthusiastically inspired by the display of the reconstruction of Paris after the Franco-Prussian war of 1870. Returning to Edinburgh he became immersed in ideas of planning and improvement, one step in which was the purchase by him of the old Observatory at the lower end of the Castle Esplanade. It housed (and still does) a camera obscura which was used to project views of the city onto a white 'projection table' for visitors to study.

Renamed the Outlook Tower and using whatever small funds and voluntary help that he could muster, Geddes began to create a kind of regional museum. He was also involved in teaching at the Edinburgh Summer Meetings or schools, linking the educational work with the displays in his Outlook Tower and excursions into Edinburgh to encourage city renewal.

Helen Meller, in Patrick Geddes: "Social Evolutionist and City Planner", shows how he absorbed ideas from the efforts of museums to collect and classify social knowledge. The Musee Sociale in Paris built on ideas which had been shown at the Paris Exhibitions of 1867, 1878 and 1889 about the study of people and their environs. The International Bibliographical Institute in Brussels was systematically collecting and classifying human knowledge in order to act as a centre of study. Geddes devised an idea for an `Index Museum' in his Outlook Tower with a kind of three-dimensional encyclopaedia of the world installed in it. Geddes again went to an Exhibition in Paris, this time in 1900, organising a huge programme of lectures and tours in a Summer School there. "Eight hundred classes were held in just 120 days, and the average attendance at these was between 40 and 502". And there at the Exhibition were pavilions and buildings from around the world. Geddes wanted to save them as a permanent `Index Museum', a centre of study of the world's cultures and societies. It failed to happen for reasons of cost and ownership.

Within the Paris Exhibition of 1900 the strands of education, tourist attraction (the displays) and inspiration for progress (the ideas communicated by the displays and the School) came together. It did not become permanent: that would happen in museums and inter-activity centres in another age, perhaps more related to heritage than to visions of the future as Geddes wanted, but the principles, firmly based in educative forms of tourism, were all there.

A different-though related-reason was behind the origins of the Scout and Guide movement, which turned mere country visiting into an organised, structured, educationally-motivated activity. "Our business is not merely to keep up smart `show' troops, but to pass as many boys through our character factory as we possibly can: at the same time, the longer the grind that we can give them the better men they will be in the end". Scouting was one of the occupations which, along with inspirational books like "Bevis: The Story of A Boy" and "Swallows and Amazons" created the idea of adventure holidays which is at the heart of modem children's activity tourism. Jefferies educated his readers about the countryside: Baden-Powell trained his, through "Scouting For Boys" into adventurers who grew inwardly through their interaction with the rural environment.

As Michael Rosenthal shows, much of scout culture drew upon the works of the Anglo-American author, Ernest Thompson Seaton. Between the 1880s and the 1900s Seton spread ideas of what he called Woodcraft' as a way for young American males to learn from, and be entertained by, life in the great outdoors. He based his philosophy on the native North American culture and outlined a national movement based on features from his reading of native life, with a liberal dash of European chivalric ideas thrown in. Baden-Powell's movement adopted some of the ideas, but Seton's Woodcraft Indians continue still as a separate organisation. There was also an influence on the European Woodcraft Folk movement which grew amongst people who wanted a youth organisation which avoided what they saw as Baden-Powell's establishmentism and military leanings. Within one sector of tourism therefore it is possible to follow the development of a clear political/philosophical strand. During the nineteenth century the growth and diversity of schooling allowed experimentation in terms of organisation and curriculum. Influenced by Rousseau's ideas about the importance of an individual's development some innovations were made which tried to relate teaching environments to the pupil's needs. In England, Cecil Reddie founded Abbotsholme School in 1889 as somewhere which could take a boy "to train him how to live". This meant daily, outdoor activities such as drill, sports, river bathing, running, carpentry and gardening.

Just after World War I Kurt Hahn co-founded Salem School in Germany with Prince Max von Baden, in which the development of character and selfdiscipline were foremost. Abbotsholme had an influence. With the arrival of Nazism Kurt Hahn was forced to leave, and he moved to Britain_ In late 1933 he opened Gordonstoun School in Scotland, with a disciplinarian programme which included ideas of service to the nearby community. From 1935 onwards boys were enrolled as HM Coastguards, and they later operated a small fire brigade. The 'Moray Badge' scheme was devised with tests in athletics, expeditions, and life-saving, partly in response to a national debate about the poor quality of fitness in young people. It is interesting to note the similarities to matching fears expressed at the turn of the century about the health and character of boys which helped lead to the Boy Scouts.

Out of the Badge scheme came three experimental; residential summer schools in Invemess-shire and Morayshire. Their success led in turn to the formation of the Outward Bound schools, this time in Wales, at Aberdovey, to which Gordonstoun had been evacuated on the outbreak of war. From 1941 an Outward Bound Sea School commenced operation, offering courses to young men from industry, not only in maritime activities, but also 30-mile mountain country expeditions. The Outward Bound movement has also grown and expanded its activities to a number of British and European centres.

In Germany the idea of the school excursion had gained ground rapidly from 1907 and the formation of the 'wandervogel' at Jena in January that year. Its aims were "to promote rambles and excursions of German boys in their own and other neighbourhoods, and thus to awaken in them a taste for the beauties of nature, and to give them opportunities of learning to know their German homeland and its people at first hand". Local associations were set up and older children encouraged to qualify as guides. Books and maps were bought and could be hired out to non-members. Travel and overnight accommodation were to be simple-fourth-class rail and country barns.

Earlier still, the Eberfeld 'Realgymnasium' was one of several schools which held indoor lessons until noon and then gymnastics or excursions. On six afternoons in the summer term the whole four hundred children at Eberfeld would march out of town behind a band, the older children going the furthest, and teachers instructing the pupils along the way. Games would round off the excursion, for which six hours was allowed. The government extended the Whit holiday to allow higher classes make longer journeys to places like the Westerwald, Taunus and Eiffel districts. Up to twenty boys and their masters might make a fortnight's visit to somewhere like Italy. The days started early and consisted of long walks followed by evening recreation ("beer and songs") and summaries by the boys of what they had done-often given in foreign languages. The pupils paid themselves in advance, with poorer boys charged less, but "for poor masters no funds were provided". It is noteworthy that German interest in exploring environments seems to have underpinned the country's ideas in gestalt psychology, to which reference will be made later.

Another organisation began in Germany in the same year, 1907, that Baden-Powell was holding his first scout camp on Brownsea Island in Poole Harbour. A teacher, Richard Schirmann, opened his school to a group of children from slum areas, so that they could enjoy a countryside holiday. Two years later Altena Town Council and a local businessman gave money to turn Burg Altena into a hostel. It was the start of the 'wandervogel' movement, anti-militarist, anti-machinery, pro-country life. Britain set up its first hostel in 1930 though a water-supply problem forced it to close soon afterwards. The YHA dates from that year, and the next year saw no fewer than twenty hostels open. Country life, exploration and adventure were the aims of all their visitors.

In Britain all of these strands became woven together after 1945 and new ones were added. The Field Studies Council in Britain opened its first centre in Suffolk in 1946, and the first local authority centre, White Hall near Buxton, opened in 1950. National Parks, open air museums, commercially-run adventure centres, stately homes and historic houses, castles and wartime defences, zoos and sea-life centres, gardens and country parks, heritage centres and inter-active science centres, factory tours and craft demonstration units made their appearances on ever larger scales. Were these just part of a heritage industry making new money, or an extension of the very long growth of educational tourism? School visits, especially when linked to the National Curriculum, can provide the bread-and-butter visitor income that they need to survive.

This account of some of the educational aspects of tourism is not complete, nor could it be within the confines of a discussion paper. Nor does it attempt to discuss in detail who benefited from each, nor just how much benefit there was, nor how prejudiced or enlightened any of it might have been. What is important here is the acknowledgement of the frequent close liaison that there has always been in tourism with education. It is fair, and appropriate, to say that all forms of information and opinion, whether expressed between individuals, through the mass media, or in education, are subject to limitations on access, quality and objectivity. The point is that tourism is just as good, or just as bad, as they are. But it has, like them, a potential for being beneficial.

Educational Tourism in Thailand

Imagine studying in a country like Thailand... Imagine rewarding yourself with a weekend on the beach after a hard week's study, or trekking through the jungle as soon as your exams are over! Whether for full blown degree programs or short vocational courses, more and more people are making Thailand part of their educational objectives and becoming 'Educational Tourists'.

With fewer Thai students studying abroad over the last decade, foreign universities opened campuses in Thailand or made agreements with Thai universities to run 'Dual' (or 'Twinning') degree programs-foreign degrees run at Thai universities. As a result, Thailand has a huge choice of international-level education options and is a major draw for students all over the world looking for world-class education.

Of course, to benefit from higher education at an 'English-medium' university, students must understand English well. For many years there has been a booming domestic market for

English language courses in Thailand; a market driven by Thai students who appreciate the benefits of studying with a native English speaking teacher. As a result, there are countless teaching jobs available to foreign teachers in Thailand, both at commercial language centres and within the state system. Such is the demand for teachers that visitors often include teaching English as part of their itinerary for a trip to Thailand. Would-be-teachers do though need training and as a result of there has been a dramatic rise in the number of English teacher training courses available in the Kingdom. Whether it's short courses that give you the basics, or detailed internationally recognized courses that offer a stepping stone into the English teaching profession, there is certainly a course in Thailand to meet your needs.

English though is not the only language you can study in Thailand. As the country takes its place on the international stage, its influence grows around the world. Increasingly, people take Thai language lessons for business and educational purposes, or simply build a short language course into their stay in the country for fun. As a result, a number of commercial Thai language centres catering for expatriates and visitors have emerged to give people an insight into the language.

Of course, with the rise of tourism to Thailand the world is now interested in all things Thai – particularly Thai food. There is an abundance of centres in Thailand teaching foreigners the intricacies of preparing Thai cuisine... and very popular they are, too! With the worldwide boom in Spas and 'Wellness', the demand for masseurs able to offer Thai massage is increasing and the number of visitors studying massage in Thailand growing. Likewise, more and more visitors take courses in traditional Thai medicine to become practitioners in their own countries. What follows is a sample of courses for 'Educational Tourists':

University Courses in Thailand

Although traditionally every young Thai person's dream has been to study abroad in a country like the USA, Britain or Australia, the realities of issues like the financial downturn of the late 1990s, '9-11' and war in Iraq forced many to reconsider their educational goals. As a result, numbers of Thai students studying abroad plummeted as many chose to stay at home.

Losing valuable revenue streams, foreign universities got creative. Rather than fighting over fewer Thai foreign students, they changed tactics and began to look at opportunities actually here in Thailand. As a result, some of the world's leading universities now either have a campus in Thailand or are attached to a Thai university where they offer 'International' degree programs. The benefits to Thai students of having world-class higher education on their doorstep are obvious, but there have been substantial benefits for Thailand as a whole – the Kingdom has become a hub for foreign students who want to receive an international-standard higher education. Students from places like China, Taiwan, former Eastern bloc countries, Scandinavia, and increasingly, Europe, the United States and Great Britain, take university courses in Thailand to enjoy the benefits of standard, lower cost (particularly in terms of cost of living and educational fees) and the ability to simply be able to enjoy Thailand while they study. Most universities require some formal indication of English language capability and increasingly this means students taking an IELTS test. Click here to learn more about the IELTS listening, reading, writing and speaking test. What follows are details of some of Thailand's leading universities offering 'International' programs.

6

Approaches in Youth Hospitality

Introduction

Recreation is an essential service in establishing and maintaining a healthy, livable community. Availability and accessibility to recreation opportunities contributes to effective crime prevention and reducing health care costs. Opportunities and facilities that promote physical and mental well being, bring citizens together in positive, supportive, and fun atmospheres, and create memorable experiences for families are primary in a positive future for our community. By proactively approaching the future needs of a growing and aging population, recreation programs and facilities contribute to a healthy community. The physical, mental, environmental, and economic contributions are great and far-reaching. Roughly 40% of the public has participated in a recreation or arts program offered by the City of Olympia during the past 12 months. The highest participation in recreation programs is by people in the age groups of 25 to 34 (50%), 55 to 64 (48.6%), and 10 to 14 (47.6%).

The most needed recreation programs, according to survey respondents, are organized sports, swimming activities and cultural arts activities.

Youth Programs

The Youth Programs Division provides a safe, positive environment for Olympia's youth by offering a variety of quality recreational activities and self esteem building experiences. These opportunities include the Middle School After School Program, a free drop-in program offered in cooperation with the Olympia School District, summer and school break day camps that target elementary aged youth, year round outdoor adventure camps and trips, and special events such as Middle School Activity Nights. Recreational opportunities focus on the development of positive, meaningful, nurturing, and supportive relationships between staff, youth, school administrators, teachers, custodial staff, parents, and other youth service agencies. Physical and emotional safety for all staff and participants is highly emphasized.

It is important to offer a diverse array of recreational opportunities that allow youth to explore, learn and develop social, physical and problem solving skills. In the After School Program this is accomplished by conducting the recreational components brought to each activity site by recreation leaders on a rotating schedule. Components include Outdoor Adventure Skills, Sports and Field Games, Fitness and Dance, Arts, Crafts, Cooking and Leadership Development and Community Service.

In addition, field trips and special guests are regularly scheduled. Day camp programs also include similar components with field trips, swimming and tennis lessons available.

Youth between the ages of 6 and 14 years of age make up the primary target population for this program area. Day camp programs are appropriate for 6 to 11 years olds, with a Leader-In-Training option for youth 12 to 14 years old.

Many of the youth participants in the After School program would be considered latchkey youth, having no adult supervision between the hours of 2:30 PM and 6:00 PM. The benefits of these programs are preventative, offering positive recreation options during after school hours. Youth participants also have opportunities to associate with positive adult role models in supervised activities where they learn and practice appropriate behaviour and build supportive relationships. Day camp participants also have many of the same opportunities, interacting in positive social situations. They also explore and experience new recreational activities.

Facilities Needed

It is important to work closely with the Olympia School District and other local agencies to access facilities for the implementation of these programs. The After School program is most effective when operating on site at each of the respective middle schools. Access to gymnasiums, home economics rooms, weight rooms, cafeterias and play fields allow for diverse program activities. Elementary schools are suitable and offer appropriate facilities for day camp activities. The Olympia Centre is widely used during school break camps with the exception of summer camps. Art rooms, cooking facilities, gymnasiums, and outdoor park areas are important in offering well-rounded program activities.

Staff Needs

Competitive salaries and benefits are vital to recruiting and hiring quality staff. It is also imperative to have funding available for quality staff training opportunities. The public demands responsible, intelligent, resourceful, and caring individuals to supervise their children. To maintain safe and appropriate staffing ratios, 1:8 for day camps, 1:6 for adventure camps, and 1:12 for after school programs, additional staffing positions will be necessary as the youth program grows.

Teen Programs

The Teen Recreation Program offers a wide range of activity choices for teens in the City of Olympia. A year round afternoon program consistently offers activities Monday through Friday. Late Night activities are offered on Fridays in conjunction with the afternoon program. Teens know that five days a week including almost every Friday night, a positive recreation alternative is available.

Teen Recreation Program Participants

Quality staff provides a listening ear and positive role models for teens. They also plan and present a wide menu of recreational activities for teens to choose from. The fun includes field trips for bowling and laser tag, professional sporting events, dances, ceramics, photography and art, kayaking and wind surfing, basketball and hacky sack tournaments, concerts and trips. Educational activities offered by local service agencies are also sponsored regularly. The Teen Recreation Program focuses on providing fun, diverse recreational activities in a safe and supportive environment.

Population Served

The teen program targets any interested teen in the City between the ages of 12-17, unless enrolled in high school. Since January 2000, 1,200 teens have registered for the program. On any given Friday, 150-200 teens seek safe and positive alternatives to parties and other high-risk activities. Staff work diligently to create an environment that honours, promotes and supports diversity. Olympia teens who need support, activity alternatives, or simply a safe place to spend their free time are welcomed at The Olympia Centre, agreeing to respect themselves, the program, the staff, and other program participants.

Facilities Needed

Currently, the Teen Recreation Program is housed at The Olympia Centre, a comprehensive recreation facility that hosts a wide range of populations and activities. Although the program has integrated well within The Olympia Centre, unique challenges such as sharing space, maintaining a reasonable noise level, and accommodating the increasingly successful growth of the program are ever present.

Staff Needs

Competitive salaries and benefits are vital to recruiting and hiring quality staff. It is also imperative to have funding available for quality staff training opportunities. The public demands responsible, intelligent, resourceful, and caring individuals to supervise their youth and teen participants. With the anticipation of future program growth, additional staffing will be necessary to maintain safe and appropriate supervisory ratio of 1:20.

Athletic Programs

The Athletic Program division provides a safe, organized and challenging environment for Olympia's citizens by offering a variety of quality leagues, tournaments, and classes. These opportunities include adult soccer, volleyball and basketball, martial arts, fitness programs and youth clinics and camps. In addition, athletic field allocations for the City and Olympia School District are managed by the Athletic Program within the Department.

Population Served/Benefits

Adults between the ages of 18 and 50 years of age make up the primary target population for adult leagues. Youth sports camp and clinics are appropriate for 6 to 11 year olds.

Preschool Gymnastics Class

Adult athletics provides opportunities for fitness, competition, social interaction, and wellness. Indirect benefits include decreased long-term health care costs and economic opportunities and expenditures diverted to more leisure activities and sports related equipment. Other economic benefits directly impact the community with revenue resources from tournaments positively impacting local hotels, restaurants, and tourism services. Youth participants also have opportunities to associate with positive adult role models in supervised activities where they learn and practice skills, appropriate behaviour and build supportive relationships. Athletic field allocation management creates an opportunity for a comprehensive and diverse approach to usage. The by-product is a fair that efficiently utilizes existing facility resources.

Facilities Needed

To meet the needs for future athletic programs, it will be important to work closely with the Olympia School District and other local agencies to provide facilities for these programs. The Adult Basketball and Volleyball leagues use middle school gymnasiums as well as The Olympia Centre gymnasium. The Adult Soccer programs take advantage of local school fields as well as Yauger Park during the fall, which provides lighted fields.

Staff Needs

Competitive salaries and benefits are vital to recruiting and hiring quality staff. It is also imperative to have funding available for quality staff training opportunities. The public demands responsible, intelligent, resourceful, and caring individuals to supervise and implement quality athletic programs, clinics, and tournaments.

Leisure Recreation Classes

Life long learning and recreational activities are taught

through a variety of class offerings. Most of the leisure recreation classes are conducted at The Olympia Centre. The offerings appeal to a population of wide interests, skill level, and talents. Classes are available to youth, adults, and families and include art, dance, landscape design, languages, cooking, preschool, dog obedience, gymnastics, yoga, computer education, and investment.

These opportunities introduce participants to new recreational activities as well as promote balance, relaxation and creative outlets for our citizens.

Under the leadership of the Parks, Arts & Recreation Department, the City should develop new programs and events to support the recreation activities that are most accessible to Olympia residents: bicycling and walking. The Department should sponsor leisure and moderate paced bicycle rides to help new riders gain strength and confidence for safe and independent riding. In addition, the City should support recreational walking and bicycling by developing maps that show the location of trails, routes, parks, and important interpretative and educational locations. The City should also consider bicycle safety and education programs for youth and adults in coordination with the Olympia Police Department and Transportation Division.

Population Served/Benefits

All segments of the Olympia population are served through recreation classes and special events. Youth, teens, adults, families, and seniors have many opportunities to choose from. Scholarships are available to families and individuals that demonstrate financial need.

Promoting healthy lifestyles through positive and creative recreational opportunities benefits the entire community. Seniors engage in uplifting social interaction, vital to physical and emotional health, while continuing or learning new recreational skills. Youth and teens have opportunities to try new activities in a positive and supportive atmosphere while learning appropriate social skills. Adults enjoy continuing education opportunities, learning skills that empower them to become more self-sufficient, environmentally conscious, and physically and creatively active.

Facilities Needed

In anticipation of population growth, increased participant interest, and furthering skill development and activity offerings, additional recreation facilities are needed. While most classes are conducted at The Olympia Centre, it does not have the capacity or functionality to host the current demand. Inappropriate flooring, classroom size, lighting and other aspects impair functional space.

This impacts the cost effectiveness and quality of classes. Limited classroom space and building scheduling conflicts create waiting lists for popular classes, disappointing many would-be participants.

To meet the current as well as anticipated needs it is vital to work closely with other facilities operators, such as the Olympia School District and other local agencies to access facilities for the implementation of these programs. While The Olympia Centre offers a centrally located activity site, local schools offer more convenient and accessible activity sites for many other residents.

Seniors and youth particularly will benefit greatly by establishing identified neighbourhood educational facilities as community schools where recreational classes will be available. This concept also allows for the expansion of program schedules into after school hours during the school year and mornings during the summer. Schools offer complete and comprehensive recreational facilities with gymnasiums, art and music rooms, home economic rooms, computer labs, weight rooms, cafeterias and play fields.

More importantly, there is a need to build and maintain facilities that are dedicated solely to conducting a comprehensive recreation menu for all ages and interests levels.

Staff Needs

Competitive salaries and benefits are vital to recruiting and hiring quality staff, contractors, and instructors. It is imperative to have funding available for quality staff training opportunities. The public demands responsible, intelligent, resourceful, and caring individuals to teach and lead a variety of recreational classes.

Special Events

Community events promote family recreation and activities. Ethnic and cultural diversity is celebrated through dance and entertainment, food, art, crafts, and educational demonstrations. Youth activities include hands on projects, games, bubble gum blowing contests, petting zoos, and sensory and large motor skill activities. Families and adults enjoy a variety of music, dance and entertainment presentations. These events are free to the public and sponsored largely by local businesses and sponsorship funding and in-kind services. For the community, special events is a time for people from all walks of life to come together celebrating, playing, and enjoying the vast recreational opportunities available.

Population Served/Benefits

All segments of the Olympia population are served through special events. Families and individuals have many opportunities to choose from. Families enjoy outings and experience a variety of recreational opportunities that they might otherwise not have access to due to limited finances, transportation or knowledge of resources. A sense of belonging to a vibrant community is a common thread throughout all of the events offered.

Staff Needs

Competitive salaries and benefits are vital to recruiting and hiring quality staff. It is imperative to have funding available for quality staff training opportunities. The public demands responsible, intelligent, resourceful and caring individuals to plan and implement a variety of special events. In addition, support staff are needed to assist with set up, supervision and take down of events.

Outdoor Adventure Programs

Olympia and the surrounding area host a tremendous number of outdoor recreation resources. Opportunities to learn about and enjoy land and water activities only require organization and programming. Muscle-powered recreational activities available include sailing, wind surfing, hiking, mountain biking, skiing, whale watching, snow shoeing, rock climbing, and beach exploring.

Population Served/Benefits

Seniors and adults enjoy mid-week or weekend activities where they get outdoors, experience positive social interactions, and engage in physical activities. A chance to explore and participate in a variety of outdoor settings – city, county, state and national parks, wildlife refuge areas, and rivers, bays, and lakes – all offer pristine natural environments for relaxing and invigorating experiences.

Youth and teens explore a variety of outdoor skill development and educational opportunities through Outdoor Adventure Camps and Adventure Days. Camp activities include theme camps, such as rock climbing, mountain biking, sailing, or beach exploration and play, or a variety of combined activities such as hiking, sea kayaking, and rock climbing. Older youth can develop outdoor leadership skills through Adventure Leadership Challenge camps. Skills and instruction in outdoor trip logistics, map and compass, outdoor cooking, low-impact camping, wilderness first aid and trip planning are the primary focus. Team building and leadership skill development enhances the camp activities.

Families enjoy winter sleigh rides, summer wagon train treks, up close tours to wildlife animal parks, and river raft trips. These offer unique and exciting experiences that strengthen and bind families to each other. These activities offer informal educational opportunities, social interaction, and exploration of the outstanding outdoor resources available.

Additional benefits include increased environmental and wildlife habitat awareness. Outdoor recreation enthusiasts that are educated and aware of their impact on wetlands, waterways, and trails contribute a great deal to protection, preservation and enhancement of outdoor resources. Citizens who participate in outdoor activities advocate and protect the very resources they use. This further contributes to an overall healthy community.

Economic benefits extend from local businesses benefiting from the sale of outdoor gear and equipment to local state and national parks. Park and trail user fees bring in revenue from entrance fees, back country permits, snow park permits, and some trail fees.

The physical, social, and emotional benefits participants gain from these activities are life long and far reaching. Mentoring and educating future outdoor stewards guarantees that local resources will be available for generations to come. The outdoor environment offers diverse classroom settings for informal education, appropriate settings for a variety of recreational activities-an exceptional atmosphere for uplifting, refreshing, and invigorating the mind and body.

Facilities Needed

While most outdoor activities are conducted in outdoor settings, there is a need for access to indoor facilities. Rock climbing gyms, swimming pools, and classroom space allows for conducting introductory classes related to rock climbing, kayaking, SCUBA diving, and outdoor cooking. Slide presentations and hands on activities such as knot tying, winter clothing and wilderness first aid classes require indoor facilities as well. Many activities and classes are held at local parks with limited shelter available in the event of inclement weather.

Sailing and wind surfing classes and camps are interrupted due to bad weather. With additional indoor facilities available alternative activities related to the camps or classes would allow for uninterrupted continuation of these programs.

Integrating Function, Aesthetics & Metaphor

The Indian Creek Stormwater Treatment Facility was constructed in 2001 as a result of a unique collaboration between the City of Olympia Public Works Department, the Olympia Arts Commission, artist Elizabeth Conner, local Tribes and the Washington State Dept. of Transportation. Although the primary role of this facility is to clean stormwater runoff from Interstate 5, its unique design also integrates public art with the functional aspects of stormwater treatment and slope stabilization. Walking trails, landscape and views of the stormwater cleansing process transform this facility into a publicly accessible site that support creative solutions, discovery and education.

Staff Needs

Outdoor recreation participant interest and skill level continues to increase, creating a demand for more opportunities for youth, teens, seniors, adults, and families. To meet this demand additional staffing is required. An Outdoor Adventure Recreation Coordinator will allow for the required research, planning, development and implementation of additional outdoor opportunities for the community. Pre-trips to new activity areas including the Cascade Marine trail for kayaking/ camping, Capitol Forest trails for hiking and mountain biking, numerous state and national parks trails for hiking and back packing as well as special tours such as Family Christmas tree cutting outings require additional hours for quality activities.

Trip leaders and staff who specialize in and meet standard certification requirements are needed to maintain safe and quality programs. Staffs who relate well to youth, teens, seniors, and families are necessary to conduct successful activities. Ratios for youth adventure camps are 1:6 while adult and family trips are 1:12. Competitive salaries and benefits are vital to recruiting and hiring quality staff, contractors, and instructors. It is imperative to have funding available for quality staff training opportunities on an on-going basis. The public demands responsible, intelligent, resourceful, safety conscious, and caring individuals to teach and lead outdoor adventure recreation classes, camps, and trips.

Conclusion

Public recreational programming is vital to a healthy community. The mental and physical well being of our citizens ensures vibrant, supportive, and safe neighbourhoods. Nurturing our youth and supporting our family structure is the most cost-effective approach to crime prevention. Individuals – youth, adults, and seniors who feel nurtured gain a sense of belonging, make great contributions, and invest in their communities.

Future Needs/Challenges

Budget Resources

To meet the level of service demand by anticipated increased participation in youth and family activities, additional budget resources are necessary. Adult programs are currently and will continue to remain self-supporting.

Facilities

A shared vision of recreational programming by the Olympia

School District with an enhanced or increased level of cooperation is needed to meet the community's needs. Schools that function as satellite or neighbourhood recreation centres after school hours between 3 and 10 p.m. will allow for the expansion, availability, and accessibility of recreation programs to a larger segment of citizens. After school youth recreation programs, classes for seniors, adults, and families, and sports programs all will benefit by this shared vision.

Modifications to The Olympia Centre building are also necessary. It is currently identified as a rental facility, senior centre, youth centre, and for recreation classes. However, limits of space, room configuration, flooring, and availability limit its use as a recreation centre.

The lack of a local community aquatic facility greatly inhibits recreational program offerings. Day camps and youth programs have limited access to local YMCA pools or others operated by outside agencies. Swimming lessons, water aerobics, pool sports, competitive swimming and open swim opportunities are in high demand. Outdoor adventure programs also will be enhanced with access to pool facilities for introductory or educational purposes.

Outdoor athletic facility needs include lighted full sized, year round soccer fields. Tournament level soft ball and soccer fields also will allow for additional recreational opportunities as well as increase the quality of participation and improve safe playing conditions.

With population forecasts showing an aging and growing population, the future of recreation in Olympia needs to be addressed. Either specific recreation facilities must be built or future school facilities need to be designed and built with the intent of meeting this future deficit.

Transportation

Limited availability of adequate program transportation negatively impacts program quality. Currently transportation is accessed through renting or leasing state, county, and private vehicles. Not only is the situation cost-prohibitive it also is often unreliable. To better serve program participants and enhance youth programs, camps, outdoor adventures, and classes, reliable transportation is needed.

Costs

The costs to run quality programs include: 1) staffing and training; 2) supplies and materials; 3) photocopies and binding; 4) uniforms and identification; 5) consumable supplies; 6) equipment; 7) transportation and fuel; 8) admission fees; 9) expert services and/or contractors; 10) marketing and promotion; and 11) photography.

Outdoor Adventure Programs

The costs to run quality outdoor adventure programs include: 1) staffing and training; 2) supplies and materials; 3) photocopies and binding; 4) uniforms and identification; 5) consumable supplies; 6) equipment; 7) expert services and/or contractors; 8) marketing and promotion; 9) photography; and 10) and consistent, reliable, and available transportation for camps and trips.

Equipment needs are numerous based upon the initial program purpose of offering introductory outdoor activities. Many participants do not own or have access to the variety of outdoor gear related to selected activities and would not expect to purchase the gear until deciding to more aggressively pursue certain activities. Equipment and gear needs include snow shoes, cross country ski equipment, kayaks, canoes, and related gear, wind surfboards, binoculars, camp stoves, back packs, tents, and mountain bikes. In order to properly maintain quality gear and equipment these items should be scheduled for replacement every 3 to 5 years.

The greatest challenge is in securing appropriate transportation means. Outdoor camps and trips are often limited due to the lack of appropriate transportation. Transportation needs include multiple 15-passenger vans with trailer hitch capacity and racks for storage containers. A kayak/canoe trailer, bicycle trailer, and enclosed gear trailer are also needed to provide quality activities.

Demographic Trends and their Impact on Holiday Tourism Demand

Demographic Trends and Their Impact on Holiday Tourism Demand: Demographic change is said to be one of the important drivers for new trends in consumer behaviour in most European countries. Two important demographic trends, often being in focus at conferences as well as in publications are:

a. an older growing society due to rising life expectancy (developed countries taking the lead),
b. a declining number of children due to sinking fertility in many industrial countries combined with the dissolution of traditional family patterns,

These are major demographic changes that are already influencing society today and that are worth a closer look on how they may have an impact on holiday travel behaviour.

Compared to other trends, demographic trends seem quite easy to identify and predict-estimated future development based on these developments therefore appears to be rather reliable. The problem is the next step: How will these demographic changes influence consumer behaviour? Are they of any importance? Will the senior generation of tomorrow behave the same way as the present one or perhaps completely different? Will a growing number of one-child-households, patchwork-families, grandparents travelling with their grand children etc. affect the expectations on family products? (How) should suppliers adjust?

To draw conclusions about a potential future reality of consumer behaviour based on statistical data not only requires a sound basis of demographic data but a reliable knowledge on the links between demographic data and the tourists' behaviour. Tourism consumer surveys can provide data

- on the importance a segment has in tourism (does change really matter in terms of volume?)
- on the specific behaviour patterns of the segment in focus (e.g. does a "new", emerging segment show a different behaviour from "older" segments?)
- on the direction and degree of change in tourist behaviour patterns related to the general trends in society

We define a trend as a development in time which can be identified in the past and is likely (with good reasons) to continue in the future. Thus, trends describe *possible* developments likely to come. They can be used as information input for marketing or social planning. According to his objectives, the marketing professional will support or fight the trend, his action of course influencing the reality as well.

This paper gives two examples from Germany on how the results of consumer surveys can be used as a tool for trend research. The first example refers to the growing number and share of "seniors", analyses the fundamental patterns of changes in holiday travel behaviour during the life span, and allows for a surprisingly simple way to have a look at the dynamics ahead. The second example focuses on the declining number of children born combined with the dissolution of traditional family patterns. What does this change mean for holiday tourism?

Database: The "Reiseanalyse" (RA) Travel Survey

The *Reiseanalyse* RA survey (travel analysis), which is conducted in Germany every year, was designed to monitor the holiday travel behaviour, opinions and attitudes of Germans and has been carried out since 1970, using the same method and a comparable set of questions in the questionnaire. The survey describes and analyses holiday trips of 5 days and more as well as short trips of 2-4 days.

The survey is organised by the F.U.R, For schungs gemeinschaft Urlaub und Reisen e.V., Kiel/Hamburg, an independent association of domestic and international users of tourism research in Germany. F.U.R is a non-profit organisation. The users cover a broad spectrum of companies and organisations in the tourist industry such as (special) tour operators, hotel chains, regional, national and international tourism organisations and ministries.

Data are based on face-to-face interviews with a representative sample (German-speaking population aged 14 years and above, living in private households in Germany) of more than 7,500 respondents, the interviews being carried out in January each year. The sample is randomly selected in several steps.

As the survey has been carried out with the same scientific standards for more than 30 years, with a large sample and a very stable set of questions it offers a sound base for long term analyses and a fine tuned segmentation. These features can be quite helpful to examine some of the effects of demographic change on tourism demand.

Holiday Trips of Seniors

Senior Citizens and Tourism

The growing number of senior citizens in the European Union, and other industrialised countries such as the USA and Japan, looks to become one of the major marketing challenges for the tourism industry to grapple with in the new millennium. This demographic shift has already been the focus of some academic tourism research and the topic for several tourism conferences-such as those sponsored by the WTO in Spain (1993), Brazil (1996) and Portugal (1999) as well as for ITB 2000 and 2003 in Berlin.

The idea that elderly need and deserve special attention is not really that recent. In Germany for example this segment has been an issue in the media for more than 40 years.

Even if societies are already experiencing the change and its impacts the fundamental shift still is to come in the next two decades.

In looking ahead, United Nations statistics predicts that the share of people being 60 or older will grow dramatically in the coming decades, and is expected to rise from 10 percent of the world population in 2000 to more than 20 percent in 2050.

Such demographic shifts will be seen on all continents whereas Europe is the major area of the world where population ageing is most advanced. Looking at the predictions for Germany, the number of persons aged 60 years or older will rise from 18.9 mn (23% of the population) in 2000 to 22.9 mn (28.5%) in 2020 and 25.2 mn (35.8%) in 2050.

Thus, there is no doubt that these changes will happen. But what do they mean for the development of tourism demand, e.g.:

- Do we have to face a change in the structure of tourists as well (which only will occur, if people don't stop to travel when getting older)?
- Will there be fewer trips (due to a lower travel propensity of elderly people)?
- Will the "new" seniors travel differently (compared to their predecessors or to the average tourist)? Will we experience a change in basic holiday behaviour patterns?

Methodological Approach: Survey Results can be Useful and May be Misleading

Of course, these questions can not be answered with population statistics and forecasts alone. Several market research projects have looked to asses future senior citizen travel patterns. Such projects have attempted to not only determine the actual number of senior citizens who will be travelling, but have also sought to evaluate and specify certain aspects of future senior travel behaviour. However, they have been based on the implicit assumption of that there is a close relationship between the travel behaviour of past, present and future seniors. But, is this a valid assumption?

Lohmann (1989), Lohmann & Merzbach (1997), and Lohmann & Danielsson (2001) have examined the problem with the help of time series data from the German "Reiseanalyse". Their approach focuses on the development of holiday travel behaviour in the course of life of cohorts, e.g.: How do Germans aged 65 to 75 years travel today, and how did they travel 20 years ago in the age of 45 to 55? As age sure is not the only variable influencing holiday travel behaviour, such an approach has its limits. But we felt it was worth a replication.

Holiday Travel Propensity and Age

Before we try to study the dynamics in the data over time, we examine the holiday participation figures for different age groups in the past and the age structure of German holiday travellers.

Travel propensity, which is defined as the share of persons in the population or a sub-group who made at least one holiday trip lasting five days or longer during a certain year, is one of the general parameters that is necessary to consider. The travel propensity in different age groups of the German population in 1972 and 2003.

As can be seen, older people travel less than younger, today as well as 30 years ago. This may lead to the assumption that people cut down on their holiday activities when getting older. The data reveals as well that today's seniors behave different compared to those 30 years ago, and that their higher travel propensity has been one of the important drivers for the general increase in holiday travel.

Table 1: Change of holiday travel propensity 1972 / 2003

	Holiday travel propensity		*Change*
age group	*1972*	*2003*	*1972/2003*
<29 years	57	80	+ 40%
30-39	53	79	+ 49%
40-59	49	81	+ 65%
60-69	41	76	+ 85%
70+ years	33	63	+91%
All	49	77	+ 57%

Figures for German population aged 14 years or older; in % of age groups

Data source: F.U.R, Reiseanalyse RA 1972-2004

In looking at the demographic situation of travellers in Germany, 2. gives an overview of the change of age structure of travellers since 1972. As the data shows, the overall age structure of holiday travellers did not vary much in the 70s and 80s. Yet, by 1995 the picture had already begun to change quite dramatically with people aged 50 years or older making up more than 40 percent of all travellers.

Table 2: Age structure of German holiday travellers

	1972 %	*1985* %	*1995* %	*2003* %
14 – 19 years	10.1	13,7	7,6	8,3
20 – 29 years	20.9	17,9	17,9	12,1
30 – 39 years	21.0	16,2	18,0	18,5
40 – 49 years	15.4	19,0	15,5	18,3
50 – 59 years	13.2	13,3	18,2	15,4
60+ years	19,4	20,0	22,6	27,5
Travellers (mn)	23.0	27,6	48,9	49,45

Obviously, there is a parallel development in the age structure of the population and of the travellers. However, the cross-sectional data is not sufficient enough to answer the question about whether any generation or cohort *changed* its travel behaviour during their life. Thus the results are of limited value when it comes to the question of future developments.

Participation in Holiday Travel during the Life-Cycle

In order to fully answer that question in-depth, a carefully prepared longitudinal cohort study (panel) would be necessary. Such a study could monitor its subjects travel patterns throughout their life-cycle.

Obviously, such a research project would have to face a lot of practical problems, be very expensive to conduct, and it would take decades to generate any data. Looking at this issue from a methodological perspective, the development of a longitudinal trend study (with a fresh sample each year) based on a series of independent surveys representing the population in different years is a possible solution. The *Reiseanalyse* RA.

Using the RA surveys of different years it is possible to take a look at the travel propensity of different generations between 1970 and 2003. Referring to this RA-data, we define a 'generation' (or cohort) as a group of interviewees who have a similar age at one time, e.g. persons from 70 to 79 years in January 2004 (= the 75 years old), 60 to 69 years in January 1994 ("65 years"), 50 to 59 years in 1984 etc. The data in a specific year for an age group always refers to the group of respondents which is defined by a ten years' range. So, in discussing the 75-year olds in 2004, the group of people then at the age of 70 to 79 years is described.

Thus, we examine the behaviour of a cohort over time by looking at the results of independent samples each representing this very generation in a given year. This approach allows us to follow these generations through their life-cycle using the RA data. While this methodological approach is not necessarily very sophisticated, it does have the important advantages of being both cost-effective and pragmatic.

The times series Lohmann & Danielsson (2001) have presented suggested that cohorts when becoming older stick to their once established travel behaviour. These findings were in line with previous publications. To examine if these findings still hold true, we have now used the same approach starting with the most recent data on the holiday behaviour of Germans based on the RA survey carried out in January 2004 and going backwards in time to trace the cohorts being 50-60 years old in the year 2003. Table 3 shows the travel propensity of these two German "generations" (cohorts).

Table 3: Holiday Travel Propensity for two German generations over time

Year	*1973*	*1979*	*1983*	*1988*	*1993*	*1998*	*2003*
population travel propensity (%)	49	57	54	65	75	76	77
cohort 25 to 55 years age	25	30	35	40	45	50	55
travel propensity	56	66	59	74	81	82	80
cohort 45 to 75 years age	45	50	55	60	65	70	75
travel propensity	52	57	56	60	66	67	65

Figures for West-Germany; % of age groups

What we see is:

a. for the first cohort an increase of the travel propensity from 25 years (56%) till 45 years (81 %, @ +45%) with a temporary decrease at 35 years and a stabilization at around 81% till 55 years.

b. for the older cohort a lower travel propensity and in total less variability, but still an increase between 45 years and 65 years (@ +27%), after 65 years little variation (travel propensity at about 65-67%).

Previous findings showed, that travel propensity increased throughout life until the age of about 50 years of age and was then kept stable until very late in life. Partly these recent results seem to contradict the previous findings as there is no rise from 45 to 50 in the new data for the younger cohort. The lack of additional growth could possibly be interpreted as a "ceiling-effect" at a travel propensity level of 80%, the 45-year-olds have simply reached the limit; The most important result is that the travel propensity of a cohort while getting older is not going down between 65 and 75 years. Of course, the overall development of this variable is influenced by a lot of other factors which are responsible for quite a variation over time. It is now possible to suggest that the general pattern of travel propensity is one of the key indicators for holiday life-cycle travel behaviour, and can be observed going though three stages:

1. Growth – tends to increase from early adulthood until 45 years old or when reaching some 80%
2. Stabilisation-from the ages of around 50 until 75 years old, starting with a soft transition phase with lower increase

3. Decrease – a slight decrease occurs once people reach the more advanced age of 75 to 85 years old.

The data indicates that while the travel behaviour of today's seniors is different from that of senior travellers in the past, it is for one simple reason-it is just another generation. Thus the development of the 'new seniors' market has come about largely because each new senior generation has a different behaviour pattern from its predecessor. Furthermore, in looking at this from another perspective, it can be seen that a particular generation's behaviour changes little. In other words, they seem to adopt a quite rigid and conservative set of pattern over a period of time, and it is this rigidity which seems to establish itself during the middle of the life-cycle and to last for about 20 years.

Holiday Destination Choice During the Life-Cycle

Such conservative behaviour is not only true for the general characteristic of travel propensity, but also-within limits-seems to hold true for the choice of holiday destinations. This can be seen in Table 4.

Table 4: Travel destinations of different generations

All travellers in %	1975	1990	2003
Domestic	46	30	28
Abroad	54	70	72
Austria	15	7	5
Italy	9	10	10
Spain	10	13	16
Other foreign countries	20	40	41
Travellers aged 55 to 79	1975 (55 yrs*)	1990 (70 yrs*)	2003 (83 yrs*)
Domestic	52	51	59
Abroad	48	49	41
Austria	18	8	2
Italy	8	10	5
Spain	7	8	10
Other foreign countries	15	23	19

The data shows a considerable change in the destination choice of Germans in general from 1975 to 2003 with domestic trips loosing market shares while outbound travel switched from Austria to the Mediterranean and a lot of destinations which have been of low importance thirty years ago. The generation becoming a senior in the period from 1975 to 1990 as a cohort fairly maintained their destination preferences at least with respect to the distribution between domestic and outgoing trips. In 2003, now in an age between 78 and 88 years, they show a slightly higher preference for domestic destinations.

Of course, there are numerous factors influencing the decision of a holiday destination, and the increasing global competition between destinations makes predictions harder than ever. The longitudinal trend-analysis preferences for certain destinations did show some change within the generations, and presumably for other reasons such as price and image. Nevertheless, a certain amount of rigidity is still evident even for the choice of holiday destination. What we see is not the picture of elderly people avoiding far away destinations. Only when reaching the (statistical) end of their life-cycle do the seniors' preferences for domestic holiday destinations increase.

The Future's Senior Holiday Travelling

Based on these empirically founded assumptions, we dare to have a look into the future. What this paper has shown is that the travel characteristics of today's new senior market largely correspond to the same patterns that they themselves exhibited some fifteen years ago. In other words, those who are currently 55-years old, will keep travelling in the way they do today for many years to come. Given such information, it is now possible to have a basis on which to make some more reliable predictions about the future.

The re-analysis of the RA-data has meant that it is possible to get an idea about how future senior generations will behave. Ignoring other possibilities (such as changing external influences), it can be assumed they will behave in a similar manner as they do at present-being today's 'pre-senior' generation. In looking to the future, Table 5. Shows some projected changes in travelling behaviour. In this case, seniors are defined as being in the age group 70-80, and the columns labelled *2008* and *2018* contain the characteristics of today's 65 to 75 and 55-65 year old travellers, and projecting them into the future. The first column shows the characteristics of tourists aged 70 to 80 in 2003. Due to a larger group of seniors in 2008, and a higher holiday travel propensity, the absolute number of travelling seniors will rise considerably, and they will more than likely prefer holiday destinations outside of Germany.

Table 5: Travel behaviour of future German senior generations

	75-year-olds in...		
	2003	**2008**	**2018**
Total in the age group mn	6.4	8.35	8.40
Travel propensity in %	65	70	78
Travellers in mn.	4.2	5.8	6.6
Destination of main holiday trip in %:			
Domestic	50	42	31
Abroad	50	58	69

Note: All figures for West-Germany only; 75-year-olds = 70-80 years of age at a certain year. Figures for 2008 and 2018 are estimations based on the rates of the age groups 65-75 and 55-65 today (2003).

Own Calculations Based on F.U.R, Reiseanalyse RA 2004

The coming up rise in the volume of senior holiday travellers in 2008 is partly due to the changing age structure in the German society and partly the result of the "rigidity", i.e. the cohort's keeping the once acquired behaviour. In 2018 the socio-demographic change impact is neglectable

Lessons Learned

The analysis of the RA-data shows that people do not change their travel behaviour just because they turn 60 or 65, or because they retire. Looking at this from a tourism suppliers point of view, these 'new' senior citizens already exist. A change in travel behaviour of seniors cannot be put down to a change in the travel behaviour of a specific generation. Just as the travel behaviour of today's current senior citizens is different from that of people belonging to this age group ten years ago, future senior generations will behave differently as well.

The notion of rigidity in behaviour is only related to the generation as a group. Of course, individuals will change their behaviour from time to time. Furthermore, the role of past experiences on future travel participation and tourism behaviour is important, but far from being the only determining factor.

Other aspects such as changes to personal circumstances, or changes in the external macro-environment, may also influence behaviour to a broad extent.

Nevertheless, what can be seen is that once people have passed the 55-year old mark, their generation tends to maintain a consistent set of travel behaviours. Their travel experiences during their formative years and the established travel patterns as an adult, will become an important influence on the behaviour in the last third of life. The rigidity-hypothesis is supported by the fact that people older than sixty tend to describe their actual travel behaviour in relation to their former travel behaviour, as not having changed much.

The 'new' senior citizens in five or fifteen years time will be different from the present senior citizens when it comes to travel behaviour. While senior travellers are already relatively active, the new senior generations to come are more than likely to surpass them.

Such future behaviour can be predicted from the present, because these travellers, if considered as a generation, are unlikely to change their behaviour for the last third of their life. Of course, this may not be the case.

It is possible that future senior travellers will be totally different from today's, by showing a complete lack of rigidity and stability in travel behaviour past 55-years of age. Therefore, it is conceivable that they might keep their unstable and less predictable patterns of travel behaviour their whole lives. While this cannot be ruled out, such a dramatic shift in human behaviour is unlikely to occur in the near term.

In conclusion, the approach described here offers an easy-to-do method to reach some rough predictions of how the target group of tomorrow's seniors may behave in the future. It is likely to be useful for marketing and planning purposes in tourism, and offers a starting point for additional future research on this topic.

Holiday Trips with Children

Family Holidays in a Changing Society

The demographic trends which we have been referring to earlier will not only have impacts on the senior segment but as well on other segments in tourism. Our second example focuses on family holiday trips, i.e. holiday trips (of 5 days or longer) of adults accompanied by children aged up to 13 years of age. The development towards an older society with fewer children combined with a growing individualisation and new patterns of living together (or apart) may lead the tourism destinations and industry to wonder, e.g.

- Is there a need to look for new segments to replace the old-fashioned family trip?
- Are offers tailored to the specific needs of single parents a strategy which may be fruitful for a significant part of the tourism industry?
- Shall we put more emphasis on products for one-kid-families?
- Will comfortable holiday trips with a touch of culture for the senior travelling with (grand) children meet a growing demand?

Before we use the tourism consumer data to check whether there really is a development to support such assumptions for holiday travel we have to take a second look at the underlying trends in society. Again we take Germany as an example.

The Demographic Trends Revisited

There is no doubt that the number and the share of elderly people will rise. In Germany the number of persons aged 60 years or older will rise from 18.9 mn (23% of the population) in 2000 to 22.9 mn. Furthermore we can assume that these new seniors will stay healthy and vital for a longer period than their predecessors. According to Opaschowski (2002) family life and being together with grand children has gained much more importance.

The declining number of children seems to be the real challenge for family holidays. For Germany Eurostat expects an 11% decline in the number of children under 15 years in the period 2000 to 2015. The number of children per woman in Europe has been clearly below the replacement level (2,1 children per woman) for years and this curve is still pointing downwards in many European countries such as e.g. Germany (currently 1,3 children per woman). This will result in smaller families on the one hand (with more one-kid-families) but the number of adults living with children will decrease to a lesser extent than the number of children in total.

The forecasting suggests that most of the Germans will live in multi person households even in the future. The way how and how long they will live together will become more colourful. For the tourism industry it is probably of low relevance whether adults travelling with children are married or not and whether these adults are the biological parents or not. The salient aspect is the structure and volume of persons living with children.

The available data for the household structure in Germany shows that within the last 30 years the share of households with children decreased from 45% to 32%. In West Germany the share of single parents with kids up to 17 years has increased from 8% of all families with kids in 1972 to 14% in 2000. Today, out of 100 families (private households with children up to 17 years) in Germany, 78% (7.3 mn) consists of a married couple with kids, 6% (0.6 mn) of unmarried couples with kids, and 15% (1.4 mn) are single parents (one adult living with kids but not with a partner). We estimate the number of single parents with kids up to 13 years to be some 1.15 mn. According to Statistics Austria one can expect a further rise in the number of single parents.

Thus, the major quantitative demographic trends with possible relevance for family holidays are (each with estimation for the degree of change from 2000 to 2010): more seniors (+ 11%), fewer children (-8%), more one-kid families (+ 8 %), more single parents (+ 12%).

Related trends in tourism behaviour – and their meaning for future development

To identify the meaning of a demographic trend for tourists' consumer behaviour one has to take into consideration the volume of the segment, the direction and degree of expected change with respect to this segment, and holiday travel behaviour data. We have used the data of the German "Reiseanalyse" as a data base and tool for segmentation. The segments are:

(1) all holiday trips with children up to 13 years, and the partly overlapping subgroups:

(2) holiday trips of single parents,

(3) holiday trips of respondents aged 50 or older,

(4) holiday trips with exactly one child.

We have looked at these segments in order to determine their actual volume, the change to be expected for the future applying the change rates derived from the demographic trends and to identify segment specific patterns of travel behaviour.

The segment of holiday trips with children (up to 13 years) has proved to be stable in Germany for more than a decade with some 22% of all holiday trips. In 2003 this share resulted in 14.4 mn holiday trips. An 8% decline would lead to a number of 13.2 mn trips, still an important segment. One can expect even a higher number when considering the fact that the decrease of the number of families will be slower as the one of the number of children. Thus, there is no need for a complete re-orientation of the tourism industry towards new target groups replacing the family holiday. But of course given not only the demographic change but also the strong competition between destinations a strong focus on the needs and expectations of this segment is recommended.

Among all holiday trips with children those of single parents are only a small group (less than 4%, some 0.5 mn trips). An increase of 12% in a decade would result in 0.6 mn trips, a change which is – given the limits of a survey – barely measurable. A closer look at the travel behaviour of this group reveals that 87% of their trips are in the company of at least one more adult, i.e. the single parents do not travel as single parents. As far as the data can be interpreted there is not much of a difference between single parents' trips and other family holidays. The small volume together with the unspecific behaviour patterns lead to the assumption that the single parent holiday trip will remain a niche segment.

The share of people aged 50 years or older within all German family trips has been 9.4 % in 2002. This is already today a significant segment which could be considered more closely by the tourism industry, especially as a further increase can be expected. In addition, this segment shows a specific behaviour as tourists, e.g. compared to all family holiday trips a lower seasonality, higher spending, longer stays and other destinations choices. Against expectations they are not very fond of culture trips and prefer holiday homes or apartments to hotels.

Finally, the one-kid-trip seems to be the standard of family holidays. So, this is not a development to come but today's reality. Again, this segment has specific travel behaviour patterns as e.g. more flight trips and more use of tour operators and as it offers further increase. In addition one-kid travellers have special needs which the tourism industry has to take into consideration. In general, we see that some of the "new" trends have already affected tourism for a long time. The one-child-family has been the standard in recent years. Other trends are of no significant importance, e.g. single parents are of low relevance for tourism (which doesn't mean: for society) due to their small volume and a holiday travel behaviour very close to other families. And some trends require closer attention as there really is a dynamic development ahead. This should have implications for product design.

These two examples have shown that the transfer of socio demographic trends to a future development needs a closer look at the real changes in society (don't over-estimate!) and that consumer survey data can be very useful in determining the trends in tourism. Or, to put it the other way around, without the data from consumer surveys we would be unable to draw realistic conclusions.

In our first example-on how future senior generations will travel-we have used the survey data to examine the patterns of travel behaviour of a generation getting older and applied the findings to draw conclusions on the future. In the second example – on the future of family trips-we have used a fine segmentation which again would have been impossible without the survey data to get a realistic picture on the travel behaviour patterns of these segments. These findings together with the statistical data on demographic change allowed for a better understanding of the coming trends in family holidays. In this paper we have only dealt with developments in consumer behaviour related to demographic change. To get a holistic picture of what will happen in the future of tourism one has to consider other influences and drivers as well, for example trends on the supply side or in consumer behaviour in general. But that is another story.

Of course, the future is predictable only within close limits, and unexpected events will always cause confusion. Still it is important (and possible) to prepare oneself for the trends that can be identified with some reliability today. This can be the starting point for the next challenge of trend research: It is not enough to know the trends; this knowledge must be transferred into products and strategies for destinations and companies. But without the survey data and a creative way of analyzing it we will never even come to this point.

Ministry for Regional Development of the Czech Republic

- Programming period 2004-2006
- Operational Program Human Resources Development
- Funding: 75% from ESF, 25% from the state budget,
- Priority 4
- Measure 4.2 Specific Education 7 projects

European Social Fund

Ministry for Regional Development of the Czech Republic

- Training and education of employees in tourism
- Vocational training of public administration officials in tourism
- Tourism information
- Destination management and creation of products in tourism
- Event marketing for tourism
- Training for public territorial administration officials and employees in tourism in the conditions of tourism development in protected landscape areas
- Improvement of the quality of vocational training and education in tourism

Projects

Ministry for Regional Development of the Czech Republic (Courses, seminars, training, publications, e-library)

Some announced courses:

- Sustainable development
- Crisis management
- Heritage care in relation to tourism
- Tourism statistics
- Destination promotion
- Golf as a specific tourism activity

Project's Activities

Ministry for Regional Development of the Czech Republic

Next announced courses:

- Practical activities of information centres, call centres and help line
- Event Marketing MICE
- Work with media in tourism
- Marketing communication regarding destination
- Local, national and international destination marketing
- Strategic development of tourism destination

Project's Activities

Ministry for Regional Development of the Czech Republic

Summary:

- A total of 68 educational programmes were created
- 12 professional publications/textbooks
- 1 teaching DVD was published in these 6 projects
- A total of about 9 000 persons were trained (businessmen, employees, officers of public sector)

Project's Activities

Ministry for Regional Development of the Czech Republic

Project "Improvement of the quality of vocational training and education in tourism"

- To analyze and to map the current status of tourism education
- To prepare comprehensive proposals and suggestions fo. introduction of an educational system in the tourism sector
- To prepare a realistic proposal for the use of finances provided by Structural Funds for the tourism sector in schools, life-long and further education of employees and employers, including support for labour market development

Project's Activities

Ministry for Regional Development of the Czech Republic in tourism education:

- Schools providing secondary education with a vocational training
- Secondary schools and colleges
- Universities
- Public administration, regional and local self-administration
- Life-long education and retraining
- Tourist guides
- Employment agencies in tourism
- Employee unions, professional associations, trade unions in tourism

Partial Evaluations

Ministry for Regional Development of the Czech Republic

- 2,301 retraining entries were generated to the tourism category
- 708 questionnaires were distributed among employers in the sector of hotels and similar facilities, travel bureaus and agencies, sports and other recreational services, cultural services
- 12 ministries were analyzed; as regards regional, city and municipal authorities, the evaluation covered all 13 regional centres, including Prague, 50 cities with more

than 20,000 inhabitants, 20 cities with 5,000 to 20,000 inhabitants, 30 rural municipalities and 11 municipalities that are centres of tourism

Partial Evaluations

Payment of the Czech Republic

- Schools providing secondary education with a vocational training (249)
- 121 secondary schools with generate certificate of education focusing on tourism and 18 colleges
- 15 universities focused on tourism were generated out of the total number of 72 university-type schools in the Czech Republic

Partial Evaluations

Ministry for Regional Development of the Czech Republic Schools providing secondary education

- Optimization of number of schools
- Increasing professional level of teachers and involvement of schools in further education of pedagogues
- Development of practical training
- Promotion of cross-border and international cooperation
- Involvement of employers in further education of employees
- Ensuring financial participation of employers in initial vocational training
- Creation of teaching aids for specialized tourism-related subjects Establishment of a system for monitoring of labour market requirements
- Creation of a life/long learning system
  - basic education programs
  - individual education

Conclusions

Ministry for Regional Development of the Czech Republic Universities

- Involvement of students in scientific research

- Supplementing study programmes with compulsory practical training by cooperation with employers
- Development of distance and combined forms of study
- Preparation of further education courses for secondary school pedagogues
- Creating a module-based solution of further education
- Introduction of regular evaluation of universities by an independent entity

Conclusions

Ministry for Regional Development of the Czech Republic

- Network of secondary schools, where courses for
- teacher will take place
- Recognition of partial qualifications in tourism
- Solution for students, who couldn´t finish theirs studies at the secondary schools (hospitality and gastronomic services, and other specializations in tourism) and back to school

Present and Future

Ministry for Regional Development of the Czech Republic Cooperation with Czech TV:

- Production of 18 episodes of an educational programme cycle
    - tourism
    - hotels, other accommodation types
    - gastronomy
    - travel bureaus and travel agencies
    - spa, wellness, rural tourism
    - guides, congress tourism, events, etc.
- Production and broadcasting of a 10-part TV cycle designated for general public
- Production and broadcasting of 3 TV spots

Tourism as Education

Tourism has emerged as an instrument for employment

generation, poverty alleviation and sustainable human development. Tourism promotes international understanding and gives support to local handicrafts and cultural activities. It is an important segment of the country's economy, specially in terms of its contribution towards foreign exchange earnings, generation of additional income and creation of employment opportunities. The foreign exchange earnings from tourism during the year 2000 were estimated at about Rs. 14,408 crores with an estimated direct employment of about 15 million, which is about 2.4% of the total labour force of the country. Tourism is the third largest foreign exchange earner for India. The International tourist traffic in the country is estimated to be 2.64 million during the year 2000.

However, according to the World Tourism Organisation (WTO), India's share in world tourism arrivals is only 0.38%, accounting for 0.62% of the world tourist receipts. This indicates that much of the tourist potential is yet to be tapped. With rapid advances in Science & Technology, tourism has acquired the status of an industry in all industrialised countries. The high influx of foreign tourist traffic has accelerated demand for certain economic production and distribution activities. Tourism has emerged as an industry next in importance only to Information Technology industry in the Services sector. By 2005, the contribution of Tourism to the world economy will be doubled. The economic liberalisation in India and consequent foreign investment opportunities, development of tourist facilities including expansion in air-line services, etc. provide an impetus for a spurt in tourist arrivals as in South

Asian Regions

Domestic tourism plays a vital role in achieving the national objectives of promoting social and cultural cohesion and national integration. Its contribution to generation of employment is very high. With the increase in income levels and emergence of a powerful middle class, the potential for domestic tourism has grown substantially during the last few years. Realising the importance of tourism, the Government of Tamil Nadu has accorded high priority to tourism promotion and has taken initiatives to improve/ create infrastructure in tourism potential centres and geared to encourage private sector investment in this regard. The many splendoured State that Tamil Nadu is has been described in the following paragraphs:

Tall palms and taller gopurams, the towering, intricately carved temple towers of a land of temples welcome the traveller to Tamil Nadu. There is no better place to begin one's discovery of the ageless South than in this colourful historic State, an ancient land of proud cultural heritage.

Tamil Nadu is a window to the modern South as much as it is a wide open archive of ancient legacies. Yet amazingly, for all its modern-day progress, Tamil Nadu retains its old-world charm. The harmony of the ancient and the new and the picturesque is truly remarkable here. Giant chimneys, symbols of an industrial upsurge that has put the land of the Tamil people in the fore-front of Indian development; stately palaces and exquisitely hewn temples of by-gone eras; beautiful unspoilt hill resorts and beaches and forest sanctuaries, massive developmental projects and new industries-they all mingle in one marvellous mosaic in Tamil Nadu. Chennai-a tiny fishing village that has mushroomed leisurely into a sprawling metropolis in the 300-odd years since it was founded in 1639-is the capital of Tamil Nadu, a land that has seen the rise and fall of many ancient kingdoms, the Cholas, the Pandyas, the Cheras, the Pallavas and many others, each leaving behind in the sands of time ineradicable cultural treasures.

Chennai a spacious city of distances, a city open to the skies, a city free of most of the ecological problems of the major cities of today, a city of beaches and parks and historic landmarks, is the pleasantest starting point for one who sets out to enjoy the delights of the South.

From Chennai no part of Tamil Nadu is too far. Excellent road and rail and air services speed travellers to any point in this ancient land. None of which is very much more than 24 hours away from the capital, each of which has something delightfully different to offer. The names of the towns are as musical as the ancient language of the people and they roll off the tongue sounding as exquisite as the sights they have to offer the beholder. Here are ancient capitals of once-proud kingdoms.

Like magnificent Madurai, its temple one of the wonders of India, and ancient Thanjavur, its Brahadeeswarar temple, a tribute to the splendour of Chola builders, among the greatest the world has ever known. Here are the ruins of historic Poompuhar, the Chola port and planned city known to Ptolemy and Pliny. Here are the Pallava towns of Kancheepuram and Mamallapuram, the former, one of Hinduism's seven sacred cities and a town of a thousand temples, the latter, famed for its sculpture but now becoming better known as one of India's finest beach-resorts. Here are Tiruchirappalli and Kanniyakumari where ancient legends live on, in rock and plaster and wood. Here are hill stations that waft the aroma of tea and coffee, eucalyptus and pine. Hill resorts that seem like little bits of England's green country that are as rugged as India's own. And here, too, are forest and sanctuaries untouched by man. Mudumalai, Vedanthangal and Point Calimere where the deer and the buffalo roam and the stork and the flamingo and egret nest.

Tamil Nadu has immense potential in tourism. The multitude of choice the State offers from beach resorts to hill stations, adventure holidays to cultural tours, heritage packages to wildlife sanctuaries should be presented to holiday makers.

Ninth Five Year Plan Review

For the Ninth Plan period, a sum of Rs. 30 crores was provided for Tourism sector. Against this the total expenditure during the Ninth Plan period is expected to be around Rs. 24.06 crores. This works out to 80.20 % of the total outlay. For the year 2001-02, the outlay for the Tourism promotion activities was stepped up to Rs. 11.82 crores. A sum of Rs. 2.95 crores was also spent on Tourism promotion projects under the Hill Area Development programme.

The following schemes were taken up during the Ninth Plan:

(i) Establishment of Tourist Information Centres at Tiruvandrum, Bangalore & Hyderabad

(ii) Conduct of Fairs and Festivals

(iii) Provision of Infrastructure facilities and important Tourist Centres

(iv) Identification of heritage towns and their preservation

(v) Grant of incentives for construction of Hostels, purchase of generators

(vi) Luxury Coaches

(vii) Encouragement to joint venture schemes.

(viii) Development of Taragambadi, Marina Beach and Children's Park at Guindy

(ix) Grants-in-aid to State Institute of Hotel Management and Catering

Technology, Thuvakkudi

The position in regard to tourist arrivals during the period from 1995-2000 may be seen from the Table below:

The home of Carnatic music and Bharata Natyam, the legacies of temple songs and dances handed down through the centuries. The home of magnificent schools of art and architecture. The home of great cultures and philosophies. This is Tamil Nadu. Gloriously ancient. Proud preserver of its traditions. Now magnificently modern. Everywhere here, there is exciting experience, splendid sights and havens away from it all.

Vision

- To make Tamil Nadu the number one State in India in respect of Tourism sector and place it on the map of International Tourism by marketing it as an important destination with heritage sites.
- Double the tourist arrivals and revenue to the Government by the end of the X Five Year Plan period.
- To address rampant unemployment problem through tourism.
- To make tourism a major economic activity in the coming years.

Goals, Objectives and Strategy

The following elements *inter alia* will influence the policies and programmes of the Tourism Department during the Tenth Five Year Plan period:

Sustainability

Hitherto the maintenance of the assets created was not taken care of adequately. In recognition of this aspect, the State

Government has taken recently earnest efforts to improve infrastructure at various destinations. In order to ensure sustainability, proper upkeep and operation and maintenance also would be made part of the projects in future. As a first step in this direction, a project directory containing all relevant details of tourism related projects implemented in the State since 1980 is being prepared. This maiden venture will not only provide an opportunity for review and evaluation of the facilities already available, the facilities required to be created etc., but also help the State plan its future activities.

Tranquility, Public Order and Tourism

The terrorist attack on world trade centre, U.S.A. on 11-9-2001 was indeed a black day in the history of tourism. The attack had a devastating effect on Tourism as fear gripped all over and, in its aftermath, several nations issued negative advisories regarding travel. The situation has, however, quickly returned to normalcy. The ethnic strife in Sri Lanka, the ongoing warlike situation in West Asia, the cross border terrorism from western borders of the country have all had a contributory role and share in affecting tourism. Tourism can thrive and prosper only if there is peace and tranquility. Tamil Nadu offers from this angle a very safe destination. However, the issues concerning safety and security of tourists and their belongings should be kept in mind.

Private Sector Participation

Recognition of the fact that tourism is essentially a private sector activity and the Government has to play only a catalytic role and that of a facilitator and to provide the platform for accelerated growth of tourism in the State. And the realisation that the Government need no longer be a service provider.

Institutional Arrangement

More effective coordination among various organisations and sectors of Government such as civic administration and adequate road, rail and air connectivity, communication, general administration etc. would be ensured.

'Product – Identification' and 'Product Development'

Keeping the clientele in view, products such as cultural and architectural heritage, pilgrims and religious destinations, eco–tourism destinations such as hill stations, beaches, rural and village tourism, arts and performing arts, crafts, and handicrafts, music, dance, the whole life-style yoga, health, Ayurveda, Siddha etc and provision of world class infrastructure/ support systems etc., would have to be on the top of agenda.

Paradigm Shift

To recognise that tourism is an economic activity and is a major engine of economic growth; for it has very extensive forward and backward economic linkages that builds upon and has impact on overall income, employment etc., especially for the vulnerable sections such as women, children, disabled etc.

Tamil Nadu as a Complete Tourist Destination

To position Tamil Nadu as a complete tourist destination for all seasons and for all.

Information Technology and Tourism

At the working level, therefore, evolve a new work culture taking note of the requirement of an environment of co-operative federation, diversification and technological advancement.

Goals/ Objectives

1. To increase the Tourist inflow to Tamil Nadu to 10-12 % per annum from the present level of 7-9 % (special focus will be on tourists from abroad as also up country domestic tourists).
2. To increase the period of stay of domestic tourists in Tamil Nadu from 7-9 to 10-12 days and in respect of foreign tourists from 4-7 days to 6-8 days; and restore the prime position Tamil Nadu had in the tourism sector in the past.
3. To evolve a Government led, private sector driven and community oriented framework at the organizational level, since tourism essentially is a private sector activity where Government has to play only a catalytic role.
4. To fully exploit tourism potentials and convert these as employment generation and poverty alleviation programmes.

5. To recognise the deep rooted innate relationship between Tourism and Culture and promote as such.
6. To promote eco-tourism.
7. To tap the tourism potential in the coastal belt.
8. To expand the product base to have more effective coordination with other States in India in general and immediate neighbours in particular.
9. To make extensive use of information technology and other technological advancements.
10. To make tourism a CORE competency sector.

The thrust areas, keeping the above goals/ objectives in view, therefore, during the Tenth five year plan period would be:

(1) Clear product identification, development and expansion, such as destination, circuits, services etc.;

(2) Creation and upgradation of required infrastructure, basic amenities etc., following an integrated and holistic approach;

(3) Human resource development and skills upgradation; and

(4) Promotion and marketing these aggressively and holistically.

Strategies

At strategy level also there would be a paradigm shift; instead of looking at various destinations & activities in isolation, attempt would be to look at Tamil Nadu and various tourism products holistically and in integrated manner.

Long Term Measures

For Increasing the Tourist Inflow

Aggressive marketing strategies will be adopted to publicise the tourist potential of Tamil Nadu both nationally and internationally. Some of the main features of this strategy are as follows:

a) Opening of Tourist Information Centres in other States.

b) Appointment of marketing agents throughout the country and also abroad.

c) Advertisement *blitzkrieg* in print and electronic media.

d) Publishing of high quality literature in Indian and foreign languages, and

e) Screening of documentaries in theatres, railway stations, airports, bus termini etc.

World Class infrastructure will be provided at all important tourist destinations. Mega tourism projects pertaining to the products/ infrastructure and destination development, of tourist circuits, large revenue generating projects like rope ways, sound and light shows, cruises etc., and capacity building (training of personnel engaged in the hospitality and related skills) will be launched. Setting up of natural therapy centres, developing village tourism, construction of jungle lodges, promotion of adventure tourism, Yoga/ transcendental meditation centres, constructing star hotels at important pilgrim centres, eradication of beggar menace, deployment of tourism police together with good civic governance would be some of the important aspects of the strategy.

For Promoting Private Participation

The Government will gradually assume the role of a catalyst/ facilitator and involve the private sector in restoring the prime position occupied by the State in tourism earlier. Besides facilitating clearances to attract the private entrepreneurs, it is proposed to adopt a multi-pronged strategy, viz.,

a) A land bank will be opened where available government and private lands throughout Tamil Nadu will be identified and pooled. Land from this bank will be made available to the private entrepreneurs on long term lease basis on concessional terms;

b) The Project proposals submitted by the private entrepreneurs will be cleared instantaneously through single window clearance system; and

c) Attractive incentives will be offered; and

d) Required technical assistance would be made available.

It is a well known fact that tourism industry is capable of generating huge employment (both direct and indirect) opportunities. It is estimated that world wide tourism industry enjoys a 10 % share in generation of employment opportunities. Therefore, steps will be taken to train educated un-employed youth in the tourism related fields. i.e., Hotels, Guide, Recreation activities, Studio services, Theatres, Communication net work, Bar, Beauty parlour etc. The unskilled rural folk will be trained in the fields of Driving, Hospitality, Costumes, Traditional arts, Handicrafts etc. Proposals are also there to include Tourism studies in the Schools and College curriculum to create awareness among youth so as to fully prepare and sensitise the coming generations.

For Promoting Tourism in the Coastal Belt

Tamil Nadu has been bestowed with a spectacular thousands kms. long coastline. With respect to tourism related activities, the Government of India also have granted certain relaxations as to the ' coastal regulation zone rules'. These would be fully utilised to establish recreational and entertainment provision by roping in the private sector in a big way.

Short Term Measures

For Promotion of Cultural Tourism

The rich culture and heritage of Tamil Nadu is renowned the world over. Foreign tourists especially from ethnic countries and non-resident Indians are specially attracted by this unique feature of Tamil Nadu. To fully exploit this potential it is proposed to conduct fairs/ festivals at more centres and also expand the product range by introducing new festivals, which will highlight the salient features of Tamil culture and heritage.

For Promotion of Eco-Tourism

Rapid advancements in science and technology are threatening to turn the world into a concrete jungle. Hence the tourists nowadays yearn to visit eco-tourism centres like hill resorts, water falls, mangrove forests etc. Therefore, in the Tenth Five Year Plan period, the endeavour will be to exploit the natural resources maintaining complete harmony with nature and without endangering the otherwise extremely fragile ecology and to introduce trekking, boating, water sports, hang gliding etc. in a big way both by refining and repackaging the available products as also by enlarging the product base.

For Co-ordination with other States

Recognizing the need for developing suitable inter-regional circuits and products as also with a view to properly packaging and marketing these, emphasis would be laid on establishing more effective coordination with other States. The first step in this direction was the signing of memorandum of understanding with Andhra Pradesh, Karnataka, India Tourism Development Corporation, Uttar Pradesh, Uttaranchal, Rajasthan, Delhi and Orissa Tourism Development Corporations. Tie-up arrangements with West Bengal, Kerala, Maharashtra, Andaman and Nicobar Islands tourism departments as also with other States are also on anvil.

To explore and Develop new Global Markets for Tamil Nadu Tourism Products

Communication scenario has witnessed a sea change, thanks to the advent of computers. Tourism Department has already established E-mail, Web site, Touch Screen and C.D. Rom facilities. Computerisation of the various units under the control of Commissionerate of Tourism and Tamil Nadu Tourism Development Corporation are underway. Once this process is completed, online booking facilities for the tours and accommodation in Hotels by TTDC will be possible by just a click on the mouse from anywhere in the world. In this scenario besides US, European and African Countries, it would also be the endeavour to make full use of good relations with the countries in the South Asia/ South East Asia regions to attract more regional tourists.

Programmes / Schemes for the Tenth Five Year Plan Product Identification

The tourists visiting Tamil Nadu can be broadly classified into three main groups viz., international, national and local.

International Tourists

The international tourists form a considerable chunk of tourist inflow into Tamil Nadu. In the year 2000, the number of foreign tourists who visited Tamil Nadu stood at 7-9 lakhs. An analysis of the international tourist traffic shows that foreign tourists usually arrive in Tamil Nadu between October and March. U.K. is by far the single largest source of tourists to India.

East and South East Asia are the most important tourist generating markets for South India. Americans and Japanese also prefer to stay far longer periods in India. Europe is the biggest tourist market globally. The strategy in respect of overseas market will be tailored to suit the above pattern. The products which can be sold to the foreign tourists mainly comprise cultural and architectural heritage, temples and historical monuments, arts, performing arts, handicrafts, festivals, wild life etc. The availability of good infrastructure at the tourist spots is critical, particularly as far as foreign tourists are concerned. Hence during 2001-2003, the Government of Tamil Nadu made a budget allocation of Rs.17 crores to update/ create infrastructure facilities. This will be sustained and stepped up in the years to come. The products, both destinations and circuits, identified for the International Tourism are:

Thanjavur, Dharasuram, Gangaikondacholapuram, Chidambaram, Pichavaram-Madurai, Thiruvannamalai, Gingee, Tranquebar, Trichy, Ooty, Kodaikanal, Yercaud, Mudumalai, Top Slip etc. In addition to the above, Velankanni in Nagapattinam district and St.Thomas Mount in Chennai could be two other important destinations, that could be developed and marketted.

Similarly the classical Bharathanatyam, folk dances, classical music both vocal and instrumental, handloom, Thanjavur painting, Swamimalai crafts etc. also form part of attractive products/ services.

National Tourists

The national tourists arrive in Tamil Nadu from all the States of India. The number of domestic tourists to Tamil Nadu in a year is around 25 crores. These tourists visit mainly hill stations, pilgrim centres, beach-resorts, dam sites, cultural & heritage destinations etc. To attract such tourists, it is proposed to fully develop and equip with required facilities all the pilgrim centres, develop trekking routes in hills and blend the product with adventure water sports, boating, fairs/ festivals etc. For the national tourism, the products (destinations and circuits) identified are: Kanniyakumari Rameswaram, Madurai, Tiruchirappalli, Thanjavur, Tranquebar,

Thiruvannamalai, Chidambaram, Pichavaram, Kancheepuram, Mamallapuram, Ooty, Kodaikanal, Yercaud, beaches along the nearly 1000 kms long coastline, wild life sanctuaries etc.

Local (Domestic) Tourists

Besides the above, marketable products (destinations and circuits) for the benefit of local tourists identified for development in the first phase are Palani, Gingee, Tiruchendur, Elagiri Hills, Courtallam, Tiruthani, Point Calimere, wild life sanctuaries, local circuits and destinations in the districts of the State.

Product Development

Development of Infrastructure Facilities at Tourist Destinations

To increase the number of tourists visiting Tamil Nadu, it is proposed to create infrastructure facilities of international standards. Under this scheme, development of Dam sites and minor water falls, like Thirparappu, Papanasam, Jalagambarai, will be taken up. It is also proposed to identify centres in the Districts with tourism potential and declare them as District Tourist Centres/ Circuits. These centres would include the places of worship, water falls, minor wild life sanctuaries and other lesser known tourist places.

The District Tourism Centres will be provided with infrastructure facilities like hotels, approach roads, toilets, street lights, drinking water, etc., of high standard. Each district may have small towns, which may not have any amusement centres. In such places, City Entertainment Centres will be set up. The attractions would include cinema halls, videogames, virtual reality games, simulators, cyber cafes, food courts, multi-purpose cultural centres, shopping mall etc. These are some of the areas and activities where large scale private investment is also expected. Initially, it is proposed that City Entertainment Centres may be put up in Tirunelveli, Kanniyakumari, Tiruchirappalli, Salem and Thanjavur Districts. More towns can be covered in the subsequent phases. During the Tenth Five Year Plan, 80 Tourist Centres are proposed for which an amount of Rs.25 crores will be provided.

Further, an amount of Rs.10 crores is proposed for the development of infrastructure facilities for tourists in important tourist attraction centres under the Coastal Area Development Programme (CADP).

Provision of Basic Amenities at Tourist Destinations

The object of this scheme is to develop and improve basic amenities such as drinking water supply, sewerage and sanitation systems, in particular "Pay and Use toilets", provision of Cloak room facilities, hygienic eateries etc. at the Tourist Centres. Initially 20 Tourism centres will be selected for this purpose during the Tenth Plan period in coordination with other Departments like Public Works Department, TWAD Board, Department of Rural Development, Town and Country Planning and a sum of Rs.10 crores would be earmarked for these. Similarly 38 towns have been identified as heritage towns and Rs. 50 lakhs has been earmarked for provision of basic infrastructural facilities in each of these towns. This amount would come from the Local Administration budget.

Sound & Light Programme

Sound & Light shows will be set up at Mamallapuram, Thanjavur Big temple and Kancheepuram to attract more tourists. Sound and Light shows at Thirumalai Mannar Palace, Madurai will be upgraded using the services of professionals and using advanced techniques in Audio visual communications and Acoustics. The cost has been estimated at Rs. 1.50 crores for each of the above three places and Rs. 0.50 crore for restoring and upgrading the programme at Madurai.

Cultural Festivals and Fairs

Tamil Nadu's ancient and rich cultural legacies and heritage and a variety of living traditions and cultures spread over throughout the State have high marketability. Therefore, for promoting cultural tourism, festivals such as Cape Festival at Kanniyakumari, Dance Festival at Mamallapuram, Tea and Tourism Festival at Coonoor, Mango Festival at Krishnagiri, Chithirai Festival at Madurai besides Pongal Festival in all tourist centres, Summer Festival in important hill stations and celebration of World Tourism Day in all tourist centres, Natyanjali Festival at Chidambaram, Indira Vizha at Poompuhar, Saral Thiruvizha at Courtallam and Kattabomman Vizha at Panchalankurichi are some of the events for which cultural package tours would be organised by travel agencies. Presently, Summer Festivals are being organised in the months of May and June every year at:

1) Udhagamandalam,
2) Kodaikanal,
3) Surili Falls,
4) Sirumalai,
5) Elagiri,
6) Kolli Hills,
7) Yercaud,
8) Nagappattinam Beach,
9) Valparai,
10) Javvadhu Hills,
11) Pachamaiai,
12) Silver Beach and
13) Panchalankurichi.

September 8th Festival at Velankanni in Nagapattinam District could be another important Festival to be marketted effectively. A new Festival at Rameswaram could also be thought of, since it could enhance its holding and retaining capacity. It is proposed to identify new festivals and showcase them throughout the country and also abroad. A calendar of the above programmes prepared and distributed well in advance to all concerned through departmental offices across the country and also the Government of India tourist offices abroad will enable dissemination of the required information to the prospective tourists. A sum of Rs.5 crores would be provided for this purpose.

Product Expansion

Setting up of New Boat Houses/ Upgradation of Existing Boat Houses

Apart from backwaters on the East Coast stretch, there are lakes, corals etc., where boating is feasible. One of the objectives in the 10th Five Year Plan is to increase the influx of tourists to Tamil Nadu by at least 10% per annum. Secondly, tourists should stay for a longer period. To achieve these objectives setting up of new boat houses and upgradation of the existing ones will be taken up for these are likely to increase the holding capacity of the place: (1) Opening of new boat houses at Adyar (Chennai), Pulicat, Nainarkulam (Tirunelveli), Alambarai, Muttukadu-II,

Iddaikazhinadu @ Rs.50 lakhs per centre, and (2) Up-gradation of the boat houses at Kodaikanal, Muttukadu, Udhagamandalam and Yercaud @ Rs. 50 lakhs per centre. Besides Introduction of Row boats, motorboats etc. upgradation will also include improvements to boat-jetty, purchase of new traditional boats & water-sports equipments @ Rs. 15.55 lakhs per centre. Similarly, such centres would be identified throughout the State and developed for local tourists.

Development of Hill Stations & Natural Falls

The Yercaud Hills: The Boating Centre and other Tourist spots will be renovated. The lake will be cleaned up for a better boat ride.

Hogenakkal Falls: Boating will be developed.

Javaddu Hills: During the Plan better boarding/ lodging facilities will be provided.

The Elagiri hills: It is proposed to develop a bird sanctuary and improve all tourist attractions in particular, the lake.

Arapalleeswarar Falls at Kolli Hills: It is proposed to improve the Hotel and Transport facilities.

Surli Falls at Kambam Valley: Basic amenities like road, restaurant, hotels (with boarding & lodging) and public toilets, park etc. will be provided during the Tenth Five Year Plan. An amount of Rs. 5 crores would be earmarked for this purpose.

Subsidy

Tourism has been declared as an Industry and realizing the importance of private sector participation in the Tourism Industry, it is proposed to continue the scheme of capital and generator subsidy for the construction of hotels, amusement parks, golf courses etc.

The Tourism Department of Government of India extends financial assistance to Tourism projects.

However, the State Government is to bear the cost of land, external amenities like approach road, parking lot etc. Hence, it is proposed to provide Rs.10 crores as the State's share for tourism projects during the Tenth five year plan on the assumption that the Government of India's allocation may be Rs.100 crores.

Tourism Police

The Safety and Security of tourists is extremely important and is a critical factor for the promotion of tourism. Tourists-foreign and domestic, have nightmarish experience at times at some of the tourist centres. Some of the tourists lose their travel documents, some encounter local anti-social elements while they visit places or during the stay in hotels. In some places they meet hostile youngsters.

The local people forget that they are expected to be tourist-friendly and to extend all possible help to make their visit and stay pleasant so that the influx of tourists increases. Therefore, the Government has proposed to introduce Tourism Police facilities in all important tourists centres like Mamallapuram, Rameswaram, Kanniyakumari, Madurai, Kancheepuram etc., as also at places like airports, railway stations, monuments etc., in a phased manner.

Other Product Expansion Programmes

Village (Rural) Tourism-The new concept of Rural and Village tourism as envisaged by the Government of India aims at providing adequate infrastructural facilities while maintaining the rural ambience. The villages for promotion of village tourism are identified by the District Tourism Advisory Committees. The tourists may meet and mingle with the village community, halt overnight and observe the life-style of the rural folk before resuming their journey to their further destinations. Many foreign tourists like the experience of visiting and having further sojourn in a simple Indian village. As this will generate rural employment and advance development of these areas, bring out the rich and un-adulterated culture, tradition, fine arts, martial arts, games, worship forms, handicrafts, herbal cures etc. which are preserved, protected and maintained only in the villages, it is aimed to bring out these inbuilt talents and expose some of the salient features of rich tradition to the outside world.

Adventure Tourism-Though, there is tremendous potential in the State to promote adventure tourism, very little has been done so far. Hence a fillip would be given to adventure tourism activities in the Tenth Plan. Trekking, hang gliding, para gliding, para sailing, balloon expeditions and water sports will be promoted with active participation from the private sector.

The trekking routes identified in Kodaikanal, Ooty and other hill stations will be developed and expeditions will be conducted regularly during the seasons.

Alamparai on the East Coast Road 120 kms., from Chennai has been identified as a ideal centre for development of adventure water sports. Water sports will also be developed at Muttukadu. The private sector will be encouraged to invest in adventure tourism projects for which speedy clearance will be ensured through the Single Window Machinery.

Eco-Tourism-Eco-Tourism is a form of "tourism that involves travelling to relatively undisturbed natural areas with the specified object of studying, admiring and enjoying the natural sceneries, wild plants, animals, as well as any existing unique aspects found in these areas " according to the World Tourism Organisation. Natural environment is the primary attraction in Eco-tourism.

Tourists especially from other countries are keen to enjoy visiting Eco-friendly environs. They never fail to include eco-friendly tourist spots in their itinerary while visiting Tamil Nadu. Out of the total number of tourists more than 25 percent visit natural surroundings in Tamil Nadu every year.

Among the biosphere reserves in India, two (*the Nilgiris and the Gulf of Mannar*) are located in Tamil Nadu. In order to explore eco-friendly tourism potential in the Kurusadai group of islands near Rameswaram, Glass Bottom Boats will be introduced and Eco-friendly adventure tourism activities could be encouraged at Kolavai lake, Muttukadu, Pichavaram etc.

Jungle Lodges-Tamil Nadu has been bestowed with dense deciduous forests in which there are abundant wildlife, rare species of birds and landscapes full of greenery. Tourists love to visit places which abound with natural wealth, e.g., jungles. As the jungles fall under the "Reserved" forest areas, where taking up any major construction activity will endanger the extremely fragile ecology of the region, it is proposed to construct jungle lodges with minimum human intervention, which will be operated and maintained by the Forest Department. The expertise and financial resources of the private sector will also be utilised in these ventures. The jungle lodges will enable the tourists to watch the wildlife, flora and fauna etc. and offer to them the luxury of a star hotel in a natural elegant setting. There are numerous places where it may be worthwhile to take up construction of jungle lodges, e.g., Mudumalai, Anaimalai, Kalakkad, Mundanthurai, etc.

Convention Centre (NRI/ Private Sector)-It is proposed to construct a massive Convention Centre with NRI / private sector support with 1500 capacity in between Chennai and Mamallapuram. This Convention Centre will have World class facilities for conducting National and International Conferences. This project will be taken up as a joint-venture in an area of around 500 acres and will contain a Five Star Hotel with 1000 rooms, Mini Conference Halls, shopping arcade, Disney land, ethnic village, handicraft emporium, children park, textile museum, swimming pool, bar, theatre, all modern communication links, wide car parking area, huge exhibition mansion, art gallery, etc. The total cost will be worked out at the time of implementation since it is to be fully entrusted to NRI / Private Sector.

Perspective Plan

Tourism is a field of human activity known to mankind from time immemorial. The State Government officially stepped into this sector nearly three decades ago by creating a Tourism Department in the Secretariat. Right from the first year of its inception, the Tourism industry in Tamil Nadu has received a big fillip. The main tasks assigned to the department were to attract more tourists to Tamil Nadu and provide the very basic requirements like transport facilities for sight seeing & Hotels for food/ accommodation etc.

To provide these facilities, the Government of Tamil Nadu and Government of India have pumped in crores of rupees. A major portion of this expenditure has gone into creation of assets like Hotels, Parks etc. the State Government has made a big allocation of Rs. 17 crores for improving the infrastructure at tourist centres]. It is necessary to ensure that the funds are spent judiciously & purposefully. This is possible only if a critical analysis is made of the facilities already available, the gaps and the maintenance of the facilities. Such a scientific study could be undertaken only by professional agencies. The Government of India has selected a private firm, M/s. Consulting Engineering Services.

The firm has also prepared its report, which has generally identified the following bottlenecks:-

- Lack of accommodation facilities.
- Poor water supply & sanitation.
- Poor connectivity.
- Inadequate power supply.
- Piling up of garbage near tourist centres.
- Lack of travel booking facilities.
- Insecurity.

The report has also suggested to introduce a number of facilities; some of the important ones being as follows:

- Kiosks at Beach.
- Haat at Chennai & few other places.
- Development of lesser known Tourist Centres.
- Airport at Kanniyakumari.
- Improvement to Roads leading to important tourist spots.
- Heli-taxi.
- Folders in foreign languages.
- New Boat Houses and
- Sound & Light shows.

According to them, the factors affecting the Tourism Industry in Tamil Nadu are:

1. High luxury tax
2. High camera entry ticket & regulations
3. Presence of Health Centres in Kerala, which may divert tourists from Tamil Nadu to Kerala
4. The report has suggested augmentation of infrastructure at National Tourist Centres of Kanniyakumari, Courtallam,

Kodaikanal & Rameswaram

During the Tenth Five Year Plan Period, the new initiatives will therefore focus on the above mentioned lines. The Consultant has also opined that to implement short term schemes, it will be ideal to prepare a master plan, which would be operational for a limited period of 4-5 years. Master plans will, therefore, have to be prepared for development of destinations, circuits, product etc.

Technical Assistance / Outsourcing

Tourism Department, since its inception has been executing several projects in and around tourist spots throughout Tamil Nadu. These projects relatively small in nature were mainly in the nature of providing basic amenities required by tourists, viz., drinking water, toilet, roads, lights, restaurant, rest shed etc. Such projects do not require much technical know-how. But in the coming years, as mentioned in earlier paragraphs since the Government would be implementing Mega Tourism Projects and the cost of such projects will run into crores and the state of the art technology will have to be employed, outsourcing of technical assistance is envisaged. As each project would require a detailed techno-economic feasibility study before the work is commenced on the project to begin with, a technical consultancy wing has been created in the TTDC. This wing will comprise of technical staff drawn from TTDC and elsewhere. This will help not only in preparation of techno-economic feasibility study for major projects like ropeways, sound and light shows etc., by outsourcing professional consultants, but would also help in management of the projects. This wing will also offer technical support to private entrepreneurs, who are likely to invest in tourism projects thereby considerably increasing the private sector participation. To facilitate this, therefore, an outlay of Rs. 2 crores has been suggested.

Tourism Circuits

Tamil Nadu is the "complete destination" for all reasons and seasons. To facilitate tourists visiting their desired destinations without any hardship as also to properly package and market the products holistically in an integrated manner, it is proposed to identify and develop 'Tourism Circuits'. The infrastructure in these circuits would be created and up-dated keeping the twin objectives of attracting more tourists and extending their stay in Tamil Nadu in view. Accordingly, the following tourism circuits have been identified:

For International Tourists

Most of the international tourists visiting India are from U.K., U.S, Japan, Australia, South Asian, Africans regions etc. These countries abound in hill and beach resorts, water falls, forests etc. Hence, such products cannot be marketed to the international tourists beyond a point. The foreign tourists however show keen interest in historical, architectural and cultural heritage, monuments and temples of Tamil Nadu. They enjoy the exquisite, unique, inspiring, extravagantly sculpted carvings in the temples. The carvings are not only delicate and distinct and at the same time integrally linked with each other but also display the ingenuity and artistic skills of the sculptors. Hence circuits linking Mamallapuram, Kancheepuram, Thanjavur, Gangaikondacholapuram, Poompuhar, Madurai Rameswaram, Thiruvannamalai etc., destinations will be the most ideal itinerary for the foreign tourists. These, however, would have to be packaged along with other products and presented in such a way so as to offer attractions for the foreign tourists of all the age groups. The tourist circuits identified for the purpose, therefore, are:-

a) Chennai-Mamallapuram-Kancheepuram
b) Chennai-Mamallapuram-Pondicherry-Gingee-Thiruvannamalai-Kancheepuram
c) Six abodes of Lord Muruga (particularly for NRI Tamils)
d) Chennai-Pondichery-Chidambaram-Pichavaram-Gangaikondacholapuram-Thanjàvur-Tiruchirappalli-Rameswaram-Kanniyakumari-Madurai-Chennai-(Tamil Nadu Tour).
e) Navagraha Sannidhi (for NRIs).
f) Thekkadi-Kodaikanal-Madurai-Rameswaram-Kanniyakumari

National Tourists

Tourists from all the Indian states visit Tamil Nadu. The top six States which account for generating the maximum number of tourists to Tamil Nadu are U.P. Andhra Pradesh, Maharashtra, Gujarat, Karnataka and West Bengal. These tourists usually visit the religious destinations, hill resorts, which are a beautiful mix of mountain ranges and plains, bays and sun drenched beaches, wild life sanctuaries, meandering rivers, water falls which provide an awesome spectacle of colossal cascade of water and pilgrim centres. The circuits most suited and popular among these tourists are:

a) Chennai-Tirupathi-Kancheepuram-Mamallapuram-Chennai

b) Mumbai-Chennai-Tamil Nadu-Tirupathi-Mumbai

c) Kolkatta-Chennai-Tamil Nadu-Tirupathi-Kolkatta-

d) Chennai - Trichy - Thanjavur - Kumbakonam - Dharasuram - Gangaikondacholapuram-Chidambaram-Pichavaram.

e) Kodaikanal-Madurai-Rameswaram-Kanniyakumari

f) Six abodes of Lord Muruga and Navagraha Sannidhi.

g) Chennai-Yercaud-Ooty-Kodaikannal-Chennai.

h) Chennai-Velankanni-Chennai.

i) Chennai-Nagore-Chennai

j) Chennai-Andaman and Nicobar-Chennai.

k) Buddhist and Jain Circuits-Showcasing Tamil Nadu

Local Tourists

The local tourists would have visited all the important tourist centres in the State. Some of them may have visited the tourist spots even more than once. However, many of them may not have visited the lesser known tourist places like small water falls, dam sites, heritage towns etc. With this target group in mind, the State Government has declared 38 towns as cultural and historical centres. Similarly 41 centres have been declared as District Excursion Centres (DECs). Intensive publicity and marketing will have to be undertaken to popularise these centres among the local tourists. The circuits will cover all the districts in which the cultural/ historical towns and D.E.C. are located. Some of the popular circuits so identified are:

a) Chennai-Coimbatore-Sabarimalai.

b) Chennai-Melmaruvathoor-Sathanur-Thiruvannamalai-Hogenakkal-Chennai.

c) Chennai-Vellore-Elagiri Hills-Chennai.

d) One day Chennai-Tourist covering temples in and around Chennai.

e) Chennai-Puttaparthi-Bangalore-Chennai.

f) Chennai-Vellankanni, Nagore-Chennai.

g) Chennai-Coimbatore-Ooty-Mysore-Bangalore.

h) Chennai-Palani-Madurai and around-Palani-Coimbatore.

i) Madurai City Tour.

j) Trichy and Thanjavur.

k) Buddhist/ Jain Circuits-showcasing Tamil Nadu.

Human Resources Development

Human Resources Development is vital for promoting tourism. This may be considered under the following three heads:

Hospitality

Hotels are places visited by almost all the tourists, either to have food or for accommodation. The hotels require qualified personnel to understand the specific requirements of tourists & fulfil them according to the taste/ spending capacity of the tourists. Ill-behaviour or discourtesy by the hotel staff will create an adverse image of the hotel, the people and the State.

To train qualified youth in hospitality, there are two Institutions in Tamil Nadu, one functioning under the aegis of Government of India, i.e., Institute of Catering Technology & Applied Nutrition, Taramani, Chennai and the other one, the State Institute of Hotel Management & Catering Technology, Tiruchi, sponsored by the Govt. of Tamil Nadu. Both the above institutions turn out graduates, young and well equipped to attend on the tourists. During the Tenth Five Year Plan, it is proposed to improve the curriculum, increase the intake & create and upgrade the facilities. Efforts will also be taken to open more such institutions, preferably with private participation.

Guides

Another area where the human factor is important pertains to Guides. Today, tourists have multifarious means like Telephones, E-mail, CD Rom, documentary film, folders, touch screen, website, press etc to apprise and upgrade themselves with information on tourist products. But inspite of all these facilities, the Guides present at the tourist spots have a very important role. They, therefore, have to be well informed, courteous and should possess good communication ability and knowledge of language and of history, art and culture of the State. Since they interact directly with the tourists, efforts would be made to bring out an elite group of guides, for which well equipped youngsters will be selected & they will be given intensive training. Such guides will be deployed in important tourist spots in a phased manner.

Skilled Workers

Un-employed youth will be trained as drivers, travel agents, beauty parlour attendants, costume designers etc., and their skills upgraded.

Promotion of Marketing

Publicity & Direct Marketing

Tourism is one of the 3 leading "socio-economic and service businesses" of the new century and "Promotion, Publicity & Marketing" play a vital role in promotion of Tourism. For an aggressive, powerful and effective marketing, dissemination of tourist information through various media is absolutely essential to motivate the potential tourists. Publication of good quality brochures, posters, picture post-cards etc., and their distribution through various outlets of the Tourism Department including Government of India Tourist offices and other means is equally important.

Airlines, travel agents, release of advertisements in leading journals within the country and abroad, production of short films and screening at important locations, conduct of press meets and familiarisation tours for leading domestic and foreign travel writers, Road shows at important centres, participation in tourist marts within the country and abroad would be strategically used to market various tourist destinations, circuits and other products. A focused, integrated & holistic publicity and marketing campaign during the Tenth Five Year Plan period would, therefore, be an important element of the strategy for promoting tourism. An amount of Rs.10 crores will be provided for the following measures during the Plan to attract tourists:

1) Creating a 'Tamil Nadu Brand ' position
2) Differentiate from the competitive destinations and develop a unique market position image.

a) Printing of brochures of high quality for free distribution at Airports, Railway Stations, Hotels, Bus terminals and at all destinations.
b) Production of 30mm short films for screening at Theatres, Railway Station, Exhibition, Airports, Flights, TVs.
c) Production of CD Rom for free distribution. CD will contain information on accommodation, tourist centres, transport facilities etc.
d) Advertisements in India and Abroad.
e) Participation in National & International Tourist Marts.
f) Erection of Glow Sign Boards and self-luminous sign boards in and around Tourist Spots.
g) Establish an effective and ongoing presence in each source market
h) Establish an internet portal in various languages for global consumption.

Opening of New Tourist Offices / Renovation of existing Tourist Offices in other State Headquarters

Tourist Offices are at present functioning at Mumbai, New Delhi, Kolkatta, Panaji, Jaipur, Agra and Tourist Information Centres at Bangalore, Thiruvananthapuram and Hyderabad. During the Tenth Five Year Plan it is proposed to open Tamil Nadu State Tourist Offices/ Information Centres in all the State Headquarters and at important Airports/ Rail junctions in a phased programme and to upgrade the existing Tourist Offices / Tourist Information Centres. The details are as follows:

(a) Opening of new Tourist Offices / Information Centres in 17 State Capitals of India, all important Airports etc
(b) Renovation and upgradation of the existing Tourist Offices/ Tourist Information Centres (7 Nos.) and
(c) Utilising these Tourists Offices/ Information Centres as marketing agents for tourist facilities in Tamil Nadu.

Institutionalised Marketing

To attract foreign tourists, marketing agents have been appointed in London & Malaysia. It is proposed to appoint marketing agents in all potential markets like Thailand, Mauritius, South Africa, France, Italy and other South / South East Asian Countries. So also, marketing agents are being appointed at least in important cities & towns within India.

Strengthening Communication Network

The Department of Tourism has under its control 20 Tourist Offices and 19 Tourist Information Centres for dissemination of information to tourists. Out of this, six Tourist Offices and three Tourist Information Centres are functioning outside Tamil Nadu. In the first phase of computerisation, 9 Tourist Offices have been computerised. It is now proposed to computerise the remaining Tourist Offices/ Tourist Information Centres, hotels of TTDC, bookings of accommodation and tour packages etc., besides total computerisation of the Head Office. All the above units will have STD, ISD, Fax/ E-mail/ Internet facilities. By employing state of the art technology, all the units will be inter-linked through Wide Area Network (WAN). As Internet is becoming an increasingly powerful vehicle for travel information, marketing & sales, to keep pace with this latest trends in communication, the Tourism Department has created an exclusive website, which contains full details of Tamil Nadu's Tourism potential & related information. The proposed Computerisation and connectivity will enable potential tourists in any part of the globe to obtain information and facilitate online booking.

Role of Tamil Nadu Tourism Development Corporation (TTDC)

Tamil Nadu Tourism Development Corporation (TTDC) was started in the year 1971 on a modest note with 2 coaches and 5 hotels. It has made rapid strides since then and has earned the distinction of owning the largest chain of hotels in South India numbering 54. The hotels are spread throughout Tamil Nadu. TTDC offers the following facilities to tourists:

1)	Hotels and Youth Hostels	34
2)	Boat Houses	10
3)	Restaurants	3

4)	Canteens	4
5)	Telescope Houses	4
6)	Parks	3
7)	Tourist Service Centre	1

Petrol Bunk, Mamallapuram Out of the 54 hotels, 12 Hotels at Tirunelveli, Mettupalayam, Mandapam, Sriperumpudur, Coonoor, Ranipet, Kotagiri, Namakkal, Mettur Dam, Sathanur Dam, Virudhunagar and Vaigai Dam have been franchised to private sector. Action is being taken to franchise the remaining hotels to private sector. Youth Hostels have been constructed to cater to the budget tourists at all the major tourist destinations, wherein dormitory type of accommodation is provided at economic tariff. Package Tours ranging from ½ day to 14 days covering several States like Bihar, Uttar Pradesh, Madhya Pradesh, Maharashtra besides covering all Southern States like Andhra Pradesh, Karnataka, Goa, Pondicherry and Kerala are being conducted. New package tours would be evolved. Necessary steps will be taken to organise new Air Package Tours. In the changing scenario as above, TTDC would be required to act mainly as an institutionalized vehicle of the State to attract, organise, lead, support, direct and facilitate private investment in the field of destination and other product developments. It would also provide technical support and assistance in the areas of Human Resources Development, project preparation, evaluation, market survey, research and related subjects and would serve mainly as a facilitator.

New Schemes for Tenth Plan for Development of Infrastructure

During the Seventh, Eighth and Ninth Plans, the Ministry of Tourism was assisting the State Governments/ UT Administrations to undertake a large number of small, isolated projects spread through out the length and breath of the country resulting in the resources being spread very thinly. The Central financial assistance had, therefore, not been able to create any major impact on the development of tourism infrastructure in the country. In order to provide a quick and substantial impact to tourism growth in the Tenth Plan, the following new schemes for the development and promotion of tourism in the country have been proposed:

1) Integrated Development of Tourism Circuits.
2) Product/ infrastructure and Destination Development.
3) Assistance for Large Revenue Generating Projects.

Whereas the GOI would meet the entire expenditure towards the development of tourism circuits, in the case of Tourist destinations, the share of the Department of Tourism, Government of India would be 90% of the project cost and 10% would have to be met by the State Government. The GOI has identified initially the following two circuits in Tamil Nadu:

1) Chennai – Mammallapuram – Pondicherry-Gingee-Thiruvannamalai – Kancheepuram-Chennai; and
2) Thekkadi – Madurai-Rameswaram-Kanniyakumari.

In respect of tourist destinations besides Mamallapuram, it is proposed to develop Kanniyakumari in the first phase. The maximum amount for the development of a tourist destination would be around Rs. 5 crores. Keeping these in view, therefore, it is proposed to earmark Rs. 10 crores as State Government's share towards Government of India assisted Schemes assuming the total share of Government of India during the entire plan period to be Rs. 100 crores.

Hill Area Development Programme

Funds are also allotted to the Nilgiris District for tourism schemes under the Hill Area Development Programme to create infrastructure facilities/basic amenities etc.

Tenth Five Year Plan Outlay

While a major part of the investment is going to come from the private sector, there are certain promotional activities that have to be undertaken, and certain infrastructure that has to be established by the State only. In view of this position and considering that efforts are being made to make Tamil Nadu the number one State in India and position it firmly on the global tourism map, programmes/ schemes for a total cost of Rs. 1202 crores would be taken up.

7

Defining and Analysing Hospitality and its Impact

An Introduction to Tourism

Tourism is travel for recreational, leisure or business purposes. The World Tourism Organization defines tourists as people who "travel to and stay in places outside their usual environment for more than twenty-four hours and not more than one consecutive year for leisure, business and other purposes not related to the exercise of an activity remunerated from within the place visited". Tourism has become a popular global leisure activity. In 2008, there were over 922 million international tourist arrivals, with a growth of 1.9% as compared to 2007. International tourism receipts grew to US$944 billion (euro 642 billion) in 2008, corresponding to an increase in real terms of 1.8%. As a result of the Late-2000s recession, international travel demand suffered a strong slowdown beginning in June 2008, with growth in international tourism arrivals worldwide falling to 2% during the boreal summer months, and this negative trend intensified as international tourist arrivals fell by 8% during the first four months of 2009. Thereafter this declining trend was exacerbated in some regions due to the outbreak of the influenza AH1N1 virus.

Tourism is vital for many countries, such as the U.A.E, Egypt, Greece and Thailand, and many island nations, such as The Bahamas, Fiji, Maldives and the Seychelles, due to the large intake of money for businesses with their goods and services and the opportunity for employment in the service industries associated with tourism. These service industries include transportation services, such as airlines, cruise ships and taxis, hospitality services, such as accommodations, including hotels and resorts, and entertainment venues, such as amusement parks, casinos, shopping malls, various music venues and the theatre.

Definition

Hunziker and Krapf, in 1941, defined tourism as people who travel "the sum of the phenomena and relationships arising from the travel and stay of non-residents, insofar as they do not lead to permanent residence and are not connected with any earning activity." In 1976, the Tourism Society of England's definition was: "Tourism is the temporary, short-term movement of people to destination outside the places where they normally live and work and their activities during the stay at each destination. It includes movements for all purposes." In 1981, the International Association of Scientific Experts in Tourism defined tourism in terms of particular activities selected by choice and undertaken outside the home.

The United Nations classified three forms of tourism in 1994, in its "Recommendations on Tourism Statistics: Domestic tourism", which involves residents of the given country travelling only within this country; Inbound tourism, involving non-residents travelling in the given country; and Outbound tourism, involving residents travelling in another country. The UN also derived different categories of tourism by combining the three basic forms of tourism: Internal tourism, which comprises domestic tourism and inbound tourism; National tourism, which comprises domestic tourism and outbound tourism; and International tourism, which consists of inbound tourism and outbound tourism. *Intrabound tourism* is a term coined by the Korea Tourism Organization and widely accepted in Korea. Intrabound tourism differs from domestic tourism in that the former encompasses policy making and implementation of national tourism policies.

Recently, the tourism industry has shifted from the promotion of inbound tourism to the promotion of intrabound tourism, because many countries are experiencing tough competition for inbound tourists.

World Tourism Statistics and Rankings

The World Tourism Organization reports the following ten countries as the most visited in between 2006 and 2008 by number of international travellers. When compared to 2006, Ukraine entered the top ten list, surpassing Russia, Austria and Mexico, and in 2008 surpassed Germany. In 2008 the U.S. displaced Spain from the second place. Most of the top visited countries continue to be on the European continent.

International Tourism Receipts

In 2008, there were over 922 million international tourist arrivals, with a growth of 1.9% as compared to 2007. International tourism receipts grew to US$944 billion (euro 642 billion) in 2008, corresponding to an increase in real terms of 1.8% on 2007. When the export value of international passenger transport receipts is accounted for, total receipts in 2008 reached a record of US$1.1 billion, or over US$3 billion a day. The World Tourism Organization reports the following countries as the top ten tourism earners for the year 2008. It is noticeable that most of them are on the European continent, but the United States continues to be the top earner.

International Tourism Expenditures

The World Tourism Organization reports the following countries as the top ten biggest spenders on international tourism for the year 2008. For the fifth year in a row, German tourists continue as the top spenders.

History

Wealthy people have always travelled to distant parts of the world, to see great buildings, works of art, learn new languages, experience new cultures and to taste different cuisines. Long ago, at the time of the Roman Republic, places such as Baiae were popular coastal resorts for the rich. The word *tourism* was used by 1811 and *tourist* by 1840. In 1936, the League of Nations defined *foreign tourist* as "someone travelling abroad for at least twenty-four hours". Its successor, the United Nations, amended this definition in 1945, by including a maximum stay of six months. The earliest forms of leisure tourism can be traced as far back as the Babylonian and Egyptian empires. A museum of "historic antiquities" was open to the public in the sixth century BC in Babylon, while the Egyptians held many religious festivals attracting not only the devout, but many who came to see the famous buildings and works of art in the cities. The local towns accommodated tourists by providing services such as: vendors of food and drink, guides, hawkers of souvenirs, touts and prostitutes.

From around the same date, Greek tourists travelled to visit the sites of healing gods. Because the independent city-states of ancient Greece had no central authority to order the construction of roads, most of these tourists travelled by water, hence seaports prospered. The lands of the Mediterranean Sea produced a remarkable evolution in travel. People travel for trade, commerce, religious purposes, festivals, medical treatment, or education developed at an early date.

Guidebooks became available as early as the fourth century BC, covering a vast area of destinations, i.e. Athens, Sparta and Troy. Pausanias, a Greek travel writer, produced a noted "description of Greece" between AD 160 and 180, which, in its critical evaluation of facilities and destinations, acted as a model for later writers. Advertisements, in the form of signs directing visitors to wayside inns, are also known from this period. However, under Romans rule is where international travel became first important. With no foreign borders between England and Syria, and with the seas safe from piracy due to the Roman patrols, conditions favouring travel had arrived. Roman coinage was acceptable everywhere, and Latin was the common language. Romans travelled to Sicily, Greece, Rhodes, and Troy, Egypt and from the third century AD, to the Holy Land.

Domestic tourism also flourished within the Roman Empire. Second homes were built by the wealthy within easy travelling distance of Rome, occupied particularly during the springtime social season. Naples attracted the retired and the intellectuals.

Before the sixteenth century, those who sought to travel had three modes in which to do so. They could walk, ride a horse or they could be carried, either on a little or on a carrier's wagon. The development of the sprung coach was a huge advance for those who regularly travelled, and by the mid 1600's, coaches were operating regularly in Britain. In the eighteenth century the introduction of turnpike roads, which provided improved surfaces for which tolls would be charged. The later introduction of the metal, leaf spring suspension also added to comfort.

Travel also requires accommodation, and at that time, it was basic. To accommodate the new demand for travel inns was provided. They provided fresh horses, and lodgings were available for rent to visitors when they arrived at their destination.

From the early seventeenth century, a new form of tourism developed as a direct outcome of the freedom and quest for learning heralded by the Renaissance. Young men who wanted positions at court were encouraged to travel to the Continent to finish their education. Others soon adopted this practice in the upper echelons of society, and it soon became customary for the education of a gentleman to be completed by a "Grand tour" of major cultural centres of Europe, accompanied by a tutor and often-lasting three years or more. The appeal soon became social, and leisure seeking young men travelled, predominantly to France and Italy, to enjoy the rival cultures and social life of cities such as Paris, Venice, or Florence. By the end of the eighteenth century, the custom had become institutionalised for the gentry.

Passports have their origins in the medieval testimonial. A letter from an ecclesiastical superior given to a pilgrim to avoid the latter's possible arrest on charges of vagrancy. Later, papers of authority to travel were more widely issued by the state, particularly during periods of warfare with neighbouring European countries.

Spas were already well established during the time of the Roman Empire, but their popularity, based on the supposed medical benefits of the waters, lapsed in the subsequent centuries. Renewed interest in the therapeutic qualities of mineral waters has been ascribed to the influence of the Renaissance in Britain, and elsewhere in Europe.

Leisure Travel

Leisure travel was associated with the Industrial Revolution in the United Kingdom – the first European country to promote leisure time to the increasing industrial population. Initially, this applied to the owners of the machinery of production, the economic oligarchy, the factory owners and the traders. These comprised the new middle class. Cox & Kings was the first official travel company to be formed in 1758.

The British origin of this new industry is reflected in many place names. In Nice, France, one of the first and best-established holiday resorts on the French Riviera, the long esplanade along the seafront is known to this day as the *Promenade des Anglais;* in many other historic resorts in continental Europe, old, well-established palace hotels have names like the *Hotel Bristol,* the *Hotel Carlton* or the *Hotel Majestic* – reflecting the dominance of English customers.

Many leisure-oriented tourists travel to the tropics, both in the summer and winter. Places often visited are: Cuba, the Dominican Republic, Thailand, North Queensland in Australia and Florida in the United States.

Winter Tourism

Major ski resorts are located in the various European countries.

Mass Tourism

Mass tourism could only have developed with the improvements in technology, allowing the transport of large numbers of people in a short space of time to places of leisure interest, so that greater numbers of people could begin to enjoy the benefits of leisure time. In the United States, the first seaside resorts in the European style were at Atlantic City, New Jersey and Long Island, New York.

In Continental Europe, early resorts included: Ostend, popularized by the people of Brussels; Boulogne-sur-Mer and Deauville (Calvados) for the Parisians; and Heiligendamm, founded in 1797, as the first seaside resort on the Baltic Sea.

Adjectival Tourism

Adjectival tourism refers to the numerous niche or speciality travel forms of tourism that have emerged over the years, each with its own adjective. Many of these have come into common use by the tourism industry and academics. Others are emerging concepts that may or may not gain popular usage. Examples of the more common niche tourism markets include:

1. Agritourism

2. Culinary tourism
3. Cultural tourism
4. Ecotourism
5. Heritage tourism
6. LGBT tourism
7. Medical tourism
8. Nautical tourism
9. Religious tourism
10. Space tourism
11. War tourism
12. Wildlife tourism.

Recent Developments

There has been an upmarket trend in the tourism over the last few decades, especially in Europe, where international travel for short breaks is common. Tourists have higher levels of disposable income and greater leisure time and they are also better-educated and have more sophisticated tastes. There is now a demand for a better quality products, which has resulted in a fragmenting of the mass market for beach vacations; people want more specialised versions, such as Club 18-30, quieter resorts, family-oriented holidays or niche market-targeted destination hotels.

The developments in technology and transport infrastructure, such as jumbo jets, low-cost airlines and more accessible airports have made many types of tourism more affordable. WHO estimates that up to 500,000 people are on planes at any time. There have also been changes in lifestyle, such as retiree-age people who sustain year round tourism. This is facilitated by internet sales of tourism products. Some sites have now started to offer dynamic packaging, in which an inclusive price is quoted for a tailor-made package requested by the customer upon impulse.

There have been a few setbacks in tourism, such as the September 11 attacks and terrorist threats to tourist destinations, such as in Bali and several European cities. Also, on December 26, 2004, a tsunami, caused by the 2004 Indian Ocean earthquake, hit the Asian countries on the Indian Ocean, including the Maldives. Thousands of lives were lost and many tourists died. This, together with the vast clean-up operation in place, has stopped or severely hampered tourism to the area.

The terms *tourism* and *travel* are sometimes used interchangeably. In this context, travel has a similar definition to tourism, but implies a more purposeful journey. The terms *tourism* and *tourist* are sometimes used pejoratively, to imply a shallow interest in the cultures or locations visited by tourists.

Sustainable Tourism

"Sustainable tourism is envisaged as leading to management of all resources in such a way that economic, social and aesthetic needs can be fulfilled while maintaining cultural integrity, essential ecological processes, biological diversity and life support systems."

Sustainable development implies "meeting the needs of the present without compromising the ability of future generations to meet their own needs"

Ecotourism

When there is a significant price difference between countries for a given medical procedure, particularly in Southeast Asia, India, Eastern Europe and where there are different regulatory regimes, in relation to particular medical procedures, travelling to take advantage of the price or regulatory differences is often referred to as "medical tourism".

Educational Tourism

Educational tourism developed, because of the growing popularity of teaching and learning of knowledge and the enhancing of technical competency outside of the classroom environment. In educational tourism, the main focus of the tour or leisure activity includes visiting another country to learn about the culture, such as in Student Exchange Programs and Study Tours, or to work and apply skills learned inside the classroom in a different environment, such as in the International Practicum Training Program.

Creative Tourism

Creative tourism has existed as a form of cultural tourism,

since the early beginnings of tourism itself. Its European roots date back to the time of the Grand Tour, which saw the sons of aristocratic families travelling for the purpose of mostly interactive, educational experiences.

More recently, creative tourism has been given its own name by Crispin Raymond and Greg Richards, who as members of the Association for Tourism and Leisure Education (ATLAS), have directed a number of projects for the European Commission, including cultural and crafts tourism, known as sustainable tourism. They have defined "creative tourism" as tourism related to the active participation of travellers in the culture of the host community, through interactive workshops and informal learning experiences.

Meanwhile, the concept of creative tourism has been picked up by high-profile organizations such as UNESCO, who through the Creative Cities Network, have endorsed creative tourism as an engaged, authentic experience that promotes an active understanding of the specific cultural features of a place.

More recently, creative tourism has gained popularity as a form of cultural tourism, drawing on active participation by travellers in the culture of the host communities they visit. Several countries offer examples of this type of tourism development, including the United Kingdom, the Bahamas, Jamaica, Spain, Italy and New Zealand.

Dark Tourism

One emerging area of special interest tourism has been identified by Lennon and Foley (2000) as "dark" tourism. This type of tourism involves visits to "dark" sites, such as battlegrounds, scenes of horrific crimes or acts of genocide, for example: concentration camps. Dark tourism poses severe ethical and moral dilemmas: should these sites be available for visitation and, if so, what should the nature of the publicity involved be. Dark tourism remains a small niche market, driven by varied motivations, such as mourning, remembrance, macabre curiosity or even entertainment. Its early origins are rooted in fairgrounds and medieval fairs.

Growth

The World Tourism Organization (UNWTO) forecasts that

international tourism will continue growing at the average annual rate of 4 %. With the advent of e-commerce, tourism products have become one of the most traded items on the internet. Tourism products and services have been made available through intermediaries, although tourism providers can sell their services directly. This has put pressure on intermediaries from both on-line and traditional shops.

It has been suggested there is a strong correlation between tourism expenditure per capita and the degree to which countries play in the global context. Not only as a result of the important economic contribution of the tourism industry, but also as an indicator of the degree of confidence with which global citizens leverage the resources of the globe for the benefit of their local economies. This is why any projections of growth in tourism may serve as an indication of the relative influence that each country will exercise in the future. Space tourism is expected to "take off" in the first quarter of the 21st century, although compared with traditional destinations the number of tourists in orbit will remain low until technologies such as a space elevator make space travel cheap.

Technological improvement is likely to make possible air-ship hotels, based either on solar-powered airplanes or large dirigibles. Underwater hotels, such as Hydropolis, expected to open in Dubai in 2009, will be built. On the ocean, tourists will be welcomed by ever larger cruise ships and perhaps floating cities.

Latest Trends

As a result of the Late-2000s recession, international arrivals suffered a strong slowdown beginning in June 2008. Growth from 2007 to 2008 was only 3.7% during the first eight months of 2008. The Asian and Pacific markets were affected and Europe stagnated during the boreal summer months, while the Americas performed better, reducing their expansion rate but keeping a 6% growth from January to August 2008. Only the Middle East continued its rapid growth during the same period, reaching a 17% growth as compared to the same period in 2007.

This slowdown on international tourism demand was also reflected in the air transport industry, with a negative growth in September 2008 and a 3.3% growth in passenger traffic through September. The hotel industry also reports a slowdown, as room occupancy continues to decline. As the global economic situation deteriorated dramatically during September and October as a result of the global financial crisis, growth of international tourism is expected to slow even further for the remaining of 2008, and this slowdown in demand growth is forecasted to continue into 2009 as recession has already hit most of the top spender countries, with long-haul travel expected to be the most affected by the economic crisis. This negative trend intensified as international tourist arrivals fell by 8% during the first four months of 2009, and the decline was exacerbated in some regions due to the outbreak of the influenza AH1N1 virus.

Tourist Product

A product may be defined as the sum of the physical and psychological satisfaction it provides to the buyer. For a tourist, the product covers the complete experience from the time he leaves home to the time he returns back. Tourist products include a comprehensive range of package and travel facilities. Three basic components of the product are attractions of the destination, facilities at the destination and accessibility to the destination.

A tourism product can be defined as the sum of the physical and psychological satisfaction it provides to tourists during their travelling en route to the destination. The tourist product focuses on facilities and services designed to meet the needs of the tourist. It can be seen as a composite product, as the sum total of a country's tourist attractions, transport, and accommodation and of entertainment which result in customer satisfaction. Each of the components of a tourist product is supplied by individual providers of services like hotel companies, airlines, travel agencies, etc. The tourist product can be analysed in terms of its attraction, accessibility and accommodation.

Attractions

Of the three basic components of a tourist product, attractions are very important. Unless there is an attraction, the tourist will not be motivated to go to a particular place. Attractions are those elements in a product which determine the choice made by particular tourist to visit one particular destination rather than another. The attractions could be cultural, like sites and areas of archaeological interest, historical buildings and monuments, flora and fauna, beach resorts, mountains, national parks or events like trade fairs, exhibitions, arts and music festivals, games, etc. Tourist demands are also very much susceptible to changes in fashion. Fashion is an important factor in the demand for various tourist attractions and amenities. The tourist who visits a particular place for its natural beauty may decide to visit some other attractions due to a change in fashion. Peter has drawn up an inventory of the various attractions which are of significance in tourism.

Inventory of Tourist Attractions

Cultural: Sites and areas of archaeological interest, Historical buildings and Monuments, Places of historical significance, Museums, Modern Culture, Political and Educational institutions, Religious Institutions

Traditions: National Festivals, Arts and Handicrafts, Music, Folklore, Native life and Customs.

Scenic: National Parks, Wildlife, Flora and Fauna, Beach Resorts, Mountain Resorts.

Entertainment: Participation and Viewing sports, Amusement and Recreation Parks Zones and Oceanariums, Cinemas and Theatres, Night Life and Cuisine.

Others: Climate, Health resorts or Spas, Unique characteristics not available elsewhere.

However, the attractions of tourism are, to a very large extent, geographical in character. Location and accessibility (whether a place has a coastal or inland position and the ease with which a given place can be reached) are important. Physical space may be thought of as a component for those who seek the wilderness and solitude. Scenery or landscape is a compound of landforms; water and the vegetation and has an aesthetic and recreative value. Climate conditions, especially in relation to the amount of sunshine, temperature and precipitation, are of special significance. Animal life may be an important attraction, firstly in relation to, bird watching or viewing game in their natural habitat and secondly, for sports purposes, eg. fishing and hunting.

Man's impact on the natural landscape in the form of his settlements, historical monuments and archaeological remains is also a major attraction. Finally, a variety of cultural features-ways of life, folklore, artistic expressions, etc. provide valuable attractions to many. Accessibility It is a means by which a tourist can reach the area where attractions are located. Tourist attractions of whatever type would be of little importance if their locations are inaccessible by the normal means of transport. A Tourist in order to get to his destination needs some mode of transport. This mode may be a motor car, a coach, an aeroplane, a ship or a train which enables him to reach his predetermined destination. If tourist destinations are located at places where no transport can reach or where there are inadequate transport facilities, they become of little value. The tourist attractions, which are located near the tourist-generating markets and are linked by a network of efficient means of transport, receive the maximum number of tourists.

The distance factor also plays an important role in determining a tourist's choice of a destination. Longer distances cost much more in the way of expenses on travel as compared to short distances. An example can be that of India. About two and a half million tourist arrivals for a country of the size of India may look rather unimpressive. However if one looks at certain factors like the country's distance from the affluent tourist markets of the world such as the United States, Europe, Canada, Japan and Australia, one may conclude that the long distance is one of the factors responsible for low arrivals. It costs a visitor from these countries, quite a substantial amount, to visit India for a holiday. It has been stated earlier that Europe and North America continue to be the main generating and receiving areas for international tourism, accounting for as much as 70% and 20% respectively, of international tourist arrivals. Easy accessibility, thus is a key factor for the growth and development of tourist movements.

Accommodation

The accommodation and other facilities complement the attractions. Accommodation plays a central role and is very basic to tourist destinations. World Tourism Organization in its definition of a tourist has stated that he must spend at least one night in the destination visited, to qualify as a tourist. This presupposes availability of some kind of accommodation.

The demand for accommodation away from one's home is met by a variety of facilities. The range and type of accommodation is quite varied and has undergone considerable change since the last half century. There has been a decline in the use of boarding houses and small private hotels.

Larger hotels are increasing their share of holiday trade, especially in big metropolitan areas and popular spots. In more traditional holiday and sea-side resorts in Europe and elsewhere, big hotels are keeping their share of holiday resorts. In recent years, some changes have been reflected in the type of accommodation. There has been an increasing demand for more non-traditional and informal types of accommodation. The latest trends in accommodation are holiday villages. In recent years there has been an increase in the popularity of such accommodation.

Accommodation may in itself be an important tourist attraction. In fact, a large number of tourists visit a particular destination or town simply because there is a first class luxury hotel or resort which provides excellent services and facilities. Some countries like Switzerland, Holland, France, Austria, and Belgium have gained a reputation for providing excellent accommodation with good cuisine. Many hotel establishments elsewhere in various countries, especially the resort hotels, have gained a reputation for their excellent cuisine, services and facilities. The French government for instance, paved the way for tourist development of Corsica by launching a big hotel development programme.

Amenities

Facilities are a necessary aid to the tourist centre. For a sea-side resort, facilities like swimming, boating, yachting, surf-riding, and other facilities like dancing, recreation and other amusements are important for every tourist centre. Amenities can be of two types; natural, eg. beaches, sea-bathing, possibilities of fishing, opportunities for climbing, trekking, viewing, etc. and man-made, eg. various types of entertainment and facilities which cater to the special needs of the tourists. Excellent sandy beaches, sheltered from sunshine with palm and coconut trees and offering good bathing conditions form very good tourist attractions. Certain other natural amenities such as spacious waters for the purpose of sailing, or the opportunities for fishing and hunting are also very important.

Characteristics of Tourism Product

By now, you must have understood what a tourism product is. Now let us look at some of its characteristics:-

1) *Intangible:* Unlike a tangible product, say, a motor car or refrigerator, no transfer of ownership of goods is involved in tourism. The product here cannot be seen or inspected before its purchase. Instead, certain facilities, installations, items of equipment are made available for a specified time and for a specified use. For example, a seat in an aeroplane is provided only for a specified time.
2) *Psychological:* A large component of tourism product is the satisfaction the consumer derives from its use. A tourist acquires experiences while interacting with the new environment and his experiences help to attract and motivate potential customers.
3) *Highly Perishable:* A travel agent or tour operator who sells a tourism product cannot store it. Production can only take place if the customer is actually present. And once consumption begins, it cannot be stopped, interrupted or modified. If the product remains unused, the chances are lost i.e. if tourists do not visit a particular place, the opportunity at that time is lost. It is due to this reason that heavy discount is offered by hotels and transport generating organizations during off season.
4) *Composite Product:* The tourist product cannot be provided by a single enterprise unlike a manufactured product. The tourist product covers the complete experience of a visit to a particular place. And many providers contribute to this experience. For instance, airline supplies seats, a hotel provides rooms and restaurants, travel agents make bookings for stay and sightseeing, etc.
5) *Unstable Demand:* Tourism demand is influenced by seasonal, economic political and others such factors.

There are certain times of the year which see a greater demand than others. At these times there is a greater strain on services like hotel bookings, employment, the transport system, etc.

6) *Fixed supply in the short run:* The tourism product unlike a manufactured product cannot be brought to the consumer; the consumer must go to the product. This requires an in-depth study of users' behaviour, taste preferences, likes and dislikes so that expectations and realities coincide for the maximum satisfaction of the consumer. The supply of a tourism product is fixed in the short run and can only be increased in the long run following increased demand patterns.

7) *Absence of ownership:* When you buy a car, the ownership of the car is transferred to you, but when you hire a taxi you buy the right to be transported to a predetermined destination at a predetermined price (fare). You neither own the automobile nor the driver of the vehicle. Similarly, hotel rooms, airline tickets, etc. can be used but not owned. These services can be bought for consumption but ownership remains with the provider of the service. So, a dance can be enjoyed by viewing it, but the dancer cannot be owned.

8) *Heterogeneous:* Tourism is not a homogeneous product since it tends to vary in standard and quality over time, unlike a T.V set or any other manufactured product. A package tour or even a flight on an aircraft can't be consistent at all times. The reason is that this product is a service and services are people based. Due to this, there is variability in this product. All individuals vary and even the same individual may not perform the same every time. For instance, all air hostesses cannot provide the same quality of service and even the same air hostess may not perform uniformly in the morning and evening. Thus, services cannot be standardised.

9) *Risky:* The risk involved in the use of a tourism product is heightened since it has to be purchased before its consumption. An element of chance is always present in its consumption. Like, a show might not be as

entertaining as it promises to be or a beach holiday might be disappointing due to heavy rain.

10) *Marketable:* Tourism product is marketed at two levels. At the first level, national and regional organisations engage in persuading potential tourists to visit the country or a certain region. These official tourist organisations first create knowledge of its country in tourist –generating markets and persuade visitors in these markets to visit the country. At the second level, the various individual firms providing tourist services, market their own components of the total tourist product to persuade potential tourists to visit that region for which they are responsible.

Forms of Tourism Product

By now you must be aware of what a tourism product is and what its peculiar features are. It is necessary to understand the components of the tourist product from the point of view of the consumer. The product for the tourist covers the complete experience from the time he leaves home to the time he returns. The tourist product today is developed to meet the needs of the consumer and techniques like direct sales, publicity and advertising are employed to bring this product to the consumer. The tourist product is the basic raw material, be it the country's natural beauty, climate, history, culture and the people, or other facilities necessary for comfortable living such as water supply, electricity, roads, transport, communication and other essentials. The tourist product can be entirely a man-made one or nature's creation improved upon by man. A consumer can combine individual products in a large number of ways. There would be many possible destinations, each with a number of hotels, each to be reached by more than one airline. Thus, the potential choice facing the consumer is very large. The large number of tourist destinations have placed at the disposal of a tourist a very large variety of tourist products in abundant quantity from a large number of competing destinations. This eventually, has led to the adoption of the new concept i.e., the marketing concept in tourism by various countries promoting tourism. Tourism, basically, is an infrastructure based service product. The nature of the service here is highly intangible and perishable offering a limited scope for creating and maintaining the distinctive competitive edge. The effective marketing of tourism needs constant gearing up of infrastructure to international standards and presupposes in its coordination with the tourism suppliers. In strategic terms, it calls for the action of an integrated approach to management and marketing. In operational terms, it means the implementation of a better defined, better targeted market-driven strategy for realizing the defined objectives.

The important point to note here is that marketing is applied to situations where the choice can be limited to a relatively small number of brands giving the consumer a reasonable choice. The process of selection thus becomes easier. In the field of tourism this process is taking place by the increased use of 'package tours'. A package tour is a travel plan which includes most elements of vacation, such as transportation, accommodation, sight-seeing and entertainment. The tourist product is a composite product, whether it is sold as a package or assembled by the individual himself or his travel agent.

There are many tourism products that are available to the consumer today. In modern times these products, whether traditional in nature like culture and pilgrimage, or modern like adventure, conventions and conferences, health, medical, etc. are being packaged, promoted and priced appropriately to woo as many tourists as possible.

Tourism products can be classified as under for a better understanding of each of their peculiar characteristics, so that they can be marketed and positioned appropriately:

Natural Tourism Products

These include natural resources such as areas, climate and its setting, landscape and natural environment. Natural resources are frequently the key elements in a destination's attraction. Let us look at some examples:

1) Countryside
2) Climate-temperature, rains, snowfall, days of sunshine
3) Natural Beauty-landforms, hills, rocks, gorges, terrain
4) Water-lakes, ponds, rivers, waterfalls, springs
5) Flora and Fauna

6) Wildlife
7) Beaches
8) Islands
9) Spas
10) Scenic Attractions

The climate of a tourist destination is often an important attraction. Good weather plays an important role in making a holiday. Millions of tourists from countries with extreme climates visit beaches in search of fine weather and sunshine. The sunshine and clear sea breeze at the beaches have attracted many people for a very long time. In fact, development of spas and resorts along the sea coasts in many countries were a result of the travellers, urge to enjoy good weather and sunshine. In Europe, countries like France, Italy, Spain and Greece have developed beautiful beach resorts. North Europeans visit the Mediterranean coast searching for older resorts like Monte Carlo, Nice and Cannes on the Riviera and new resorts in Spain and Italy. Beautiful beaches of India, Sri Lanka, and Thailand, Indonesia and Australia and some other new destinations are more examples of how good weather can attract tourists. All these areas capitalise on good weather.

Destinations with attractive winter climates, winter warmth and sunshine are also important centres of tourist attraction. Many areas have become important winter holiday resorts attracting a large number of tourists.

Around these winter resorts, winter sport facilities have been installed to cater to the increasing needs of tourists. People from warm climates travel especially to see snowfall and enjoy the cold climate. In countries with tropical climates, many upland cool areas have been developed as 'hill stations'. Hence climate is of great significance as a tourism product. The scenery and natural beauty of places has always attracted tourists. Tourists enjoy nature in all its various forms. There are land forms like mountains, canyons, coral reefs, cliffs, etc. One of the great all time favourite tourist destination is the Grand Canyon, Arizona. Mountain ranges like the Himalayas, Kilimanjaro, and Swiss Alps, etc. There are water forms like rivers, lakes waterfalls, geysers, glaciers, etc. The Niagara Falls shared by Canada and the United States is an example of how scenic waterfalls attract tourists. Lake Tahoe in California and the, deserts of Egypt are other examples of great tourist products. Other great natural wonders that attract tourists are the Giants Causeway of Northern Ireland, the Geysers of Iceland, the glaciers of the Alps, the forests of Africa etc. Vegetation like forests, grasslands, moors deserts, etc. has all been developed as tourist products.

Flora and Fauna attract many a tourist. Tourists like to know the various types of plants and trees that they see and which trees are seen in which seasons. There are many plants which are specific to certain regions and many times students and travellers visit those areas especially to see those varieties of plants. Thick forest covers, attract tourists who enjoy trekking and hunting activities. Fauna attracts tourists who like to watch birds, wild mammals, reptiles and other exotic and rare animals. Countries in South East Asia have crocodile gardens, bird sanctuaries, and other tourist products that display the fauna of their region.

Spas are gaining popularity as modern tourism products all over the world. While most parts of the world have their own therapies and treatments that are effective in restoring the wiliness and beauty of people. New kinds of health tours that are gaining popularity are spa tours. Spas offer the unique advantages of taking the best from the West and the East, combining them with the indigenous system and offering best of the two worlds. For example Swedish massages work well with the Javanese Mandy, lulur, aromatherapy, reflexology and traditional ayurvedic procedures. Now various spa products are being combined with yoga, meditation, and pranayama, giving a holistic experience to tourists. Spa treatments are now combined with other medical treatments to treat blood pressure, insomnia, depression, paralysis and some other diseases. People are now travelling to spas and clinics for curative baths and medical treatment. In some countries like Italy, Austria and Germany, great importance is given to spa treatments. In Russia along the Black Sea coast and in the foothills of the Caucasus Mountains, there are many world famous sanatoria where millions of Russians and international tourists throng every year. Beach tourism is very popular among the tourists today. Tourists of all age groups, backgrounds, cultures and countries enjoy this tourism product. Besides attraction and saleability, beach holidaying has lead to overall development of tourism in many parts of the world. The basic importance of beaches is that they provide aesthetic and environmental value of the beach such as beautiful natural scenery with golden sands, lush green vegetation and right blue sky. The water should be clear, free of currents and underwater rocks. Beach tourism activities include water and land resource use. The water usage involves swimming, surfing, sailing, wind surfing, water scootering, Para-sailing, motorboat rides, etc. The land use has multifacets like sunbathing, recreational areas for tourists (parks, playgrounds, clubs, theatre, amusement parks, casinos, cultural museums, etc.), accommodation facilities, car and bus parking areas, entertainment and shopping complexes, access roads and transportation network. Due to its multidimensional requirements the beach product needs special care. A beach resort needs to be developed as an integrated complex to function as a self-contained community. Environmental management should also ensure the availability of necessary infrastructure in the immediate hinterland to the coastal region in support of the development on the coast to maintain its ecosystem.

Islands abound with natural beauty, with the rare flora and fauna and tribes. This makes islands an ideal place for adventure, nature and culture lovers to visit. This tourist product has great scope as these islands are being developed as tourist paradises. For example, Hawaii, Maldives, Mauritius, Tahiti, Andaman and Nicobar Islands, etc. has developed with tourism activity over the past few decades. The topography is generally undulating and they offer natural scenic beauty with exotic flora and fauna. Most of these islands have places of worship like churches, temples, etc. As an added attraction some of these islands have developed as tax havens thereby encouraging commercial development of these economies. They offer social and cultural attractions as tourists can experience the local lifestyle, local food, fairs and festivals, etc. Scenic attractions, like good weather, are very important factors in the development of tourism. Breath-taking mountain scenery and the coastal stretches exert a strong fascination on the tourist the magnificent mountain ranges provide an atmosphere of peace and tranquillity. Tourists visiting the northern slopes of the Alps in Switzerland and Austria and the southern slopes in Italy and also the Himalayan slopes of India and Nepal for the first time, cannot but be charmed by their physical magnificence.

Man-Made Tourism Products

Man-made tourism products are created by man for pleasure, leisure or business. Man-made tourism products include:

a) Culture

b) Sites and areas of archaeological interest

c) Historical buildings and monuments

d) Places of historical significance

e) Museums and art galleries

f) Political and educational institutions

g) Religious institutions

Cultural tourism is based on the mosaic of places, traditions, art forms, celebrations and experiences that portray the nation and its people, reflecting the diversity and character of a country. Garrison Keillor, in an address to the 1995 White House Conference on Travel & Tourism, best described cultural tourism by saying, "We need to think about cultural tourism because really there is no other kind of tourism. It's what tourism is...People don't come to America for our airports, people don't come to America for our hotels, or the recreation facilities....They come for our culture: high culture, low culture, middle culture, right, left, real or imagined — they come here to see America." Two significant travel trends will dominate the tourism market in the next decade.

- Mass marketing is giving way to one-to-one marketing with travel being tailored to the interests of the individual consumer.
- A growing number of visitors are becoming special interest travellers who rank the arts, heritage and/or other cultural activities as one of the top five reasons for travelling.

The combination of these two trends is being fuelled by technology, through the proliferation of online services and tools, making it easier for the traveller to choose destinations and customize their itineraries based on their interests. Today we can witness large masses of people travelling to foreign countries to become acquainted with the usages and customs, to visit the museums and to admire works of art. One way of hastening the beneficial effects resulting from tourism is to bring the cultural heritage into the economic circuit, thus justifying the investments made at the cost of the national community, for its preservation.

Taking an economic view of the cultural heritage of a nation may not altogether be justified, considering that the preservation of its culture is one of the basic responsibilities of any community. But considering the financial obstacles especially for the developing countries, this may appear to be a rational approach. Hence mass tourism can contribute unique benefits to the exploiting of the cultural heritage of a nation and can serve indirectly to improve the individual cultural levels of both citizens and travellers.

Cultural resources have another specific characteristic, which many tourists want to experience the exotic. There will be a great urge on the part of the tourist to visit and become acquainted with the ancient civilization in their quest for novel human knowledge. Culture means the prospect of contact with other civilizations, their original and varied customs and tradition with their distinct characteristics. This entire process creates a powerful motivator towards travel.

Various Museums also attract tourists like Madame Tussauds Museum in London, the Louvre Museum in Paris, Smithsonian Washington Museum, Museums of famous painters like Salvador Dali, Pablo Picasso, Natural History Museum, British Museum, Museum of Modern Art are also popular tourist products. Sites of archeological interest like remains of Mohenjodaro and Harrapan civilizations, museums for fossils and dinosaurs.

Sites for historical interest like city of Hiroshima and Nagasaki, sites of holocaust in Germany, tombs of various leaders and emperors. Historical buildings like Warwick Castle, Tower of London, Stratford-on-Avon which is Shakespeare's birthplace, the Roman Baths are all popular with tourists. Even historical cities like Varanasi in India get a lot of tourists due to its status as one of the oldest cities of the world. Stonehenge in United Kingdom, The White House, Buckingham Palace and other places of political significance, are also great tourist draws.

Traditions Pilgrimages

- Fairs and festivals
- Arts and handicrafts
- Dance
- Music
- Folklore
- Native life and customs

A pilgrimage is a term primarily used for a journey or a search of great moral significance. Sometimes, it is a journey to a sacred place or shrine of importance to a person's beliefs and faith. Members of every religion participate in pilgrimages. A person who makes such a journey is called a pilgrim. Secular and civic pilgrimages are also practiced, without regard for religion but rather of importance to a particular society. For example, many people throughout the world travel to the City of Washington in the United States for a pilgrimage to see the Declaration of Independence and the Constitution of the United States. British people often make pilgrimages to London to witness the public appearances of the monarch of the United Kingdom. A large number of people have been making pilgrimages to sacred religious places or holy places. This practice is widespread in many parts of the world. In the Christian world, for instance, a visit to Jerusalem or the Vatican is considered auspicious. Among Muslims, a pilgrimage to Mecca is considered a great act of faith. In India there are many pilgrimage centres and holy places belonging to all major religions of the world.

India is among the richest countries in the world as far as the field of art and craft is concerned. Tourists like to visit and see the creative and artistic treasures of various countries. Every country has certain traditional arts like soap sculptures and batik of Thailand; gems and jewellery, tie and dye works, wood and marble carving in Indonesia; ivory, glasswork, hand block printing, sandalwood, inlay work; are some of the examples of traditional art that attract tourists.

Modern forms include Blues, Rock, Pop, Jazz, Rap, Techno and Hip-Hop. Music also adds to the attraction of a destination. Fairs and Festivals capture the fun loving side and bring out the joyous celebrations of the community. Festivals like Christmas, Easter, Thanksgiving, Eid, Ramadan, Diwali, and Holi and so on, also bring people to destinations where the celebration can be enjoyed. Some popular Fairs which cater to fun and work are Pushkar Mela in Rajasthan, Pret fair in Paris, Magic Fair in Vegas for garments, Hong Kong Fashion Week and various job fairs where people are recruited.

Entertainment

* Amusement and recreation parks
* Sporting events
* Zoos and oceanariums
* Cinemas and theatre
* Night life
* Cuisine

Tourist products that have entertainment as their main characteristic are many. Just to name a few there are amusement and recreational parks like Disneyworld in United States, Hong Kong, Paris, Singapore and theme parks in various countries and cities like Appu Ghar and Fun and Food Village in Delhi, Essel World in Mumbai and so on. Tourists may come to attend sports events and it is also an opportunity to explore the country. The fundamental concept is that all tourist activities have an influence on providing economic benefits and have a powerful influence in some definite locality, like the Olympics in Athens has given immense benefit to all in tourism business in Athens in particular and Greece in general.

Many countries organise year round sports events like swimming meets, athletic meets, weight lifting events, cricket matches, baseball and football events and many more such events which encourage tourism. India will be hosting the Common-Wealth Games on 2010 and it is anticipated to give the tourism industry a big boost. Night Life is one of the prime attractions in a holiday. Tourists like to especially visit areas in cities where the night life activity is promoted. These areas are usually lit up with street stalls like flea markets and food areas. Bars, night clubs, casinos and very often open air bands attract and add to the psychological satisfaction and experience of tourists.

Cuisine is very often an understated but highly important part of any holiday. Now-a-days there is cuisine from all areas of the world which is found at most tourist destinations. Speciality restaurants serve Indian, Continental, Chinese, Italian, Japanese, Thai, Indonesian, Fast food, Mexican, Mediterranean, and Arabic and so on. However, tourists usually like to eat the local food of the areas they visit.

Business

- conventions
- conferences

People who travel in relation to their work come under the category of business tourism. However such travel for business purposes is also linked with tourist activity like visiting places of tourist attraction at the destination, sight seeing and excursion trips. Business travel is also related to what is termed today as convention business, which is a rapidly growing industry in hospitality and tourism.

A business traveller is important to the tourism industry as it involves the usage of all the components of tourism. He travels because of different business reasons-attending conventions and conferences, meetings, workshops etc. Participants have a lot of leisure time at their disposal.

The conference organisers make this leisure time very rewarding for participants by organising many activities for their pleasure and relaxation. The spouses and families accompanying the participants are also well looked after by the organisers. The organisers plan sight seeing tours and shopping tours for the participants and their families.

In India, cooking classes for learning Indian food cooking from the various states, visits to the craft bazaars where tourists see how artisans make clay pots and other handicrafts, they visit tie and dye units to see Indian printing eg. Batik printing etc. Women tourists enjoy henna demonstrations. Conferences are events which require meticulous planning and efficient implementation, co-coordinating various activities so that the right things happen at the right time. There are a number of players in the convention business. On one hand are the customers or the consumers and on the other hand are the principle suppliers like hotels, transporters, convention centres, tour operators and travel agencies, tourism departments, exhibition organisers, sponsors etc.

Symbiotic Tourism Products

Some tourism products do not fall into the above categories. Wildlife sanctuary, Marine parks, Aero products and Water sports, Flower festivals are the example of tourism products which are a blending of nature and man. Nature has provided the resource and man has converted them into a tourism product by managing them. National parks for example, are left in their natural state of beauty as far as possible, but still need to be managed, through provision of access, parking facilities, limited accommodation, litter bins etc. Yet the core attraction is still nature in this category of product. These products are symbiosis of nature and man.

In case of adventure sports tourists can be participants. The basic element of adventure is the satisfaction of having complete command over one's body, a sense of risk in the process, an awareness of beauty and the exploration of the unknown. Adventure tourism can be classified into aerial, water based and land based.

Aerial adventure sports include the following activities-

A) Parachuting, which involves jumping off from an aircraft or balloon and descending by means of a parachute. The infrastructure required, includes an aircraft, parachutes and large landing zones.

B) Sky Diving, which involves a sky diver jumping off an aircraft or balloon at a much greater height without deploying his parachute initially and opening it after some interval at a pre determined height.

C) Hang Gliding, which involves running off a mountain or being towed by a winch and essentially flying like a glider where the directional control is achieved by a shift in his own weight by the pilot.

D) Para Gliding, is the latest aero-sport which has taken the world by storm. A Para Glider is a specially designed square parachute, along with a harness attached by lines.

E) Para Sailing is a simple sport that involves towing a parachutist to a height of a few hundred feet in the air and then descending by means of a parachute. As a year round activity, Para sailing can be done on land and water.

F) Bungee Jumping, which requires no equipment except a 'bungee cord' made of nylon fiber of enough elasticity to be able to absorb the shock at the end of the jump. The jumper makes a headlong jump into empty space and the resultant rush of adrenalin makes the experience very exhilarating.

G) Ballooning, where a balloon is attached to a basket by steel wire ropes. By regulating hot and cold air, the pilot can steer the balloon along any charted course.

Water based adventure sports include the following-

A) White water rafting which is one of the most important and exciting water sports, which involves riding down water rapids in an inflatable raft which is used to negotiate fast flowing rivers.

B) Canoeing and Kayaking are adventure sports which begin upstream where the water is wild and white. The gradient best suited for canoeing is the stage near the river's entry into the plains where the trip can be combined with a natural holiday in a forest. Kayaking is appealing as it enables innovation on the river by one or two oarsman seated in tandem.

C) Adventure sports in the waters of the sea like wind surfing, scuba diving, snorkeling, yachting, water skiing, etc. also offer thrilling activities to the tourists.

Land based adventure tourist products include the following-

A) Rock climbing which originated as a means of practicing techniques for ascending high mountains. It was earlier provided as training to mountaineers but has now evolved into a highly developed sport. The climber moves up, using knowledge of rope handling, climbing, securing one to another, etc. Very sophisticated techniques and equipments are used nowadays to ascend or descend on very steep terrain.

B) Mountaineering requires trained physical ability and suitable equipment. The higher peaks need better equipment which is also costly. The challenges which mountains like the Indian Himalayas pose attract mountaineers from various countries.

C) Trekking the mighty Himalayas which spread across five Indian states form a sweeping arc and compress in its expanse a wide geographical variety and contrasting cultures.

D) Skiing is the practice of sliding over snow on runners, called skis, attached to each foot. There are three types of ski resorts, the first are large towns, second type are alpine villages and the third resorts built for skiing.

E) Heli skiing is a type of alpine skiing where the skier is dropped to the top of a mountain by a helicopter and then he slides down on his own.

F) Motor Rally is a sport that tests the navigational skills of man and his endurance with the machine. Motor rallies, grand prix racing, hill climbing rallies, vintage car rallies, sports car racing, etc. are some forms of this tourism product.

G) Safaris were earlier taken on camel, horse and elephants as an excursion for hunting or a journey. As a modern tourist product now safaris are taken on jeeps and in the form of caravans. Viewing and enjoying nature, meeting the local villagers, seeing their traditions, customs and lifestyle, entertainment and camp fires are some of the characteristics of modern safaris. Eg, Egypt desert safaris. Horse and elephant safaris are arranged in most of the national parks and wildlife sanctuaries.

Event Based Tourism Products

Where an event is an attraction, it as an event based tourist product. Events attract tourists as spectators and also as participants in the events, sometimes for both. The Ocktoberfest organised in Germany, Dubai and Singapore shopping festivals, the camel polo at Jaisalmer, Kite flying in Ahmedabad attracts tourists, both as spectators and participants. Whereas in case of the Snake Boat race of Kerala can be enjoyed witnessing it.

Event attractions are temporary, and are often mounted in order to increase the number of tourists to a particular destination. Some events have a short time scale, such as the Republic Day Parade, others may last for many days, for example Khajuraho Dance Festival or even months like the Kumbh Mela. A destination which may have little to commend it to the tourist can nevertheless succeed in drawing tourists by mounting an event such as an unusual exhibition.

Site Based Tourism Products

When an attraction is a place or site then it is called a site based tourist product. Site attractions are permanent by nature, for example Taj Mahal, The Great Wall of China, The Grand Canyon in Arizona, Eiffel Tower, Statue of Liberty, Temples of Khajuraho, etc. A site destination can extend its season by mounting an off season event or festival.

A large number of tourists are attracted every year by the great drawing power of Stratford on Avon in England because of its association with Shakespeare, the city of Agra in India with its famous Taj Mahal, Pisa in Italy for its famous Leaning Tower. Some new features have been added to the same product to keep the tourist interest alive in the products. For example now visitors can see Taj by night, music shows have been organised with Taj as the backdrop so that there are repeat tourists.

Other Tourism Products

Health Tourism

Holidaying is generally considered as an investment in health, a subject that presents opportunities of cost-benefit analysis. The medical expertise of various countries has added a new product to the existing tourism products.

People are travelling to various countries for treatment of various ailments and medical procedures like Cardio care, Bone Marrow Transplant, Dialysis and Kidney transplant, Neuro surgery, Joint Replacement Surgery, Urology, Osteoporosis, and numerous other diseases. Even cosmetic surgery, alternative medicines like homeopathy, acupressure, ayurvedic medicines and naturopathy are also becoming tourism products wherein travel companies are offering Yoga and Rejuvenation packages. Tourists travel for what is illegal in one's own country, e.g. abortion, euthanasia; for instance, euthanasia for noncitizens is provided by Dignitas in Switzerland. Tourists travel also for advanced care that is not available in one's own country, in the case that there are long waiting lists in one's own country or for use of free or cheap health care organisations.

Ecotourism

Tourism that combines local economic development, protection of the quality of the environment and promotion of the natural advantages and the history of an area. The combination of all or some of the above mentioned kinds of tourism could contribute significantly to the development of tourism in any country. The availability of tourist packages involving gastronomy, entertainment and information about the cultural wealth of a country should be regarded as a priority issue for tourist agents, as it will reduce the concentration of tourist activity in certain areas and will improve and enrich the tourist.

Rural Tourism

Any form of tourism that showcases the rural life, art, culture and heritage at rural locations, thereby, benefiting the local community economically and socially as well as enabling interaction between the tourists and the locals for a more enriching tourism experience an be termed as rural tourism. It is multifaceted and may entail farm/agricultural tourism, cultural tourism, nature tourism, adventure tourism, and ecotourism.

The stresses of urban lifestyles have lead to this counter-urbanisation approach to tourism. There are various factors that have lead to this changing trend towards rural tourism like increasing levels of awareness, growing interest in heritage and culture and improved accessibility and environmental consciousness, Tourists like to visit villages to experience and live a relaxed and healthy lifestyle.

Ethnic Tourism

Ethnic tourism is travelling for the purpose of observing the cultural expressions of lifestyles of truly exotic people. Such tourism is exemplified by travel to Panama to study the San

Blas Indians or to India to observe the isolated hill tribes of Assam. Typical destination activities would include visits to native homes, attending traditional ceremonies and dances, and possibly participating in religious rituals.

Senior Citizen Tourism

A newly emerging trend in tourism, basically for senior citizens or old people who live in isolation, especially in the west, because of daily busy schedules of their children and more importantly the attitudes. The characteristic feature of this type of tourism is that the senior people are less demanding in the form of facilities and services, besides leaving minimum impact on the destination community and their main consideration is on personalised service.

Spiritual Tourism

Many people when living under conditions of stress turn to spirituality. The Eastern world is considered to be very spiritual with many of the new age Gurus and their hermitages. This takes the form of another tourism product, that is, spiritual tourism. Tourists visit places to attend spiritual discourses and meditation workshops. For example, The Osho Foundation, Art of Living Foundation which have centres all over the world, Buddhist Monasteries and Ashrams.

Golf Tourism

Golf has been enjoyed by many for a long time. Earlier it was enjoyed as a sport but in recent times it has developed into a hot tourism product. Many tourist organizations plan promotional packages to woo the golf tourist especially from Japan where the green fees are very high. These tourists take exclusive golfing holidays wherein their accommodation is also arranged near the course and they return after serious golf playing.

Nature of Tourism

The United Nations classified three forms of tourism in 1994 in its Recommendations on Tourism Statistics: Domestic tourism, which involves residents of the given country travelling only within this country; Inbound tourism, involving non-residents travelling in the given country; and Outbound tourism, involving residents travelling in another country. The UN also derived different categories of tourism by combining the 3 basic forms of tourism: Internal tourism, which comprises domestic tourism and inbound tourism; National tourism, which comprises domestic tourism and outbound tourism; and International tourism, which consists of inbound tourism and outbound tourism.

Intrabound tourism is a term coined by the Korea Tourism Organization and widely accepted in Korea. Intrabound tourism differs from domestic tourism in that the former encompasses policy-making and implementation of national tourism policies.

Recently, the tourism industry has shifted from the promotion of inbound tourism to the promotion of intrabound tourism because many countries are experiencing tough competition for inbound tourists. Some national policy makers have shifted their priority to the promotion of intrabound tourism to contribute to the local economy. Examples of such campaigns include "See America" in the United States, "Get Going Canada" in Canada, and "Guseok Guseok" (corner to corner) in South Korea.

Before people are able to experience tourism they usually need disposable income; time off from work or other responsibilities; leisure time tourism infrastructure, such as transport and accommodation; and legal clearance to travel.

Individually, sufficient health is also a condition, and of course the inclination to travel. Furthermore, in some countries there are legal restrictions on travelling, especially abroad. Certain states with strong governmental control over the lives of citizens (notably established Communist states) may restrict foreign travel only to trustworthy citizens. The United States prohibits its citizens from travelling to some countries, for example Cuba.

Tourist Destination

A tourist destination is a city, town, or other area that is dependent to a significant extent on the revenues accruing from tourism. It may contain one or more tourist attractions and possibly some "tourist traps (A tourist trap is an establishment, or group of establishments, that has been created with the aim of attracting tourists and their money. Tourist traps will typically provide services, entertainment, souvenirs and other products for tourists to purchase, and these will often be at inflated prices.

While the term may have negative connotations for some, such establishments may be viewed by tourists as fun and interesting diversions. The term is somewhat ambiguous; the sort of tourist trap common in the US, for example, is slightly different from that found in Europe.

Tourism is distinguishable from travel undertaken in the past by its mass character, and is now not a luxury only for the upper classes.

Tourism is a luxury, with most people in the developed world and increasing numbers of people living in developing countries engaging in tourism at some time in their lives. Tourism is accepted and accustomed, and has become a good indicator of economic status and is considered necessary for good health and personal being.

Defining Tourism

Tourism is a productive activity that encompasses human behaviour, use of resources, and interaction with other people, economies and environments. It involves physical movement of tourists to locations other than their normal place of living. It involves consumption of goods and services provided by organizations in the process, and generate a mass productive activity, employment and income.

Tourism is a highly complex productive activity. It involves the activities and interests not only of large transport undertakings, owners of tourist sites and attractions, and of various tourist services at the destination but also of all levels of government. Each of these serves the resident population and visitors. For countries delivering the tourist product it makes a significant contribution to GDP, employment, investment and FOREX earnings. It is a major catalyst for economic growth and structural change. It also diversifies employment prospects.

Tourism is dependant on a large number of economic activities supplying inputs to the industries that directly cater for tourists and producing consumer durables used for tourist activity.

Characteristics of tourism are:

- Constantly operating industry, seasonal fluctuations
- Labour-intensive industry
- Lack of barriers to entry
- Small business predominates
- Important medium for educational and cultural exchange
- Sheer numbers
- Growing levels of consumer expenditure
- A few producers dominate
- New tourist attractions are regularly opening
- Mass tourists products have little differentiation.
- The impacts of tourism are broad ranging (economic, social, environmental)

Two forms of tourism:

- International Tourism

Travel to country outside residence.

- Domestic Tourism

Travel within tourist country.

Spatial Pattern

Travel and tourism is the world largest industry. Western Europe and North America dominate global tourist flows. Total world tourism grew throughout the 1980s and 1990s at around 4% per annum. The range of destinations now encompasses virtually all countries in the developed world and many of those in the developing world. There has been spectacular growth in the Asia-Pacific region. Countries which are good destinations have sufficient environmental safeguards and a trained work force.

Tourism has developed in many contexts. Modern mass tourism has origins in affluence of industrialized countries of West Europe, North America, and Japan. Tourism has also expanded significantly in East Europe, Asia, Africa and the Caribbean. It has developed in liberal and western societies and in a variety of physical environments.

Tourism has also developed in a wide variety of physical environments, with many different environments within a country becoming favourable tourist destinations. These environments may include:

- Islands
- Alpine
- Coasts
- Countryside

Factors Affecting Tourism

The tourism industry is multi faceted. Many components of tourism are inextricably bound to other economic sectors, and other forms of accommodation to commercial development. The spatial interaction that arises out of the tourist's movement from origin to destination and factors affecting it lend themselves to analysis.

The Biophysical and Built Environment

- A countries biophysical environment, cultural heritage and artistic life represent integral components of its tourist industry. Various types of tourism have differing requirements for favourable development and some countries will be more favourable for development than others.
- The industry is ultimately located according to the spatial distribution of attractions and access to them, which is largely determined by environmental factors. The tourist destination must offer tings the tourist seeks and needs.
- Tourist behaviour patterns are influenced by environment conditions, and they may place constraints on types of developments. Natural characteristics are highly desirable and should complement infrastructure and attractions.
- Climate is a special consideration, and favourable weather conditions are essential. For each tourist activity there is an optimal climate, and climate often determines the length and profitability of the holiday season at a resort.

Technological Change

- One of the most important variables affecting tourism is technological change. In the twentieth century, transport technology allowed the spread of mass tourism to a widespread array of destinations, which were previously not reachable by rail or ship.
- Manufacturers are constantly developing the capabilities of vehicles. Such developments influence places which can be reached, in terms of social and cost constraints.
- The development of wide-bodied long haul jets i.e. Boeing 747 was a major impetus to the growth of tourism.

Socio-cultural Influences

- Participation in tourism is affected by a number of demographic and social factors, such as age distribution, family life cycle, level of education, occupation structure, and population concentration. Demographic and social changes should profoundly affect the propensity of populations to indulge in tourism in the future.
- Increased life expectancy and changing work force composition is also important. Increasing participation rates of women have provided a boost to tourism, because two income families have higher discretionary income. There is also a growing number of DINK's who frequently travel.

Economic Factors

- Tourism is among the strongest performing sectors of the global economy. Tourism is a major source of employment with the provision of accommodation, catering, transport, entertainment and other service industries important. There is also an enormous amount of productive activity generated indirectly by tourism. It is an important instrument for facilitating economic growth because of its wide multiplier effects.
- Tourism is Australia contributes 17.3Bn in export earnings to the Australian economy.
- Changing economic circumstances largely determine the magnitude of the tourist industry. With higher levels of

development, the employment structure changes, and a more affluent society creates a demand for tourists products.

Cultural Influences

- Features of historical or cultural interest exert a powerful attraction for tourists. Three major forms of culture attract visitors:
- Forms of culture that are inanimate such as monuments
- Forms of culture reflected in the normal daily lives of a destination
- Forms of culture at are especially animated and may involve events such as festivals.
- Tourism is often accompanied by cultural exchanges and cultural enrichment. These contacts can have harmful effects where native cultures and traditional ways of life are weakened or destroyed.

Political Influences

- Governments at all levels and of all persuasions have recognized that while tourism is basically private sector, its impact requires government involvement.
- Government profoundly affects the economic climate in which tourism operates. The government's principal role is to foster the development of the industry that can best prosper consistent with broad economic, social and environmental objectives.

The Relationship Between Production and Consumption

Tourism as a productive activity consists of three major components: the country of origin of tourists; destinations; and routes travelled between locations.

Tourism Generating areas

Represent homes of tourists. These areas represent the main tourist markets in the world and major marketing functions of tourism are found here.

Tourism Destination Areas

Attract tourists by offering what isn't available at home.

Transit routes link these two areas of productive activity and are key elements. They are the main transport component of productive activity. As tourists travel they acquire an experience made up of many different parts. These activities are extremely interdependent.

The Changing Nature of the Production Process

The growth of tourism throughout the twentieth century was closely associated with rising living standards in the developed world. In the first half of the twentieth century the opportunity to travel remained largely the privilege of the wealthier people in society, but periods of rapid growth following WW2 enabled more people to travel. The car and aircraft became the main mode of transport.

A number of important changes are associated with the development on the industry:

- Internationalization of tourism: Tourism has become globalised. The global transportation infrastructure is rapidly becoming an interconnected pathway all over the world. The level of globalization has increased as more countries participate in international travel.
- Organizational developments: The organization of tourism comes from two sources: the government and private sectors.

Recognizing the contribution tourism makes towards a countries economic and social well being nearly all governments have organizations to promote tourism. The extents of their responsibilities vary.

The opportunities which exist in tourism give rise to a mix of large and small scale operations catering for all the tourist needs from origin to destination. As with other productive activities there has been a significant growth of corporate involvement in tourism. Much of the growth in large tourism companies arises from the very competitive nature of many tourist markets and destinations and a drive for greater market share and economies of scale.

Social Impacts of Tourism

Tourism is driven by individual consumer decisions.

Package Tours

The package tour is sold for an all inclusive price, and this is usually cheaper bringing holidays in reach of a much larger section of the market. Consumers have a wise variety of choice. Contiki tours are a good example of a company catering for 18-35 year olds world wide. Contiki has an arrangement with Cathay Pacific.

Small Group Tours

Small group tours are a popular alternative. They utilize local resources and services wherever possible.

Individual Travel

Many tourists are actively planning their own travel experience. They prefer to individualize their own itinerary rather than be locked into a group tour. Experienced travellers are seeking to fulfil specific desires. This reflects the desire of travellers for new and different experiences. More specialized demands has seen tourism as a productive activity respond.

Economic Impacts of Tourism

Increasing the Scale of Production

The profit motive has encouraged development of large scale operations and an increase in the size of the companies involved. Increasing scale is especially evident in the accommodation sector.

The scale of operations in the hotel sector continues to expand. While large hotel chains can exploit economies of scale, the small independents can compete on the basis of cost, and personalized service.

Horizontal and Vertical Integration

Growth in the scale of production and increases in the concentration of ownership and control have generally come about through horizontal and vertical integration. A business may expand or develop by itself or seek to combine with other businesses.

Transnational Operations

Integration in tourism has continued to point where operations become multinational or transnational in nature.

The pattern of multinational development varies. Clearly a global marketplace provides greater market potential and opportunities to secure a competitive advantage. Companies wishing to diversify their portfolio will expand activities overseas.

Technological Impacts of Tourism

Tourism receives substantial research funds to facilitate the development of new technology. They change every area of this productive activity.

Consumer Choice

Tourist motivation and decision making are increasingly shaped by changing technology. The Internet has allowed a wealth of information to become available to tourists. Hotel facilities, reservations, and attractions to name a few.

Transport Technologies

Aircraft

Future developments in aircraft will favour larger capacity aircraft, but still subsonic speed. The amount of power to propel aero-planes increases with speed.

Therefore new aircraft are unlikely to travel any faster than existing, but they will have a greater range and more seating reducing the costs of travel.

Land Transport

Transport is now faster and more competitive over long trips. This has come hand in hand with infrastructure development.

Sea Transport

The cruise industry is growing particularly fast. The world's cruise fleet has doubled in the last decade of the 20th century.

Keeping Track of People and Possessions

Computerization allows transport operators to work more efficiently, and generates a wealth of data which can be used for planning marketing activities. Global satellite networks have provided powerful new marketing tools. Technology has transformed the distribution process.

Political Impacts of Tourism

Most governments now actively seek to promote tourism to and within their countries and take steps to coordinate public and private tourism activities and to foster industry growth. Government support has been less forthcoming in some parts of the developed world. In many developing countries tourism is seen as a way of accelerating economic development. Some governments have also encouraged the development of international tourism to further their own political objectives.

The changing political and economic environment

- Collapse of the soviet union and opening up Eastern Europe
- Switch from centralized economies to free market economies in China and India
- Creation of NΛFTA.

Bibliography

Barnett, T. : *Sociology and Development,* London: Hutchinson, 1988.

Bhatia, A.K. : *Tourism Development: Principles and Practices,* New Delhi, 1982.

Bianchi, R. : *Tourism Development and Resort Dynamics: An Alternative Approach,* Wiley, 1994.

Brown, L.A. : *Innovation Diffusion: A New Perspective,* London and New York, 1981.

Brunt, Paul: *Market Research in Travel and Tourism,* Oxford, Butterworth Heinemann, 1997.

Buhalis, D., A.M. Tjoa : *Information and Communication Technologies in tourism,* Istanbul, Springer-Verlag, Wien-New York, 1998.

Chakravarti B.K. : *Hotel and Hospitality Management,* A.P.H., Delhi, 2011.

Clark, Colin: *Tourist Services and Guidance: Heritage and Information,* Strasbourg, Council of Europe Press, 1989.

David L: *International Tourism Policy, New York,* Van Nostrand and Reinhold, 1990.

Davidoff, Donald M.: *Customer Service in the Hospitality and Tourism Industry,* Englewood Cliffs, Prentice Hall, 1994.

Donald E. : *Public Personnel Management: Contexts and Strategies,* Upper Saddle River, NJ: Prentice Hall, 1998.

Donald M.: *Customer Service in the Hospitality and Tourism Industry,* Englewood Cliffs, Prentice Hall, 1994.

Eckel, Peter J.: *College & University Foodservice Management Standards,* Westport, AVI Pub. Company, 1985.

Fesenmaier D., Klein, S. : *Information & Communication Technologies in Tourism,* Springer-Verlag, Wien-New York, 2000.

Fowler, Peter: *Heritage and Tourism: In the Global Village,* London, Retailed, 1993.

Frechtling, Douglas C: *Practical Tourism Forecasting*, Oxford, Butterworth Heinemann, 1996.

Horn, C. and Simmons, D. : *Community Adaptation to Tourism: Comparisons between Rotorua and Kaikoura*, New Zealand. Tourism Management, 2002.

Judi Radice: *Restaurant & Food Graphics*, Glen Cove, PBC International, 1994.

Kim, J.M. : *An Analysis of Korean Residents Attitudes toward the Impact of Tourism*, Washington: The George Washington University, 1986.

Larkham, P J: *Building a New Heritage: Tourism, Culture & Identity in the New Europe*, London, Routledge,1994.

Leivadi, S: *Sociology of Tourism, The: Theoretical And Empirical Investigations*, London, Retailed, 1996.

Lucas, Rosemary E.: *Managing Employee Relations in the Hotel and Catering Industry*, London, Cassell, 1995.

MacCannell, Dean: *Tourist, The: A New Theory of the Leisure Class*, London, Macmillan, 1976.

Madhukar Manoj : *Hospitality Industries in Next Millennium*, Rajat, Delhi, 2001.

Marcussen, Carl H. : *Internet Distribution of European Travel and Tourism Services*, Research Centre of Bornholm, Denmark, 1999.

Martin, B.S. : *The Efficacy of Growth Machine Theory in Explaining Resident Perceptions of Community Tourism Development*, Clemson University, 1996.

McNicol, B.J. : *Views of Residents, Developers and Government Planners About Tourists and Tourism Resort Developments in Canmore, Alberta*, The University of Galgary, Alberta, 1996.

Murphy, P.E. : *Perceptions and Preferences of Decision-making Groups in Tourist Centers: A Guide to Planning Strategy*, Washington, DC: George Washington University, 1980.

Murphy, P.E. : *Tourism: A Community Approach*, London: Methuen, 1985.

Nijkamp, Peter: *Sustainable Tourism Development*, Aldershot, Avebury, 1995.

Norman G.: *Hotel, Restaurant, and Travel Law: A Preventive Approach*, Albany, Delmar Publishers, 1993.

Pearce, P.L. and Moscardo, G. : *Tourism Community Analysis*, London and New York: Routledge, 1999.

Prentice, R: *Conceptualising The Experiences of Heritage Tourists*, 1997.

Ratti Manish : *Hospitality Management : Theories and Practices*, Rajat Pub, Delhi, 2007.

Richards, G. : *Culture, Crafts and Tourism: A Vital Relationship*, Tilburg: Atlas, 1999.

Rogers, H Anthea and Slinn, Judy A: *Tourism: Management of Facilities*, London, Pitman: M & E, 1993.

Sabharwal Rajiv : *Tourism and Hospitality Management in Liberalised Era*, Pacific, Delhi, 2011.

Sethna, R.J. : *Social Impact of Tourism in Selected Caribbean Countries*, Washington, DC: George Washington University, 1980.

Sharma Sunil : *Planning and Development of Tourism and Hospitality*, Rajat Pub, Delhi, 2007.

Shrivastava Atul : *Modern Hospitality and Tourism Management*, Centrum Press, Delhi, 2010.

Singh Raj Kumar : *Modern Trends in Hospitality Industry*, Aman, Delhi, 2006.

Smith, V.L. : *Hosts and Guests: The Anthropology of Tourism*, Oxford: Blackwell, 1978.

Swarbrooke, J.: *Marketing Tourism, Hospitality and Leisure in Europe*, London, International Thomson Business Press, 1996.

Timothy R.: *Cases in Hospitality Management: A Critical Incident Approach*, New York, Wiley, 1995.

Tribe, John *Corporate Strategy for Tourism, London*, International Thomson Business Press, 1997.

Var, Turgut: *Tourism Planning*, London, Retailed, 2002.

Wahab, S A: *Tourism Management*, Tourism International Press, 1975.

Weiler, B: *Ethnic Tourism*, Belhaven/Wiley, 1992.

Index

A

B

C

D

E

❑❑❑